Also by Jerome Rothenberg

SHAKING THE PUMPKIN

TRADITIONAL POETRY

DOUBLEDAY & COMPANY, INC., GARDEN CITY, NEW YORK

SHAKING THE PUMPKIN

OF THE INDIAN NORTH AMERICAS

JEROME ROTHENBERG

Grateful acknowledgment is made to the following for permission to re-
print material copyrighted or controlled by them:

"Alcheringa," Volume 1, Number 1, Autumn 1970. Copyright 1970 by
Jerome Rothenberg & Dennis Tedlock. For excerpts from "Shaking
the Pumpkin," "Crow Versions," "The Deadly Dance," "song of
the old woman," "spring fjord," "the old man's song about his
wife," "a woman's song, about men," and "a man's song, about his
daughter" and "From Ceremony of Sending: A Simultaneity for
Twenty Choruses."

"Alcheringa," Number 2, Summer 1971. Copyright 1971 by Jerome
Rothenberg & Dennis Tedlock. For "Wolf Songs and Others of the
Tlingit" and "Rabinal Achí: Part IV."

The Alternative Press for excerpt from "Shaking the Pumpkin" and for
"Crazy Dog Events," published as broadsheet, through Ken & Ann
Mikolowski.

The American Folklore Society for "Text of the Raingod Drama" from
Seeking Life by Vera Laski, published in 1958.

American Philosophical Society for "Archaic Song of Dr. Tom the
Shaman," Song 99, in "Songs of the Nootka Indians of Western
Vancouver Island" by H. H. Roberts and Morris Swadesh from
Transactions of the American Philosophical Society, Vol. 45, Pt. 3
(1955).

Homero Aridjis for "First Peyote Song," "Second Peyote Song," "Song of an Initiate," "Third Peyote Song," and "How the Violin Was Born: A Peyote Account" from *Correspondencias*, No. 1, 1966, ed. by Homero Aridjis.

Stephen Berg for "More Eskimo Songs about People & Animals" from Boas Eskimo Songs. Copyright 1971 Stephen Berg, from the Boas Collection of the American Philosophical Society. Reprinted by permission of the author.

Charles L. Boilès and *Ethnomusicology* for "Tepehua Thought-Songs." Reprinted by permission of the author and publisher.

Carl Cary for "The Origin of the Skagit Indians According to Lucy Williams," "Lullaby," "One for Coyote," and "Two Divorce Songs."

The Dial Press for excerpts from "Shaking the Pumpkin," "The 12th Horse-Song of Frank Mitchell," and "The 13th Horse-Song of Frank Mitchell" from *Poems for the Game of Silence*. Copyright © 1960, 1961, 1966, 1967, 1968, 1969, 1970, 1971 by Jerome Rothenberg.

Ediciones Era for "The Evil Song of Taweakame Peyote God of Lush," excerpt from *En la tierra mágica del peyote* by Fernando Benítez, published by Ediciones Era, Mexico, 1968, p. 251.

Editions Seghers for "song of the old woman," "spring fjord," "the old man's song about his wife," "a woman's song, about men," "a man's song, about his daughter," and "dream" from *Poèmes Eskimo* by Paul Emile Victor, Editions Seghers, 1958.

Editorial Porrua, S. A. for "The Deadly Dance" from *Llave del Náhuatl* by Angel María Garibay K., published by Editorial Porrua, 1961.

Munro S. Edmonson for "Popol Vuh: The Destruction of the Dolls" and "Popol Vuh: Alligator's Struggles with the 400 Sons" from *The Book of Counsel: The Popol Vuh of the Quiche Maya of Guatemala*, Middle American Research Institute, Publication 35, Tulane University, in press.

Etnologiska Studier, Göteborg Etnografiska Museum for "Muu's Way or Pictures from the Uterine World" from *The Complete Mu-Igala in Picture Writing* by Nils Homer & S. Henry Wassén, Etnologiska Studier 21.

Edward Field and Education Development Center for "Magic Words," "Magic Words for Hunting Caribou," "Magic Words to Feel Better," "Travel Song," "Magic Words for Hunting Seal," "The Invisible Men," "Orpingalik's Song," "Hunger," and "Heaven and Hell" from *Songs and Stories of the Netsilik Eskimos*, Copyright © 1967 and 1968 by Education Development Center, Inc., Cambridge,

Vantage Press for "The Sorcerer" by Eloise Street from *The Songs of Y-Ail-Mihth* by K'HHalserten Sepass, published by Vantage Press in 1963.

Alberto Vásquez for "Archer's Dance Song" from *El Libro de los Cantares de Dzitbalché*, published by the Instituto Nacional de Antropología e Historia in 1965.

A portion of the author's proceeds from the sale of this book have been set aside for the Cold Spring (Seneca) Longhouse in Steamburg, New York.

FOR AVERY JIMERSON & RICHARD JOHNNY JOHN

Dane'ho niyo nengen' hojagowen'nondaat onen
di' nai hononho'n' gaiwayen'dahgon ne' yaden'nota
ennyenongai'daat.

So this is how many words there are.
Now once again it rests with the two singers
to go on down to the end.

CONTENTS

"Come not thus with your gunnes &
swords, to invade as foes. . . .

"What will it availe you to take that
perforce you may quietly have with love,
or to destroy them that provide your
food? . . .

"Lie well, & sleepe quietly with my
women & children, laugh, & I will be
merrie with you. . . ."

— *Powhatan, to Capt. John Smith*

1.

The awkwardness of presenting translations from American Indian
poetry in the year 1971 is that it has become fashionable today to deny
the possibility of crossing the boundaries that separate people of
different races & cultures: to insist instead that black is the concern of
black, red of red, & white of white. Yet the idea of translation has
always been that such boundary crossing is not only possible but
desirable. By its very nature, translation asserts or at least implies a
concept of psychic & biological unity, weird as such assertion may
seem in a time of growing dis-integration. Each poem, being made
present & translated, flies in the face of divisive ideology. The question
for the translator is not whether but how far we can translate one
another. Like the poet who is his brother, he attempts to restore what
has been torn apart. Any arrogance on his part would not only lead
to paternalism or "colonialism" (LeRoi Jones's term for it from a few
years back), it would deny the very order of translation. Only if he
allows himself to be directed by the other will a common way emerge,
true to both positions.

To submit through translation is to begin to accept the "truths" of
an other's language. At the same time it's a way of growing wary of
the lies in one's own, a point of vigilance that translators & poets

should be particularly keyed to. I learned, for example, that the Senecas with whom I lived call the whites "younger brothers" & themselves "*real*" people." To understand the Seneca experience (including where I stand with relation to them) I have to submit to terms like these & to get to a truth about them which includes the Seneca truth. As I do, it becomes clear to me that the very nature of "Indian" & "white" (words basic to the process I'm describing) is itself a question of language & translation.

If the term "younger brother" would later be neutralized or come to suggest contempt, what relationship did it originally express in a culture that didn't practice primogeniture & individual ownership of land—in which forests & clearings (the men were hunters, the women gardeners) were a common ground for brothers as children of one mother & members of one clan? Whether by birth or adoption didn't matter either: descended from a single mother (ultimately the Earth), "older" & "younger" was for them a matter of precedence in time & place, their relative experience of the shared environment. Thus the Senecas as older brothers recognized the rights of both to start with, but the whites (children also of the "old world" patriarchy) came to the land prepared for dispossession & fratricide. In the overthrow of the older—refusing adoption to the real-personhood of the Indian way, while asserting their own great-white-fatherhood—they triggered a disruption of the natural (ecological) order that's now making all of us its victims.

A "real" person in these terms is one who hasn't forgotten what & where things are in relation to the Earth. Earth-rooted, he is royal too, not by precedence of birth, but insofar as he has & shares a knowledge of the realm. He has only to maintain a true eye for his surroundings & a contact with the Earth, to recognize himself as the inheritor of reality, of a more real way of life. At any rate that seems to be the claim implicit in the language & confirmed by the events that have followed its denial.

The issue, writes David Antin, is reality. The *real* person (reality-person, in fact) lives, like the "primitive" philosopher described by Radin, "in a blaze of reality" through which he can experience "reality at white heat." This is a part of the tribal inheritance (not Indian only but world-wide) that we all lose at our peril—younger & older alike. Remember too how many elements are active in that situation, where we would concentrate on the words as being particularly the "poem" (many Indian poems in fact dispense entirely with words): elements, I mean, like music, non-verbal phonetic sounds, dance, gesture & event, game, dream, etc., along with all those unstated ideas & images the participants pick up from the poem's context. Each moment is charged: each is a point at which meaning is coming to surface, where nothing's incidental but everything matters terribly.

Now, put all of that together & you have the makings of a high poetry & art, which only a colonialist ideology could have blinded us into labeling "primitive" or "savage." You have also the great hidden accomplishment of our older brothers in America, made clear in the poetry & yet of concern not only to poets but to all (red, white & black) who want to carry the possibilities of reality & personhood into any new worlds to come. The yearning to rediscover the Red Man is part of this. It acknowledges not only the cruelty of what's happened in this place (a negative matter of genocide & guilt) but leads as well to the realization that "we" in a larger sense will never be whole without a recovery of the "red power" that's been here from the beginning. The true integration must begin & end with a recognition of all such powers. That means a process of translation & of mutual completion. Not a brotherhood of lies this time but an affiliation based on what the older had known from the start: that we're doomed without his tribal & matrilocal wisdom, which can be shared only among equals who have recognized a common lineage from the Earth.

2.

The question, then, was how to deliver the poetry of the first discoverers of America & civilizers of themselves. I had previously been retranslating (I wasn't unique in this among American poets) & anthologizing Indian & other tribal &/or "primitive" poetries mostly from the abundant volumes of myths & texts gathered over the previous hundred or so years by scores of Boasian anthropologists & others. That work had resulted in a worldwide anthology called *Tech-*

nicians of the Sacred (subtitle: *A Range of Poetries from Africa, America, Asia, & Oceania*), which included, in addition to my own contributions, workings by such poets as Pound, Williams, Tzara, Waley, Merwin, Sanders, Kelly, & R. Owens, plus very solid translations by anthropologists, etc. like Densmore, Berndt, Quain, Matthews, Bleek & Lloyd, McAllester, Beier, & many others. Not to mention all the workers (some better known than these) whose gatherings from around-the-world served as sources for the poems that emerged in English.

There are a couple of points from *Technicians* that I want to reiterate here. First it seemed clear to me that the range-&-depth of the materials previously collected was astonishing, & that the levels of the poetry were in no obvious relationship to the economic or industrial development of the cultures from which they derived (or if they were, that the powers of the poetry declined as those of technology & the political state increased)—clear, I mean, in spite of considerable mistranslation in even the "literal" & interlinear texts, & the fact that many of the translated poems were practically unreadable as first presented. Second, the range of the tribal poets was even more impressive if one avoided a closed, European definition of "poem" & worked empirically or by analogy to contemporary, limit-smashing experiments (as with concrete poetry, sound poetry, intermedia, happenings, etc.). Since tribal poetry was almost always part of a larger situation (i.e. was truly intermedia), there was no more reason to present the words alone as independent structures than the ritual-events, say, or the pictographs arising from the same source. Where possible, in fact, one might present or translate *all* elements connected with the total "poem"—a concern that continues into the present book.

From 1968 on, I followed a number of such concerns into a concentration on Indian tribal poetry, which seemed for obvious reasons most relevant to where-we-all-are in U.S.A. As poet I was able to experiment with more direct approaches to translation: (1) in collaboration with Seneca songmen, who acted at the very least as intermediary translators, & from whom I could get a clearer picture of how the poetry (songs, prayers, orations, visions, dreams, etc.) fitted into the life; & (2) through working with ethnomusicologist David McAllester on cooperative translation from Navajo of *The 17 Horse-Songs of Frank Mitchell*. With McAllester & on my own, I became interested in the possibility of "total translation"— a term I use for translation (of oral poetry in particular) that takes into account any or all elements of the original beyond the words. All of which (plus a growing sense of the grandeur & significance of Indian poetry & thought whether partially or totally translated) led me to the idea of a book that would offer a new look at all that in the light of the possibilities of poetry opening to us in this very time & place.

Unlike *Technicians* this gathering is almost completely a poet's book, & that in itself is an important step toward the larger work of translation & recovery I'd been hoping to develop. Several included herein had already been working in this area: Bill Merwin for at least the previous decade but with more recent emphasis on Plains Indian texts out of Lowie; Edward Field going the length of a book of adaptations from Rasmussen's Eskimo collections; Carl Cary working from anthropological texts & also from his earlier Skagit contacts; & James Koller naturalizing works from Tlingit & Sioux toward an immediate grasp of some of the levels of vision they represent. Some others responded directly to my request for help—Schwerner, Berg & Hollo with greatest energy; Tarn equally so, but bringing to it also a considerable personal acquaintance with the contemporary Mayans of Guatemala—working from earlier translations into French, Spanish & German, or from English versions that had failed to match the life of their sources. But new works by anthropologists were important too, especially where they disclosed actual structural possibilities or ways of showing those in translation: Dennis Tedlock's total translations of Zuni narratives, say, which forever did away with the idea that "prose" could be the medium of a spoken narrative, or Munro Edmonson's verse reconstruction of the *Popol Vuh*. To say nothing of McAllester's Navajo horse-songs, which were the solid basis for whatever workings I was then able to perform.

In each case the translator's voice is very different—which is the way it should be. For the translator—if he's to match the interest of the original—must extend its meanings into his own language & by means of his own voice. (This assumes a poet's voice to begin with.) He needn't lose his personhood but may extend that too & make it real—in translation as well as in any of his other workings. This has always been the way of the great poet-translators—Catullus or Chaucer or Marpa or Pound—& its beginnings here may hopefully mark the real emergence of Indian poetry into the consciousness of the non-Indian world.

Hopefully too it may coincide with Indian efforts to hold, expand or (for many) to return to the sources of their own power—even to understand that power as not only particular to its immediate place-of-origin, but as part of an historically proven & worldwide manifestation of such poetic & trans-poetic powers.

3.

As an arrangement of "classical" American poetry (i.e. of poetry in the first languages of America & representing modes or models for tribes present & to come), this anthology isn't more than a beginning. It tries above all to show the range of such poetries in the Americas north of Panama, but shies away from a division by region & tribe or from representing the major tribes & nations in anything like just proportions. (The reader who wants to see how the book breaks down along such lines can check the tribal index on page 402.) Even so, I hope the gathering is a true reflection of Indian poetry (at least of some of its faces) that would be of use to those alive & growing in the 1970s.

With a sense too that the best minds in our own culture & counter-culture will be freely rearranging any such collection, I've deliberately avoided an organization into very tight compartments. Certain works (particularly those that involve new approaches to translation or act as mini-anthologies of specialized kinds) I've isolated under separate headings; otherwise the poetry appears in four miscellaneous sections or services ("service" in the sense of a religious ritual), with each one corresponding to an evening's public reading under those circumstances in which we commonly share poetry with one another. Any other organizing principles are either self-evident or dealt with in the "commentaries" section, in which I also try to establish contexts for the poems where possible or useful, & to carry forward discussions of Indian & tribal poetry, philosophy or history as lightly touched on in this introduction. Unlike the parallel section in *Technicians*, I've here chosen not to make much of the considerable analogies between the native American classics & the work of our contemporary poets. (I do, on the other hand, say more about the poetry's relation to our own social & environmental dilemmas.) This is partly because *Technicians* already exists as a guide to all that, but mostly from a sense that these levels of poetry are so fundamental & deep-seated in human consciousness that they need no justification by resemblance to anything else in this world. Not once the old definitions have been laid to rest.

After which, it only remains to acknowledge the help I've gotten along the way & to stress again the cooperative nature of most of what's going on here. The suggestion for a pan-Indian book came from Ann London, who had hoped to do it as the first issue of a poetry magazine she was starting in Buffalo, & many of the pieces I'm printing here were originally gathered for that effort. My own experiments with oral translation were helped by a grant-in-aid from the Wenner-Gren Foundation, which followed in turn from Stanley Diamond's suggestion that I try an in-the-field translation project. I'm grateful to him for that, but also for the conscience & intelligence he's brought to bear both on anthropology & poetry—& the same holds true for David McAllester, without whose generosity the most experimental of these pieces would never have happened. Then, too, I owe great thanks to Richard Johnny John & Avery Jimerson (both for what they gave & what they withheld), as I do to all the poets & translators who are included in these pages & to many (but particularly Gary Snyder, Simon Ortiz & Larry Bird) who aren't. Anne Freedgood, Mary Dick & Janet Kafka were my editors at Doubleday; Fran Gazze was my designer; Lennie Neufeld & Kathy Acker read the script with me; Loren Shakely & Dan Dyer typed it; Matthew helped me sing the songs; & Diane shared her empathy & knowledge.

But the deepest gratitude I have is for those sacred poets, named & unnamed in this book, who first saw the visions & who spoke & sang the words.

Jerome Rothenberg

1969/1971

PRELUDES

what the informant said to Franz Boas in 1920

Keresan

long ago her mother
had to sing this song and so
she had to grind along with it
the corn people have a song too
it is very good
I refuse to tell it

— *English working by Armand Schwerner*

THANK YOU: A POEM IN SEVENTEEN PARTS

Seneca

1.

Now so many people that are in this place.
In our meeting place.
It starts when two people see each other.
They greet each other.
Now we greet each other.
Now he thought.
I will make the Earth where some people can walk around.
I have created them, now this has happened.
We are walking on it.
Now this time of day.
This is the way it should be in our minds.

2.

Now he thought.
There should be grass & weeds should be all over the Earth.
Now this has happened.
Now he thought.
From this.
There should be some that will be used for medicine.
Now it blocks the way of it.
We aren't here forever.
Now this time of day.
We give thanks for grass & weeds.
This is the way it should be in our minds.

3.

Now he thought.
I will make Springs.
Where water will be coming from.
On this Earth.
There will be Springs.
The Rivers & the Lakes.
He thought.
There will be no trouble finding them.
Wherever you are on this Earth.
Now this time of day.
We give thanks for the things we named.
This is the way it should be in our minds.

4.

Now he thought.
There should be bushes & also the Forest.
He thought.
The people can keep warm from it.
Now a certain tree is there.
He gave authority for it to be the Head One.
In the Forest.
People will call it Maple.
There is a certain time here.
When water will be coming from it.
He thought.
The people could make use of it.
Now this has happened.
The water was flowing when the warm weather came to Earth.
Now this time of day.
We give thanks for the bushes, Forest & Maple.
This is the way it should be in our minds.

5.

Now he thought.
I will do this.
He left it for us.
Something that should be for the people's happiness.
They will be strong in body from it.
He left us all this food.
He scattered this all over the Earth.
Now we will give *one* thanks.
That he has left us all this food to live on.
On this Earth.
This is the way it should be in our minds.

6.

Now where the grass grows.
The first berry that ripens will be called the short strawberry.
He thought.
They should give thanks among themselves & also give thanks to him.
For all persons that are left on this Earth.
Now this time of day.
We give thanks for the Strawberries.
This is the way it should be in our minds.

7.

Now on this Earth.
He found out.
The Earth was so barren.
He made the animals & for them to be running around.
This is for the people to enjoy.
Now this has happened.
We give thanks for the animals running around on this Earth.
This is the way it should be in our minds.

8.

Now another thing   In the Air-&-Wind
He made the fluttering of the birds there.
& the different sounds of the birds.
This is for the people to hear.
This is for them to enjoy who I made for it.
Now this time of day.
Now we give thanks for the Birds that are fluttering in the air.
This is the way it should be in our minds.

9.

Now he thought.
At a certain place.
From which the air is moving around everywhere.
They will breathe easily by it.
While walking around on this earth.
Now this is happening.
Just the way he thought it to be happening.
Now this time of day.
We give thanks for the Air.
For the place with the net on it.
Which is making the Air move everywhere on Earth.
This is the way it should be in our minds.

10.

Now he thought.
I will give authority to them to carry the dampness & the Rain
    with them.
They will take care of rivers also to dampen the gardens.
Now this has happened he has these servants now.
He also made it
so that we are relatives.
The people should call them Our Grandparents.
The Thunderers.
Now this time of day.
We give thanks to the Thunderers.
For they come from the West.
This is the way it should be in our minds.

11.

Now he thought.
There should be a sky over their heads.
So they can look up at it.
Now this has happened.
We look up to see the sky over our heads.
Now this time of day.
We give thanks for the Sky.
This is the way it should be in our minds.

12.

Now in the sky.
He created two things.
That they should be in the sky.
They are the ones to give light.
So the people could see where they are going.
The people I created.
Now this has happened.
At this time of day.
There is plenty of light.
He has given authority.
To the one who gives light for the days to have light.
Now this time of day.
We give thanks to our Brother the Sun.
This is the way it should be in our minds.

13.

Now when the Sun has rested.
Because there is a length of time that he passes over the Earth.
The shadow will pass over the earth.
Now he has authorized another.
She will be the one to give light
so that everything will go on all right if something should happen
    to the families by night.
Now he has given her more things to do.
He has authorized her to take care of the months.
She just changes from one end of the month to the other.
Also there are little ones being born.
The people count it by these months.
Now this time of day.
We give thanks to our Grandmother the Moon.
This is the way it should be in our minds.

14.

Now in the sky.
He thought.
I will create all around her.
The stars will be all over the sky.
In the past.
They all had names also directions so that nothing would go wrong
   wherever you were on this earth.
It is still the same way that he made it.
Now we will set our minds yes we will give thanks for all the
   Stars in the sky.
This is the way it should be in our minds.

15.

Now.
He found out.
On this Earth.
All kinds of evil had come to it.
From a small item even.
Even just thinking it you were creating this evilness.
Now he thought
I will come in through this person.
He will be the one to tell them what I think of it.
He picked out Handsome Lake.
Yes he is to tell these people.
What they should follow.
Now this has happened.
Now we hear the Word of our Creator.
Now this time of day.
We give thanks to our Big Man
Handsome Lake.
This is the way it should be in our minds.

16.

Now he thought yes I should have servants.
Yes four Beings should be enough.
To protect the ones I had created.
Now this is in their power.
They are doing the job that he handed them.
Now we give thanks to the Four Beings.
This is the way it should be in our minds.

17.

Now he thought.
At a certain place.
I will stay there.
All that I made will be finding its end in it.
Now this time of day.
We have given our word & our thanks for it.
For whatever he gave us.
Now this time of day.
We will give him our thanks for it.
At this time of day.
This is the way it should be in our minds.

— English version by Richard Johnny John

THE ARTIST

Aztec

The artist: disciple, abundant, multiple, restless.
The true artist: capable, practicing, skillful;
maintains dialogue with his heart, meets things with his mind.
The true artist: draws out all from his heart,
works with delight, makes things with calm, with sagacity,
works like a true Toltec, composes his objects, works dexterously,
    invents;
arranges materials, adorns them, makes them adjust.

The carrion artist: works at random, sneers at the people,
makes things opaque, brushes across the surface of the face of things,
works without care, defrauds people, is a thief.

    — *English version by Denise Levertov*

song of the bald eagle

Crow

we want what is real
we want what is real
don't deceive us!

SHAKING THE PUMPKIN

SONGS & OTHER CIRCUMSTANCES
FROM THE SOCIETY OF THE MYSTIC ANIMALS
Seneca

ENGLISH VERSIONS BY
JEROME ROTHENBERG & RICHARD JOHNNY JOHN

. . . but if everything's all right
the one who says the prayer tells them:
I leave it up to you folks & if you want to have
a good time, have a good time!

12 SONGS TO WELCOME
THE SOCIETY OF THE MYSTIC ANIMALS

(1)

T
h
e

The animals are coming by

n
i
m
a
l
s

H E H E H H E H

H E H E H H E H

H E H **U** **H** H E H

H E H E H H E H

H E H E H H E H

(2)

```
T
h
e
                    o
The doings were beginning
                    e
o
i
n
g
s
```

H E H E H H E H

H E H E H H E H

H E H U H H E H

H E H E H H E H

H E H E H H E H

(3)

```
T
h
e
            t
The doings were begun
o         o
i
n
g
s
```

H E H E H H E H

H E H E H H E H

H E H U H H E H

H E H E H H E H

H E H E H H E H

(4)

A

A she-loon too soon
  h
  e
  -
  l
  o
  o
  n

H A H A H H A H
H A H A H H A H
H A H U H H A H
H A H A H H A H
H A H A H H A H

(5)

A

A he-loon soon too
  e
  -
  l
  o
  o
  n

H A H A H H A H
H A H A H H A H
H A H U H H A H
H A H A H H A H
H A H A H H A H

(6)

```
T
h
e
'
e
       o
She drifts on the water
r         e
i
f
t
s
```

H O H O H H O H
H O H O H H O H
H O H **U** **H** H O H
H O H O H H O H
H O H O H H O H

(7)

```
T
h
e
          t
He drifts on her water
r          o
i
f
t
s
```

H O H O H H O H
H O H O H H O H
H O H **U** **H** H O H
H O H O H H O H
H O H O H H O H

T
h
e
Caw caw the crow comes at us
  r   n
  o   e
  w

```
H E Y E Y H E Y
H E Y E Y H E Y
H E Y U Y H E Y
H E Y E Y H E Y
H E Y E Y H E Y
```

(9)

T
h
e
Caw caw the crow who's there
  r w
 ·o o
  w

```
H E Y E Y H E Y
H E Y E Y H E Y
H E Y U Y H E Y
H E Y E Y H E Y
H E Y E Y H E Y
```

(10)

```
S H E   W A S
C  s h e s n a  R
A  w a s h n m  U
M  r r r e i e  N
E  r r u w n i  N
I  n n i a n n  I
N  n n g s g H  N
H  a s s r a I  G
I  h e c r s G  A
G  a m e r s H  S
H  i n H r h H  S
H  I G H r e E  H
E  H E Y u c Y  E
Y  H E Y H E Y  Y
```

(11)

```
H E   W A S
C  h e w h n m  R
A  a s r e n e  U
M  r u n w i i  N
E  n n n a n n  N
I  n i n s g H  I
N  g a s r a I  N
H  h e c r s G  G
I  a m e u h H  A
G  i n H n e H  S
H  I G H n c E  H
E  H E Y n a Y  E
Y  H E Y H E Y  Y
```

THE SONGS

```
I   t h e t r i   B
S   s o n h e r   E
T   g s b e P n   G
H   e g i s U a   I
E   n h e o M m   N
I   r e P n P e   H
R   U M P g K H   E
N   K I N s I I   R
A   S i s b N G   E
M   t h e e S H   P
E   i r n g i H   U
H   a m e i s E   M
I   H I G n t E   P
G   H H E h h e   K
H   E E Y e e y   I
H   E E Y e e y   N
```

. . . Now I'm dumping the whole bag of songs in the middle,

& each of you can sing whichever ones you want . . .

A SONG OF MY SONG, IN THREE PARTS

It's off in the distance.

&

It came into the room.

●

It's here in the circle.

CAW CAW THE CROWS CAW CAW

(1)

the crows came in

(2)

the crows sat down

TWO MORE ABOUT A CROW, IN THE MANNER OF ZUKOFSKY

(1)

Yond cawcrow's way-out

(2)

Hog (yes!) swine you're mine

h   h
i   o   o   i
g   o   o   g
h   o   h
h   h
o   o
y   THE OWL (1)   y
a   whose home was in   a
         the hemlock
h   h
o   o
o   o
o   THE OWL (2)   o
o   could cure   o
o   by poison   o
o   o
o   o
o   THE OWL (3)   o
o   a hollow tree   o
o   & whistling   o
o   o
o   o
h   h

HE ASKED THEM WHAT DID THEY KNOW & THEY TOLD HIM

i know all
about these
different
villages is
all i know

highyohoweyyehheyhighyohoweyyehheyhighyohoweyyeh

i know
all about these
different
hills is
all i know

highyohoweyyehheyhighyohoweyyehheyhighyohoweyyeh

i know all
about
these different
rivers is
all i know

highyohoweyyehheyhighyohoweyyehheyhighyohoweyyeh

```
hiiiiiiiiiiiiiiiiiiiiiiiiiiiiiiiiiiiiiiiiiiih
e                                            e
e        THREE WAYS TO SCREW UP              e
e      ON YOUR WAY TO THE DOINGS             e
e             THREE WAYS                     e
e                                            e
hiiiiiiiiiiiiiiiiiiiiiiiiiiiiiiiiiiiiiiiiiiih
```

(1)

I fell down

(2)

I got lost

(3)

I lost my bucket

h	ganeewa ganeewaha	i
e		f
r		
		s
h	ganeewa ganeewaha	h
o		e
u		
s		s
e	ganeewa ganeewaha	h
		o
		u
c		l
o	ganeewa ganeewaha	d
u		
l		m
d		o
	ganeewa ganeewaha	c
b		k
u		
r		u
n	(i mean this woman)	s

OF THREE FRIENDLY WARNINGS THIS IS THE FIRST

A POEM ABOUT A WOLF MAYBE TWO WOLVES

he comes running
across the field where
he comes running

he comes running
along the hill where
he comes running

HEY WHEN I SING THIS SET OF 4 SONGS
LOOK WHAT HAPPENS!

hey when i sing
hey it can help her
yeah it can yeah it's so strong
hey when i sing
hey it can raise her
yeah it can yeah it's so strong
hey when i sing
hey her arm gets straighter
yeah it can yeah it's so strong
hey when i sing
hey her body gets straighter
yeah it can yeah it's so strong

WHERE THE SONG WENT WHERE SHE WENT
& WHAT HAPPENED WHEN THEY MET

the song went to the garden	(heh heh heh)
the song poked all around the garden	(heh heh heh)
she went to the garden	(heh heh heh)
she went to the garden	(heh heh heh)
she went like crazy in the garden	(heh heh heh)
that's where she went	(hah hah hah)

A SONG ABOUT A DEAD PERSON—OR WAS IT A MOLE?

YOHOHEYHEYEYHEYHAHYEYEYHAHHEH
I was going thru the big earth

    YOHOHEYHEYEYHEYHAHYEYEYHAHHEH
                 I went thru this big earth

    YOHOHEYHEYEYHEYHAHYEYEYHAHHEH
        I was going thru the big earth

    YOHOHEYHEYEYHEYHAHYEYEYHAHHEH
           I went thru this big earth

    YOHOHEYHEYEYHEYHAHYEYEYHAHHEH
           I was going thru the big earth

    YOHOHEYHEYEYHEYHAHYEYEYHAHHEH
I went thru this big earth

    YOHOHEYHEYEYHEYHAHYEYEYHAHHEH
                    I was going

    YOHOHEYHEYEYHEYHAHYEYEYHAHHEH
th

    YOHOHEYHEYEYHEYHAHYEYEYHAHHEH

    YOHOHEYHEYEYHEYHAHYEYEYHAHHEH

    YOHOHEYHEYEYHEYHAHYEYEYHAHHEH

ANOTHER SONG ABOUT THAT SAME DEAD PERSON
OR MOLE–WHICHEVER IT WAS

YOHOHEYHEYEYHEYHAHYEYEYHAHHEH
I was going thru the big smoke

YOHOHEYHEYEYHEYHAHYEYEYHAHHEH
I went thru this big smoke

YOHOHEYHEYEYHEYHAHYEYEYHAHHEH
I was going thru the big smoke

YOHOHEYHEYEYHEYHAHYEYEYHAHHEH
I went thru this big smoke

YOHOHEYHEYEYHEYHAHYEYEYHAHHEH
I was going thru the big smoke

YOHOHEYHEYEYHEYHAHYEYEYHAHHEH
I went thru this big smoke

YOHOHEYHEYEYHEYHAHYEYEYHAHHEH
I was g

YOHOHEYHEYEYHEYHAHYEYEYHAHHEH
oke

YOHOHEYHEYEYHEYHAHYEYEYHAHHEH

YOHOHEYHEYEYHEYHAHYEYEYHAHHEH

YOHOHEYHEYEYHEYHAHYEYEYHAHHEH

OF THREE FRIENDLY WARNINGS THIS IS THE SECOND

```
h      g a n e e w a      g a n e e w a h a      i
e                                                f
r
                                                 s
s      g a n e e w a      g a n e e w a h a      h
h                                                e
o
e                                                s
s      g a n e e w a      g a n e e w a h a      h
                                                 o
c                                                u
o                                                l
u      g a n e e w a      g a n e e w a h a      d
l
d                                                m
                                                 o
       g a n e e w a      g a n e e w a h a      c
b                                                k
u
r                                                u
n      ( i   m e a n   t h i s   w o m a n )     s
```

```
YO OH HEYA YAH
YO OH HEYA YAH
YO HO HEYA YAH          We made a mistake in this song
YO OH HEYA YAH
YO OH HEYA YAH


YO OH HEYA YAH
YO OH HEYA YAH
YO HO HEYA YAH          We'll have to straighten it out
YO OH HEYA YAH
YO OH HEYA YAH


YO OH HEYA YAH
YO OH HEYA YAH
YO OH HEYA YAH          This time we'll do it right
YO OH HEYA YAH
YO OH HEYA YAH
```

WE GOT EVERYTHING WE NEEDED HERE
& AINT IT SOMETHING!

herezsometobaccozhere
herezsometobaccozhere
herezsometobaccozhere
herezsometobaccozhere
herez**sometobacco**zhere
herezsometobaccozhere
herezsometobaccozhere
herezsometobaccozhere
herezsometobaccozhere

herezsomepigmeatzhere
herezsomepigmeatzhere
herezsomepigmeatzhere
herezsomepigmeatzhere
herez**somepigmeat**zhere
herezsomepigmeatzhere
herezsomepigmeatzhere
herezsomepigmeatzhere
herezsomepigmeatzhere

herezsomeketttlezhere
herezsomeketttlezhere
herezsomeketttlezhere
herezsomeketttlezhere
herez**someketttl**ezhere
herezsomeketttlezhere
herezsomeketttlezhere
herezsomeketttlezhere
herezsomeketttlezhere

herezsomemusssshzhere
herezsomemusssshzhere
herezsomemusssshzhere
herezsomemusssshzhere
herez**somemusssh**zhere
herezsomemusssshzhere
herezsomemusssshzhere
herezsomemusssshzhere
herezsomemusssshzhere

WHEN HF SAYS SO WE DANCE IN ALL DIRECTIONS—WOW!

YOHOWEYAH
YOHOWEYAH
YOWEYHEEE
YOWEYHEEE
YOWEYHIGHEEEHEH
YOHOWEYAH
YOWEYHEEE
FROM THE
SWAMPS IS
WHERE ? I
COME FROM
YOWEYHIGHEEEHEH
YOHOWEYAH
YOHOWEYAH
YOWEYHEEE
YOWEYHEEE
YOWEYHIGHEEEHEH
YOHOWEYAH
YOWEYHEEE
BEHIND THE
EARTH IS
WHERE ? I
COME FROM
YOWEYHIGHEEEHEH
YOHOWEYAH
YOHOWEYAH
YOWEYHEEE
YOWEYHEEE
YOWEYHIGHEEEHEH
YOHOWEYAH
YOWEYHEEE
BEHIND THE
HILLS IS
WHERE ? I
COME FROM
YOWEYHIGHEEEHEH
YOHOWEYAH
YOHOWEYAH
YOWEYHEEE
YOWEYHEEE
YOWEYHIGHEEEHEH
BEHIND THE
EARTH IS
WHERE ? I
COME FROM
YOWEEI'MDANCING
WOW

OF THREE FRIENDLY WARNINGS THIS IS THE THIRD

her leggings could burn

ganeewa   ganeewaha

ganeewa   ganeewaha

ganeewa   ganeewaha

ganeewa   ganeewaha

ganeewa   ganeewaha

(i mean this woman)

if she should mock us

PLENTY OF FLOWERS
h   h
i   e
i   e
i   e
i   PLENTY OF FLOWERS   e
i   WHERE I'M WALKING   e
i   i
g   g
h   h
WHERE I'M WALKING

CAT TAILS ARE GROWING
h   h
i   e
i   e
i   e
i   CAT TAILS ARE GROWING e
i   WHERE I'M WALKING   e
i   i
g   g
h   h
WHERE I'M WALKING

I WAS SURPRISED TO FIND MYSELF OUT HERE
& ACTING LIKE A CROW

i didnt think i'd
shake the pumpkin
not just here & now
not exactly tonite
yahooondaaaaaheee
yohaaaaheeeeyooho
hohgaahaaaayeyhey
yohaaaaheeeeyoohoho

i didnt think i'd
rip some meat off
not just here & now
not exactly tonite
yahooondaaaaaheee
yohaaaaheeeeyooho
hohgaahaaaayeyhey
yohaaaaheeeeyoohoho

A FIRST SERVICE

> *Directions:* Use the language of shamans. Say "he turned my mind around" & mean "he told me something."
>
> *Eskimo*

MAGIC WORDS & MORE MORE MORE MAGIC WORDS

Eskimo

Magic Words (after Nalungiaq)

In the very earliest time,
when both people and animals lived on earth,
a person could become an animal if he wanted to
and an animal could become a human being.
Sometimes they were people
and sometimes animals
and there was no difference.
All spoke the same language.
That was the time when words were like magic.
The human mind had mysterious powers.
A word spoken by chance
might have strange consequences.
It would suddenly come alive
and what people wanted to happen could happen—
all you had to do was say it.
Nobody could explain this:
That's the way it was.

Magic Words to Feel Better (by Nakasuk)

SEA GULL
who flaps his wings
over my head
       in the blue air,

you GULL up there
dive down
      come here
take me with you
       in the air!

Wings flash by
my mind's eye
and I'm up there sailing
in the cool air,
      a-a-a-a-a-ah,
        in the air.

Magic Words for Hunting Caribou

You, you, caribou
yes you
      long legs
yes you
      long ears
you with the long neck hair—
From far off you're little as a louse:
Be my great swan, fly to me,
big bull
      cari-bou-bou-bou.

Put your footprints on this land—
this land I'm standing on
is rich with the plant food you love.
See, I'm holding in my hand
the reindeer moss you're dreaming of—
so delicious, yum, yum, yum—
Come, caribou, come.

Come on, move them bones,
move your leg bones back and forth
and give yourself to me.
I'm here,
I'm waiting
      just
        for
          YOU
you, you, caribou
APPEAR!
COME HERE!

Magic Words for Hunting Seal

O sea goddess Nuliajuk,
when you were a little unwanted orphan girl
we let you drown.
You fell in the water
and when you hung onto the kayaks, crying,
we cut off your fingers.
So you sank into the sea
and your fingers turned into
the innumerable seals.

You sweet orphan Nuliajuk,
I beg you now
bring me a gift,
not anything from the land
but a gift from the sea,
something that will make a nice soup.
Dare I say it right out?
I want a seal!

You dear little orphan,
creep out of the water
panting on this beautiful shore,
puh, puh, like this, puh, puh,
O welcome gift
in the shape of a seal!

— English workings by Edward Field, from Knud Rasmussen

moon eclipse exorcism

Alsea

come out come out come out
the moon has been killed

> who kills the moon? crow
> who often kills the moon? eagle
> who usually kills the moon? chicken
>   hawk
> who also kills the moon? owl
> in their numbers they assemble
> for moonkilling

come out, throw sticks at your houses
come out, turn your buckets over
spill out all the water don't let it turn
bloody yellow
from the wounding and death
of the moon

o what will become of the world, the moon
never dies without cause
only when a rich man is about to be killed
is the moon murdered

look all around the world, dance, throw your sticks, help out,
look at the moon,
>   *dark as it is now, even if it disappears*
it will come back, think of nothing
I'm going back into the house
>   and the others went back

— English working by Armand Schwerner

poem to ease birth

Aztec

in the house with the tortoise chair
   she will give birth to the pearl
               to the beautiful feather

in the house of the goddess who sits on a tortoise
   she will give birth to the necklace of pearls
               to the beautiful feathers we are

there she sits on the tortoise
   swelling to give us birth

on your way on your way
   child be on your way to me here
             you whom I made new

come here child   come be pearl
              be beautiful feather

— English version by Anselm Hollo

CROW VERSIONS

1

I am making
 a wind come here

 it's coming

2

Child listen
 I am singing

 with my ear on the ground

 and we love you

                    (by White-arm)

3

Your way
 is turning bad

 and nobody but you
 is there

4

If all of me is still there
 when spring comes
 I'll make a hundred poles

and put something on top
sun

for you
you

right there I'll make a small sweat lodge
it's cold
I'll sprinkle charcoal

at the end of it
my death

sun
it will all be for you

I want to be still there
that's why I'll do it

thank you

I want to be alive

If my people multiply
I'll make it for you

I'm saying
may no one be sick

so I make it

so

(by Plenty-hawk)

5

If there is someone above
who knows what happens

You

today I have trouble
give me something to make it
not so

if there is someone inside the earth
who knows what happens

I have trouble today
give me something
to make it not so

whatever makes these things
now just as I am
I have enough

give me just for me
my death

I have enough sadness

(by Double-face)

6

He was there
    Old Man Coyote

Water all over the earth
no animals

He looked around
    grabbed

    and there was a little bird

    a swallow
    they say

He told it Go down
    bring earth

    it brought none

Then a crow
    Go down
    get some mud

    it brought none

Wolf
    you bring it

    it brought none

Old Man said
    Nothing I can do

    grabbed a duck
    then duck gone

    it's gone

he said to himself it won't be back
    he brought earth

    made this world
    here

    then mud people
    mud man
    mud woman

at that time
    with only that much mud
    that was how

Afterward there was a baby
    a boy

then he had a baby
    a girl

so

    as they say again and again
    now there was
    being born

    more people
    came to be

    you get married
    you make others

                    (by Medicine-tail)

7

I am climbing
    everywhere is

    coming up

— *English versions by W. S. Merwin, after Robert Lowie*

A POEM FOR CATCHING TURTLES

(Tule/Cuna)

1.

I am going to shoot a little bird
to tame the turtle with it
now I bring it home & hide it
put it in a little clay stove until it burns to ashes
mix the ashes with red medicine
(medicine I made up from some tree sap)
then cut a little round gourd in two cutting the top off very neatly
with my knife I scrape its insides
smooth & clean just like a cup
& put the medicine into this cup—
ashes of bird mixed with red tree sap
now I tie the cover on tightly
put it in my trunk & don't tell anybody

And every night for eight nights I take the gourd out of my trunk
smooth round gourd with top tied on so tightly
I put cocoa beans onto a little fire & smoke the gourd
singing this song while the smoke curls around it
      "Little bird, I saw you
      "& I knew you'd be a good bird for catching turtles
      "which is why I shot you
      "So now if you don't tame the turtle
      "everyone will say you're not a good bird
      "but I know that you'll tame the turtle
      "then I'll make lots of money
      "I'll buy a gun a shirt & lots of things I like"
After the eighth night of singing my partner comes
we go down to my canoe
I put the gourd down carefully in the middle of the canoe
I've got a long pole a spearhead & a line
spearhead will be fastened on the pole
with which I'll spear the turtle

2.

Now I'm talking to the medicine in the gourd
& saying
        "When we get out to the ocean
        "I'm going to send you down under the water
        "I'm going to send you down to attract the turtle
        "& when you get to the water bottom
        "that's when you'll put on your pretty blue dress
        "to make that turtle come to you
        "Change your dresses often
        "if the turtle's got a yellow dress
        "you've got to put on a yellow dress
        "if the turtle's got a white dress
        "you've got to put on a white dress
        "if the turtle's got on a blue dress
        "you've got to put on a blue dress
        "you've got to do that to attract him
        "& when you get the turtle
        "bring him up to the canoe & let me spear him
        "Tell the turtle that the man who sent you isn't going to
           spear him
        "I'm only going to take his shell off & send him back where
           he came from
        "So you can catch lots of turtles for me
        "& everyone will say that you're a good bird"

—*Translation by Frances Densmore, with working by Jerome Rothenberg*

ARCHAIC SONG OF DR. TOM THE SHAMAN

Nootka

I know thee. My name is Tom.
I want to find thy sickness. I know thy sickness.
I will take thy sickness. My name is Tom. I am a strong doctor.
If I take thy sickness thou wilt see thy sickness.
My name is Tom. I don't lie. My name is Tom. I don't talk shit.
I am a doctor. Many days I haven't eaten.
Ten days maybe I haven't eaten. I don't have my tools with me.
I don't have my sack with me. My name is Tom.
I will take thy sickness now & thou wilt see it.

—Working by Jerome Rothenberg, after James Teit

MAGIC WORDS from RUN TOWARD THE NIGHTLAND

Cherokee

1.

Now! The Red Tobacco has come to strike your soul.

I have just come from the treetops: I have just come to step over you.

Ha! Do not think it too far: face your feet this way.

Ha! Without knowing it, you have just come to my door: let your soul be anxious.

Seven! You will be leaving your home, leading your soul toward me.

Now tonight—Seven!—you will be thinking of me: you will think that I am the only one living.

And I will let you go when the sun rises.

going to the bank at dawn he smokes the tobacco toward where the desired woman lives, after which he washes his face four times: he then smokes again at noon & at dusk: the smoking is done for four days

2.

I came from up there Above.
Now I have just come down from where You rest, You Ancient White One.

I have just come around a bend in the Pathway over there: I am not a lonely Crow.
I have just come around the bend: it is good on this side.
Let my soul be let down from Above: let you be the one who greets it.

compelling his runaway wife to return

Ha! You White Woman, you hunt your lonely soul, which will be moving about here and there.

Ha! In a friendly fashion the Sparrow Hawk has just flown in.

Ha! They will be offering you the body of a Crow. *"Gha:!"*

He corners me! *"Mi:?!"*

They have just come to tell me that your soul is very lonely.

Now and then lonely Eyes will be living with you.

I am a man! I hunt your very lonely soul that lives about here and there.

I am a good one! My soul will not be appearing about, lonely.

My body is not lonely: you will find rest in my body.

3.

Your Pathways are Black: it was wood, not a human being!

Dog shit will cling nastily to you.

You will be living intermittently. *"Grr!"*
You will be saying along toward the Nightland.

Your Black Guts will be lying all about. You will be lonely.

You will be like the Brown Dog in heat. You are changed: you have just become old.
This is your clan.

In the very middle of the Prairie, changed, you will be carrying dog turds. *"Grr!"* you will be saying.

Your Pathway lies toward the Nightland!

for making an enemy insane: one merely states the name & clan of the victim, delivers the incantation four times, & then blows one's breath toward him after each rendition

4.

Now! *Ha*! It was our Mother in front of You & me: a smooth tree leaf.

You and I have just come to cut the eyes and the souls of the people in the Seven Clan Districts.

A great wind has just thundered over our souls four times.

Thought has just descended in a column, face downward, and has just joined their souls that have just sunk into the sea.

for making them forget, to lessen argument, etc.

5.

The Black Men, those great Wizards who just arose in the Nightland, have just come to take away your soul. Seven!

a spell for remembering

They have just gone in through the Nightland, so that you will not know it.

They have just finished putting Seven Shadows over the Very Yellow Water.

They have just arrived, carrying your soul. Seven!

They are not to help you climb over. Seven!

The Black Men, those great Wizards, have just carried away your soul. Seven!

— *Translations by Jack Frederick Kilpatrick & Anna Gritts Kilpatrick*

THE KILLER
(after A'yunini)

Cherokee

Careful: my knife drills your soul
        listen, whatever-your-name-is
        One of the wolf people
listen   I'll grind your saliva into the earth
listen   I'll cover your bones with black flint
listen   *"   "   "   "   "   "* feathers
listen   *"   "   "   "   "   "* rocks
Because you're going where it's empty
        Black coffin out on the hill
listen   the black earth will hide you, will
        find you a black hut
        Out where it's dark, in that country
listen   I'm bringing a box for your bones
        A black box
        A grave with black pebbles
listen   your soul's spilling out
listen   it's blue

— Jerome Rothenberg's working, after James Mooney

THE ARCHER'S DANCE SONG

Maya

Look,
    stalker, mountain hunter,
  once,
      twice
we're going to dance/hunt
    up to where the trees begin
three times in all.

Keep your head up
  look around
      don't make any mistakes that
      will lose you the game.

Were you careful to?
  1. file down your arrowhead
  2. stretch your bowstring tight
  3. resin the feathers with *catzim*
      down to the endknob of your arrowshaft
  4. smear the fat from a stag in rut
      on the power of your arm
      on the power of your foot
      on your knees
      on your balls
      on your ribs
      on your chest
      over your heart

NOW

    dance three times around
    the painted stone shaft

where the young man is
lashed
virile, virgin, perfect

first time around

second time around

take your bow
fit the arrow
aim at his chest
but don't shoot with all your strength
or tear into his flesh too deep

let him suffer a little while

because this is the way

Lord God
wanted it.

The next time
you dance around the (painted blue) shaft
shoot him
again

you must do this thing without
a break in the dance because
that is how the good fighters,
the ones with shields, do it

men who were chosen
to please
the eyes of
Lord God

        As soon as the sun looks out
    over the eastern woods
  comes
the song of the archer

They do it all
            the shieldbearers
            the fighters

            — *English version by Ann London*

SNAKE MEDICINE POEM FOR A TOOTHACHE

Creek

coiled up on the road
on a long stick   coiled up
at the water's edge
he was coiled up
& coiled up around a branch
& was coiled up on a hollow tree
he kept on hissing
waiting   making a noise
he was a stone in the grass
coiled up there &
waiting   making a noise
on a long stick
coiled up there &
waiting   making a noise
in the sun / on the road
coiled up there &
hisssssSSSSssSSssssSSSsss

—Working by Jerome Rothenberg, after Frank Speck

SNAKE MEDICINE POEM FOR A SNAKE

Yokuts

says the kingsnake to the rattler:
don't you touch me Jack
there's nothing you can do to me
the way you're lying
                           with your belly full
big rattler on the rockpile
just don't touch me
no there's nothing you can do to me
your belly's too full
lying where the squirrel holes are thick
don't you dare & touch me
what you thinking you can do to me?
big rattler in the tree clump
stretched out in the shade
there's nothing you can do to anyone
don't touch me Jack
big rattler in the valley
white eye
the sun is shining on
just you don't touch me!

— English version by Jerome Rothenberg, after Alfred Kroeber

A SONG FROM *RED ANT WAY*

Navajo

The red young men under the ground
decorated with red wheels
& decorated with red feathers
   at the center of the cone-shaped house
   I gave them a beautiful red stone—
   when someone does the same for me
   I'll walk the earth
The black young women under the ground
decorated with black wheels
& decorated with black feathers
   at the center of the flat-topped house
   I gave them an abalone shell—
   when someone does the same for me
   I'll walk the earth
From deep under the earth they're starting off
the old men under the earth are starting off
they're decorated with red wheels & starting off
at the center of the cone-shaped house they're starting off
because I gave them a beautiful red stone they're starting off
when someone does the same for me I'll walk the earth like them &
   starting off
on the red road & on the road they're starting off

The black old women under the earth are starting off
they're decorated with black wheels & starting off
decorated with black feathers & starting off
at the center of the flat-topped house they're starting off
because I gave them an abalone shell they're starting off
when someone does the same for me I'll walk the earth like them &
   starting off
from deep under the earth they're starting off

— Translation by Harry Hoijer, with working by Jerome Rothenberg

THE DEADLY DANCE

Aztec

That shaman, owl man,
　　　　　　　　dressed himself in shining yellow feathers
once he had won.
　　　　　　　Then he planned that the people
should come together and dance.
　　　　　　　　　　So the cryer went to the hill
and announced it,
　　　　　　　and called to all the people.
Everyone in the country around heard him
　　　　　　　　　　　and left quickly for
Texcalapa, that place in the rocky country.
　　　　　　　　　　They all came,
both nobles and the people,
　　　　　　　young men and young women,
so many they could not be counted,
　　　　　　　　　there were so many.
And then he began his song.
　　　　　　　　　He beats his drum,
again and again.
　　　　　　　They begin to join in the dance.
They leap into the air,
　　　　　　　they join hands weaving themselves together,
whirling around, and there is great happiness.
The chant wavers
　　　　　　up and breaks into the air,
returns as an echo from the distant hills
　　　　　　　　　　and sustains itself.
He sang it, he thought of it,
　　　　　　　and they answered him.
As he planned, they took it from his lips.

It began at dusk
               and went on halfway to midnight.
And when the dance
               they all did together
reached its climax,
               numbers of them hurled themselves from the cliffs
into the gulleys.
               They all died and became stones.
Others, who were on the bridge over the canyon,
                                    the shaman broke it
under them
          though it was stone.
They fell in the rapids
               and became stones.
The Toltecs
          never understood what happened there,
they were drunk with it,
                    blind,
and afterwards gathered many times there to dance.
Each time,
          there were more dead,
                         more had fallen from the heights
into the rubble,   .
               and the Toltecs destroyed themselves.

— *English version by Edward Kissam*

A BOOK OF NARRATIVES (I)

A MYTH OF THE HUMAN UNIVERSE

Maya

. . . to be a man and a woman as Sun was, the way he had to put up with Moon, from start to finish the way she was, the way she behaved, and he up against it because he did have the advantage of her, he moved more rapidly. In the beginning he was only young and full of himself, and she, well, she was a girl living with her grandfather doing what a girl was supposed to be doing, making cloth. Even then he had the advantage of her, he hunted, instead, and because he could hunt he could become a humming-bird, which he did, just to get closer to her, this loveliness he thought she was and wanted to taste. Only the trouble was, he had to act out his mask, and while he was coming closer, one tobacco flower to another toward the house, her grandfather brought him down with a clay shot from a blow gun. And sun fell, right into moon's arms, who took him to her room to mother him, for she was all ready to be a wife, a man's second mother as a wife is in these parts where birds are so often stoned and need to be brought back to consciousness and, if they have their wings intact, may fly away again. As sun was. Only he could also talk, and persuaded moon to elope with him in a canoe. But there you are: there is always danger. Grandfather gets rain to throw his fire at them and though sun converts to turtle and is tough enough to escape alive, moon, putting on a crab shell, is not sufficiently protected and is killed.

Which is only part of it, that part of it which is outside and seems to have all of the drama. But only seems. For dragonflies collect moon's flesh and moon's blood in thirteen hollow logs, the sort of log sun had scooped his helpless runaway boat out of, thinking he had made it, had moon finally for his own. Foolish sun. For now here he is back again, after thirteen days, digging out the thirteen logs, and finding that twelve of them contain nothing but all the insects and all the snakes which fly and crawl about the earth of man and pester people in a hot climate so that a lot die off before they are well begun and most are ready, at any instant, for a sickness or a swelling, and the best thing to do is to lie quiet, wait for the poison to pass. For there is log 13, and it reveals moon restored to life, only moon is missing that part which makes woman woman, and deer alone, only deer can give her what he does give her so that she and sun can do what man and woman have the pleasure to do as one respite from the constant hammering.

But you see, nothing lasts. Sun has an older brother, who comes to live with sun and moon, and sun has reason to suspect that something is going on between moon and the big star, for this brother is the third one of the sky, the devilish or waspish one who is so often with moon. By a trick, sun discovers them, and moon, dispirited, sitting off by herself on the river bank, is persuaded by the bird zopilote to go off with him to the house of the king of the vultures himself. And though a vulture is not, obviously, as handsome a thing as the sun, do not be fooled into thinking that this bird which can darken the sky as well as feed on dead things until they are only bones for the sun to whiten, has not his attractions, had not his attractions to moon, especially the king of them all. She took him, made him the third of her men, and was his wife.

But sun was not done with her, with his want of her, and he turned to that creature which empowered her, the deer, for aid. He borrowed a skin, and hiding under it—knowing as hot sun does the habits of vultures—he pretends to be a carcass. The first vulture comes in, landing awkwardly a distance off, hobbles his nervous way nearer until, as he is about to pick apart what he thinks is a small deer, sun leaps on his back and rides off to where moon is. He triumphantly seizes her, only to find that she is somewhat reluctant to return.

At which stage, for reasons of cause or not, sun and moon go up into the sky to assume forever their planetary duties. But sun finds there is one last thing he must do to the moon before human beings are satisfied with her. He must knock out one of her eyes, they complain she is so bright and that they cannot sleep, the night is so much the same as his day, and his day is too much anyhow, and a little of the sweetness of the night they must have. So he does, he puts out her eye, and lets human beings have what they want. But when he does more, when, occasionally, he eclipses her entirely, some say it is only a sign that the two of them continue to fight, presumably because sun cannot forget moon's promiscuity, though others say that moon is forever erratic, is very much of a liar, is always telling sun about the way people of the earth are as much misbehavers as she, get drunk, do the things she does, in fact, the old ones say, moon is as difficult to understand as any bitch is.

— *English working by Charles Olson*

From THE POPOL VUH

Maya

The Destruction of the Dolls

. . . So in fact they were finished off again.
  They were destroyed
And they were broken up
  And killed again,
The dolls
  Carved of wood.
Then their flood was invented by the heart of Heaven.
  A great flood was made, and descended on the heads
Of those who were dolls
  Who were carved of wood.
Of tz'ite was the body of the man
  When he was carved
By Former
  And Shaper.
Woman reed was the body of the woman
  Who was carved
By Former
  And Shaper.
They did not think,
  And they did not speak
Before their Former,
  Their Shaper,
The Maker of them,
  The Creator of them,
And so they were killed;
  They were overwhelmed.
There came a great rain of glue
  Down from the sky.

There came the Rippers of Eyes, as they are called,
  And tore their eyes from their sockets.
There came Killer Bats
  And snatched off their heads.
There came Lurking Jaguar
  And ate their flesh.
There came Aroused Jaguar
  And tore them open,
And shattered their bones
  And their cartilage.
Ground up,
  Crumbled fine
Were their bones.
  The grinding up of their faces was
Because they didn't think before their Mother
  And before their Father,
The Heart of Heaven.
  1 Leg by name.
By them the face of the earth was darkened
  And there began a rain of darkness,
Daytime rain
  And nighttime rain.
There came out the little animals,
  And the big animals.
Their faces were abused by the trees
  And rocks.
And there spoke up all their jars,
  Their griddles,
Their plates,
  Their pots,
Their dogs,
  Their mortars—
However many things—
  Everything
Abused their faces.
  "Pain you have caused us.

You have eaten us,
    And now we are going to eat you back,"
Said their dogs
    And their chickens to them.
And then the grindstones:
    "We have been shattered by you
Every day—
    Every day—
Night and day,
    All the time—
Crunch!
    Crunch!
Scrape!
    Scrape!
On our faces
    You went.
If that was formerly our service to you
    When you were people
Then you can now try
    Our strength.
We shall grind up
    And we shall scrape your flesh,"
Their grindstones said to them.
    And then it was their dogs
That said further
    When they spoke:
"Why was it that you didn't give us our food?
    We just looked on, and you just ate us up.
Whether we lay down here
    Or got up there
We were beaten by you
    While you ate.
You just used to lecture us then;
    We couldn't talk,
And we got nothing from you
    Unless you didn't know about it,

And then when you found out later,
    Then we were lost.
So now you can try
    Our bones
That are in our mouths:
    We shall eat you,"
Their dogs said to them,
    And their face was destroyed.
And so their griddles
    And their pots spoke further to them:
"Pain it was
    You inflicted on us.
Sooty our mouths—
    Sooty our faces.
Aways we were dumped on the fire.
    You burned us.
We felt no pain, so you try it.
    We shall burn you,"
Said all their pots,
    And their face was destroyed.
And there were their rocks
    And their hearthstones
Stretched
    And came from the fire,
Pounding on their heads
    And hurting them.
They tried to run away.
    They were forced to scatter completely then.
They tried to climb on the houses,
    But the houses collapsed and down they fell.
They tried to climb the trees:
    They were thrown off by the trees.
They tried to crawl in the holes,
    But the holes closed in their faces.
And thus was the destruction of the formed people,
    The shaped people.

They were destroyed.
  They were overthrown as people.
They destroyed,
  They crushed
Their mouths,
  Their faces entirely.
And it is said that the remainder
  Are the monkeys that are in the forests today.
That must be the remainder
  Because their bodies were only fixed of wood
By Former
  And Shaper.
So the fact that the monkeys
  Look like people
Is a sign of one generation of formed people,
  Of shaped people,
Only puppets
  And just carved of wood.

— English version by Munro Edmonson

From THE POPOL VUH

Maya

Alligator's Struggles with the 400 Sons

. . . So these then are the deeds of Alligator in turn,
  The first son of 7 Parrot.
"I am the maker of mountains,"
  Said Alligator.
And so Alligator
  Was bathing at the edge of the water
When there passed by
  Four hundred sons,
Hauling a tree,
  A post for their house.
Four hundred of them were walking along,
  And they had cut
A great tree
  For the cross-beam of their house.
And there came Alligator
  And arrived where there were four hundred sons.
"What are you doing,
  You boys?"
"It's just a tree—
  We can't lift it."
"Shoulder it.
  I'll carry it.
Where does it go?
  What sort of use do you want from it?"
"It's just the cross-beam
  Of our house."
"All right,"
  He said then.

And when he had lifted it
  He put it on his shoulder and took it
To the door of the house
  Of the four hundred sons.
"Why don't you stay with us,
  Son?
Where are your mother
  And your father?"
"I have none,"
  He said then.
"Let us perhaps press you then
  To get some more chopped tomorrow,
Another of our beams,
  A post for our house."
"Good,"
  He said again.
And then they took counsel,
  The four hundred sons.
"Here is this boy: what should we do with him?
  Let us kill him,
Because it is not good what he does:
  He lifts the beam all by himself.
Let us dig a big hole here,
  And then we'll make him go down there in the hole.
Go get it;
  Lift the dirt out of the hole, we'll tell him.
And when he is bending over down in the hole,
  Then we can throw a big beam down there
And thus he will die in the hole,"
  The four hundred sons said.
And so they dug a big hole that went very deep
  And then they called Alligator.
"We beg of you,
  Go and dig some more earth.
We can't do it," he was told.
  And he said, "All right,"

And then went down in the hole.
   "Call up
When the dirt is all dug up
   So that you have got really deep,"
He was told.
   "Yes," he said,
And began to dig the hole.
   Only the hole he dug was to save himself.
He knew he was to be killed,
   So he dug a branch in the hole to one side.
The second hole he dug
   Was to save him.
"Well, how far along are you?"
   The four hundred sons shouted down then.
"I'm digging it fast,
   So I'll call you just as soon
As the digging is finished up,"
   Said Alligator from down there in the hole.
But he was not digging the bottom of the hole
   Which was to be his grave,
But rather he was digging his own hole
   As a shelter for himself.
And so when Alligator finally called up,
   He was safe in the earth there in the hole when he called up.
"Come on then.
   Come.
Take the earth,
   The dirt from the hole.
It is all dug.
   I have made it really deep.
Can't you hear my call maybe?
   There it is now, your call,
Only down here
   It echoes
As though you were one remove
   Or two removes away,

It sounds like,"
  Alligator called up from the hole.
But he stayed hidden down there,
  Shouting up from down in the hole.
And so their big beam was dragged over by the boys
  And then they dropped the beam right down into the hole.
"He isn't there.
  He doesn't say anything.
Let's listen now while he groans
  Until he dies,"
They said to each other,
  But they whispered quietly,
And they just hid themselves, each one separately
  When they had dropped the beam down.
And so he spoke.
  Then he groaned.
He called out just once more,
  The moment the beam was dropped.
"Ahah! It is done!
  Very good!
We've done it to him!
  He's dead!
What if further
  He had continued
What he was doing,
  What he was working at?
Why he would have become
  In fact the first,
And imposed himself with us
  And among us!
Even us,
  The four hundred sons!"
They said then,
  And again they rejoiced.
"It will be, for the making of our wine, three days,
  And three days having passed

Let us drink to our home,
  Our house,
Even we,
  The four hundred sons!" they said.
"So tomorrow we'll see,
  And the next day we'll see,
If the ants don't come
  From the ground.
When he is rotted,
  When he is decomposed,
Then it will console our hearts
  When we drink our wine," they said.
And Alligator, there in his hole, heard
  When the boys said "the next day."
And on the second day,
  Then the ants assembled.
They ran about.
  They swarmed around,
And then they got together
  Under the beam.
Quickly they took in their mouths the hair
  And they took in their mouths the nails of Alligator,
And when they saw it,
  The boys said,
"Isn't that devil finished off?
  Just look at the ants!
They have already gathered there.
  They have swarmed there.
They have quickly seized his hair.
  Those are his nails that you can see!
We did it!"
  They said to each other then.
But Alligator was still alive.
  He had just cut the hair off his head.
He had just bitten off his nails
  In order to give them to the ants,

So that the fact that he had died
    Would be known to the four hundred sons.
And so they started on their wine on the third day
    And then all the boys drank heavily,
And all the four hundred sons got drunk
    Until they knew nothing further.
And then their house was pulled down
    On their heads by Alligator.
They were finished off
    And all of them destroyed.
There were not even one
    Or two of the four hundred sons who were saved.
They were killed by Alligator,
    The son of 7 Parrot.
And since they died,
    These four hundred sons,
They are said to have gone to be stars.
    "The Group" is the name for them,
Though that may only be a play on words.

— *English version by Munro Edmonson*

THE ORIGIN OF THE SKAGIT INDIANS ACCORDING TO LUCY WILLIAMS

Suelick is the greatest Indian power.
He is like your God.
When the world was flooded
he created four powers.
Schodelick.
Swadick.
Hode and Stoodke.
We call them the brothers of Suelick.
The oldest brother is something round.
Maybe canoe anchor.
Maybe something else.
Hode is fire.
Stoodke, knife.
I don't remember Swadick
but he's a big name around here.

One day Suelick tells his brothers
to create land and people.
So the boys leave home.
Schodelick comes to Skagit country.
Creates a man and woman
and some land.
He puts fish in the rivers and lakes.
Then he shows the man and woman
how to catch the fish
how to clean the fish
how to eat them.
Schodelick creates all living things.
Trees.

Animals.
Plants.
And Schodelick shows the man and woman how to use them.

When his work is done
Schodelick is at the waterfall above Marblemount.
He tells his brothers that his work is done.
He points to the big rock in the middle of the falls.
I'll be right here in the water near the big rock
he tells his brothers.
He dives into the water.
Sings and swims for a long time.
Nothing in his stomach.
Schodelick still lives there in the water
the greatest power of Skagit Indians.
If you walk by this place early in the morning
you hear the song of Schodelick.

Quaquach is the rock
he stands on before he goes into the water.

My people believed in the power search.
They lived by it.
They went for many days without eating
before they dived into water to receive words
from Schodelick.
Without power the Indian is no good.
No long lives.
No purpose.
All our young men and women went in search of this power.

Schodelick's brothers traveled into the Okanagan.
They created land and people.
They created trees, animals, plants.

Just like Schodelick did here.
They showed the people how to use everything.
Those Indians worship fire.
They play with hot rocks.
They become crazy men
and the only way they return to this world
is beating their heads in the fire.

This is all I know.
This is the true story of the beginning of my people.

— *Adaptation by Carl Cary*

THE CREATION OF THE WORLD ACCORDING TO CHARLES SLATER

Cuna

God came from under the earth for himself. And then stood up from under the earth, and he started to thought himself how to make a woman. Because he could not stayed by himself; and whether he take palm of his hand to make a body of woman that he can compose the world. That time earth was without form and darkness. But god claimed that if he take him palm of his hand could not do because a hand will hurt a woman and if he take bottom of his feet would not do because the feet he will kick a woman. That time the earth was without form and firmament. And then God started to thought himself that if he take a heart that will do; because the heart is memory to the woman and then he take heart of string that which is gone down straight to blader, that which will make a woman way to come out of womb to form a child. And he take kineys blader, lungs, womb and liver. And then he take a soul to form of a white cloth. And then he spread out the white cloth on the table and then he put every things in it. And then he found a case to put every things in it and a key to lock every things in it. And then he carried into the four empty house and hide these and then God lay down on the bed and waiting for her to come to him. And then on 12 a clock in the night some one came crying and saying "Where is are you father? And on four days God heard a some one crying inside the case of the empty house. And then he took a key to opened the case. When he opened the case the child come from the womb and then she stood on the God key hole; and then she came upstairs and come crying and saying. "Where is my father"? God said: "here am I." And then she came and lay down with him on the bed. And then God to her My dear child my dear daughter and my dear wife and you is my heart and then I will name by the heart because you come forth of my heart and he called her name *Puna Olocueguintile.* And then God became two; and he started to thought himself to created the earth for the children to put therein. And then mother started to see white soul, yellow soul, black soul, dark soul, spotted soul, green soul and purple soul, blue soul, soft soul and red soul. And then God want it to form golden table out of his wife body. And he took bone part of just her below her neaple to form the golden table and then she start to see white soul and red soul. And then he form eight cups of it to find the soul how would became, then she spread out white soul on the golden table and then she wipe off to find the soul. And then he started to form a chair. And then mother started to see the soul again and then father called at her eight times and the last she saw the soul was round soul, and what he form chair of it and the mother never saw any more soul. And then he saw his wife bearing fruit. And then father saw it was so good to him. And he started to thought what he going to form first for his children and grand children. And then mother became sick on her day: and then God said am going to form first the earth. And then mother saw soul again and she first saw white soul and he form a different clays out of it. golden table and then she wipe off to find the soul. And then he could not bear it; but still she laugh; and God asked her how you feel" and she said alright". And a grand children will be circumcise after me. And then mother saw soul again. When she saw soul a golden eel come auf of it. When the eel come down eel go crooked and twist: and then mother saw soul again and a gueb-gueb came out of it again. That time the earth was soft. And then God took a stomach out of the woman and also he took soul out of the mother to form a eight barrels of water. And then mother saw soul again and the father called to her again And then he start to thought by himself what am going to make for my children again. And their mother became sick again on her day; and then he form a water and put it in the barrels to make a river for us. And then God saw when a river flood that the earth could not stand from river flood; because the earth was to soft; and then God created stones and Ivory rock and sanctify rock and then God started to create a clays and he created sticky clay to defend the earth from river flood and he also created falls to defend the earth: trees to prevend the earth from falling. And then god created flint to make a looking glass with it. So he also putted in the river to prevent the earth from falling. And then mother started to see soul again: and she saw white soul and then father called to her. And then the girl child come forth for her mother's womb just come like a surenge; and then mother form a surenge out of it, and she put a surenge on top up of tanks; and the water start drop down on the tanks. And when a girl come forth from her mother's womb and the father said to her: "My dear child, my dear daughter and my dear wife". And then mother said to herself am going to created thunder. And then mother stand up on top up of tanks. And on the top of tanks and inside of the mother belly a great sound was heard and roared and from that mother form a thunder. And then mother begin swell her belly and then she stood up on top of eight tanks and then she drop every kind a soul, white soul, black soul, dark soul, blue soul and red soul, yellow soul to filled the eight tanks with it. And when the every kind soul drop upon the tanks; then the smoke rise up in the air to form a cloud and to come down to sinenage. And then mother going to let water run out of the barrels and then she lay down on top up of barrels lay wide opened and when she lay down and then mother start to see a soul again; and then the soul start to run out of the mother's belly to the mouth of the river. And the lord started to think to dress the mother body. And then God lay with his daughter and then he called on her and then she start to see her soul red soul and God says I will make red cloth of it, And then she start to see her soul again a yellow soul; and God says, I will make yellow cloth of it. And then she saw her soul again it was a red dish in the middle and the white soul was round of it and then God says whitish part it will make a cotton out it and the reddish part he make pink pouder out of it. And then she start to saw her soul again a white soul and God says, I will make white cloth out of it, and then daughter says it give me a pain; but she still feel good but she keep on going and then she start to see her soul again and it was spotted soul spotted dots and with crooked line and straight line that I will make apron out of it and then she start to see her soul again it was a blue soul and God says I will form blue drill out of it. And then she saw soul again come in form just like strings just beside the tubes thats to form a twine line out of it and just to make form a bridge. And then she start to see her soul again a round soul different kind of colours and that I will form eight different colours of a beads, yellow, red, white, green, blue, pink, yellowish an reddish beads out ot it. And then she start to see a soul again and came in a form yellowish looking piece out off her womb; that is to form a gold; goldnecklace; and gold-cross necklace and then she saw her soul again it came in a form reddish an yellowish colour under her neaples and God says that I will form earrings out of it. And then she saw her soul again it came in a form just like a net reddish and yellowish and dots and crooked lines and God says I will form a handkerchief out of that. And then she saw her soul again it came in a form same as a net and bluish and yellowish and dots and God says it will form a sarpo out of that. And then she start a see a soul again it came in a form a blood just like a netish thing a thing that which is on top of the heart and it came from her womb. And God says I will form bead necklace out of it. And then she see a soul again it came in a form whitish and shine just like a crystal and God says I will form a money out of it. And then God says I will take a bone part of it to form a looking glass out of it. And then she see her soul again came in a form just like a two hook and he form a scissors out of it. And then God got up and saw her dressed up and says Oh my I never saw a good looking woman in this world and I thought lay down her side again once more, and then God saw every things what he made it was a good to him. And then God says what am going to make for my children to eat for foods and for meats; and then he consider of her what he could do. And then he asked the mother what he will do. And then he put the mother on the top up of the golden table and he said to her my dear daughter, my child and my dear wife and then God stoop her down the golden table her down the golden table and he started to back scutle her and the very minute . . .

THE SORCERER
(by K'HHalserten Sepass)

Okanagan

Deep in the forest
See-yah-na, the sorcerer,
Lived with his two sisters,
Sit-dat-til and Skhakh . . .
The old one . . . and the young one. . . .

While Tsee-ah-khum, the sun,
Walked in S-Way-Hil, the sky,
He lived
As any other warrior of the tribe
But when S-pah-lah-hum, the evening mists,
Drifted like smoke
From the fires of Kwah-sil, the pale stars,
See-yah-na
Went out from the camp
And was gone,
As the mists go
When Tsee-ah-khum, the sun,
Wakes from his sleep
And comes through O-ah-bitz, the red door,
To stand again,
In S-Way-Hil, the sky.

See-yah-na was gone,
And his sisters
Waited through the dark,
Troubled for their brother
Who was not at the camp fire.
Many moons passed,

And each night
The sisters crouched together,
Feeding the fire
And waiting for See-yah-na.

One day
As Tsee-ah-khum, the sun,
Came through the red door
Of O-ah-bitz, the dawn,
See-yah-na stood in the camp.
In his hand was Tchow-kwis,
The white hollow bone.

He said to Sit-dat-til:
"I bring you a gift from K'HHalls,
Chief of Tsee-ah-khum, the sun.
Wear it through your nose;
This bone will make you rich."

    But Skhakh wept,
    Because there was but one bone.

That night
When See-yah-na had vanished into the forest,
The two sisters
Set out to search,
Tree by tree,
Rock by rock,
To find the white bone treasure of See-yah-na.

At last they found the hidden place,
A round stone
And a great pile of bones,
The white hollow money-bones of K'HHalls.

Skhakh took one,
And the sisters fled
In fear of what they had done.
The forest was bright
With the golden gleam of morning
When they came back to the camp.

See-yah-na stood there,
Sorrowing
To see the white nostril-bone of Skhakh.
He said: "Take the bones;
Give them to the tribe;
They are money-bones,
The gift of K'HHalls . . .
But because you have done this,
I must leave you. . . .
You will see me no more."

The two sisters
Were in despair at what they had done.
They said:
"We must not lose our brother
Because of a pile of white bones;
We will look for him
In the forest;
We will take Skuh-mai to help us."

So Skuh-mai, the little dog,
Ran happily
And played
And sniffed out the trail
Of See-yah-na, his master.

Day and night,
Through the dark forest paths,
Sit-dat-til and Skhakh
Looked for See-yah-na.

At last,
Weary with walking,
They sank down to rest
On a flat stone.

Skuh-mai
Ran around the stone,
Digging in the earth and barking.
Sit-dat-til said:
"He is trying to tell us something.
Let us lift the stone."

So the two sisters,
Sit-dat-til and Skhakh,
Pushed and pulled at the stone.
It slid away,
And there was a hole
Leading to a land that is below the earth.
They leaned over
And looked down the hole.

Below them,
On a flat plain,
Young men played Tsee-khwal-eh,
The game of ball.

There was See-yah-na,
Each strand of his hair pulled through a white bone,
After the fashion of that land.
Sit-dat-til and Skhakh
Looked down,
Weeping.

See-yah-na came to stand beneath them,
And he felt their tears
Falling on his head.
He looked up. . . .
At once he was beside them.
He took Sit-dat-til on his back
And Skhakh on his shoulder;
"Shut your eyes," he said;
"I will take you to that land."

They went a long way.
Skhakh thought:
"I can hear no sounds of the forest,"
And she opened her eyes,
Just a little.

    At once
    They were back at the round stone.

See-yah-na was troubled.
He said:
"We will try again;
Do not open your eyes."

They went a long way. . . .
Sit-dat-til thought,
"I can hear no sounds of the forest,"
And she opened her eyes,
Just a little.

    At once
    They were back at the round stone.

See-yah-na said:
"We will try one time more."
The sisters

Once again opened their eyes
To see what must not be seen.

See-yah-na said:
"This is the end.
I must leave you.
Take the bones to the tribe;
You will never see me again."

He was gone,
And though they pushed and pulled at the stone,
It would not move.
It stood firm,
Fastened into the earth
Like mountain rock.

Weeping,
The two sisters
Made their way back to the tribe,
Taking with them
The white hollow money-bones
The gift of K'HHalls.

There was buying and selling,
Feasting and gift-giving;
The bones passed from hand to hand.
Some were rich and some were poor,
Each according to the brain
And craft that was in him:

    Tchow-kwis, money,
    Had come to Schwail, the earth.

—*Translation by Sophia Street and K'HHalserten Sepass*

Coon cons Coyote, Coyote eats Coon, Coyote fights Shit-Men, gets immured in a rock-house, eats his eyes, eats his balls, gets out, cons Bird-Boy for eyes, loses them to the birds & gets them back

Nez Percé

his younger brother Coon said to Coyote Here's how I get this good fried fish. I use my skunk cabbages for a pillow, the morning sun shine turns them to fish. Coyote did that, he sat against the cabbages. At sunrise they were skunk cabbages

and Coon said Not that way! What I do, I put my prick into a nest of ants, they bite it, maybe hard, and there's a big fried fish, a little bite, I get a small fish. Well Coyote did it, he found the ants & put his prick in them, it really hurt when they bit; Coyote thought about his fish and pulled out his prick all red and sore. Home with no fish Coyote said to Coon They bit my thing and hurt it but I got no fish

and Coon said Not that way! What I do, I go to the trail and ask whoever's passing by. So Coyote went too and each got food. And Coyote stole from them and Coon told and ran with his own food. They beat up Coyote and took everything back and swelled up his eyes so he couldn't see. He went home feeling sick

Coyote said to Coon When you go crabbing watch out, black beings at the river shoot people. You can know them they say Spitspam Spitspam. Coyote charcoaled himself all up and went to the river and shot an arrow into Coon. Saying Spitspam Spitspam. Coon came home in pain. I told you said Coyote, let me take care of you. And Coyote bit his fatty places, he bit them out. O Coon screamed You hurt me. No Coyote said I cure you, and Coyote ate him. Coyote had a lot of food then Coyote went here and there and couldn't decide and he said I wish I could have a fight with Shit-Man. Right away the Shit-Men hit him until he was unconscious. When he got up he smelled like shit all over and washed himself in the river

I wish I had a stone house, Coyote said, to protect me. And he had one. They couldn't get in or him out. After a long time there he got hungry and there was no food. So he pulled out his eyes and ate them, but he became thin and there was no food so he ripped out his balls and ate them

a person outside pecked and hammered; when Coyote cried out Sapsucker came. Coyote said Tell brown woodpecker, bluejay and red-headed woodpecker to break open this house and they did, and carried him out. He gave them the finest clothes and all those men went away happy

well Coyote was blind now. He heard Bird-Boy and called to him and he put flowers in his own eye-sockets. Coyote said Why don't you shoot that pheasant over there? your eyes are bad, let's trade. And each took the other's eyes. The boy ran here and there and he could see far but his eyes that were flowers wilted and dried and he was blind

Coyote would take one eye out and toss it up into the air saying Great it's mine. Birds passed by and noticed him they plucked his eyes from the air. Coyote said Great it's mine, he said it five times, but they had the eyes

Coyote reached an old one-eyed woman. O aren't they having a time with Coyote's eyes she said. She was grinding fern roots and he clubbed her to death and put on her clothes and ground fern roots. Then women came back and said to Coyote O aren't they having a time with Coyote's eyes!

the next day they took the old woman with them and she said to all the women Carry me on your back, a little lower down granddaughter. Then Coyote said That's just the right place down there. And the bearer said You're hurting me, you're sticking a thing into me. How, said Coyote, I have nothing to stick you with. But the youngest woman wouldn't put Coyote lower down and Coyote said It hurts granddaughter, a little lower down! But she threw Coyote down and they all went to the place of Coyote's eyes

they passed the eyes around and Coyote got them again and threw them into the air crying Great they're mine and Bluejay said to the others What's the old woman saying? and both eyes fell down and were his again. He took off the old woman clothes and ran away

—Working by Armand Schwerner, after Melville Jacobs

Coyote borrows Farting Boy's asshole, tosses up his eyes, retrieves them, rapes old women & tricks a young girl seeking power

Nez Percé

1

When Coyote was traveling around, he came on Farting Boy. Farting Boy had an arrow in one hand & a target in the other, & everytime he threw the target, Farting Boy would fart, pyu! he also farted when he shot at it. Pyu! went Farting Boy, he had five arrows, pyu! he shot them at the target, pyu! when he had shot them & had hit the target with five arrows he moved on. Pyu! pyu! pyu! pyu! pyu! pyu! pyu! Then he stopped, pyu! he threw it, pyu! he shot at it, pyu! he shot all five arrows at it.

2

When Coyote met him, Coyote said to him, Your thing is certainly a great thing for a lot of people. Let me have it.

— Oh no, said Farting Boy, I want mine for my own. He said that when he moved, the thing went pyu!

— Aw let me have it now, he pleaded.

— Alright, said Farting Boy to him. All that farting was only tiring the boy, & so he let Coyote have it all, the bow, the arrows, the target, all of it.

3

— Come on & throw it! he said.

Coyote threw it. Pyu!

— Come on & shoot at it! he told him.

Then Coyote shot at it. Pyu! All five arrows. Pyu! pyu! pyu! pyu! pyu!

Then the boy said to Coyote, Keep it coming.

Coyote just was going pyu! pyu! pyu!

Well, the boy said, I suppose I should be leaving. So the boy ran off, he ran as fast as he could go.

4

Each time Coyote would be making a move, the thing went pyu! He threw the target, pyu! he shot at it, pyu! he shot all five arrows at it, pyu! pyu! pyu! pyu! pyu! And when he tried just walking, pyu! pyu! pyu! pyu! pyu! pyu! So it didn't take much longer before his asshole was being sore. Then the thing exploded prrrrrrrrr, & Coyote ran off to where the boy had run. Pyu! pyu! pyu! he followed him, he called to him: Where are you? I want to give you back your farts. But though he shouted & shouted, the boy still didn't answer. By now Coyote was certainly feeling sick about his asshole. He tried keeping perfectly still, but every time he moved, prrrrrrrrr!

5

Then Coyote was sitting down, yes he thought, I think I will shit now & get this figured out. He had two younger sisters, Pine Nut & Huckleberry, & so he shat them out. Now then, he said to them, you tell me how this happened.

— Figure it out for yourself, said his sisters. You'll only end up saying, That's the one thing I forgot.

— Aw, said Coyote, tell me, tell me, tell me. What he really said was Shhluck!

— Better be careful, said his sisters, because that was how Coyote summoned rain. Then they said to him, That big strong bloke is Farting Boy. Now you must throw away your arrows, bow & target.

— That is the one thing I certainly forgot, Coyote said. So he threw them away. Now he went on without farting.

6

Coyote went on walking. Then he stopped, he was poking an eye out on one side, then he poked out both of them, then he played, then he stopped, then he put them in again. That was exactly how he did it. And while he was playing with his eyes, Buzzard was circling high above him. Then Buzzard caught his eyes & carried them away. So Coyote was standing there for a long time, but his eyes were gone.

7

Each place Coyote went he would grab hold of a stick. Who are you anyhow? he asked it.

— Only me, it answered. All the sticks he spoke to here were trees, but when he would be asking them, each one would answer, Only me.

Coyote grabbed one with his hand. Who are you anyhow? he asked it.

— Such & such a flower, said the stick.

Then Coyote pulled out two of them & stuck them in his head. Coyote made eyes of them & saw things clearly with them. Then he walked on, who knows how long a time, & then they wilted. Coyote threw them away. He pulled out fresh ones, stuck them in his head, was making eyes of them.

8

When he came to where a man named Bird was hunting, Coyote said to him: I'll trade you eyes.

— Alright, said Bird.

Coyote had also said to Bird, There are mountain goats there standing in a bunch. But when he was pointing them out for him, Bird didn't see. Then Coyote said to him, You look with my eyes & let me have yours. So Coyote gave his eyes to Bird & put on Bird's eyes. He said to him, Hey, lookie! There they are, hey lookie! So Bird did & went off hunting. Then: well, I'll be waiting for you here. You shoot a few & I'll come hollering. But Bird-Boy had no sooner gone than Coyote split, ran right off with that Bird-Boy's eyes. Then it didn't take much time, those eyes of Bird's wilted, Bird was stuck in a thicket, lost his way because he could not see where he was going.

— Bye, bye, Birdie.

9

Coyote went on walking & as he did, he heard a certain sound like floosh. Now smoke was coming from a house. When Coyote reached that house, an old woman sat there grinding roots. She was blind, she had no eyes, her body had some kind of cloak on it.

— Hey, old woman, said Coyote, I see you're grinding roots & all that there.

Old woman answered, Yes.

— And no one with you here?

— No one, certainly no one. Why, my five granddaughters have all certainly gone away from here. Why, Buzzard took Coyote's eyes, so all the people are playing with them now. That is assuredly where my granddaughters have been going.

After this Coyote beat & murdered that old woman. She had on a small hat & now Coyote carried her away & hid her. Next Coyote put that old woman's cloak on & all that clothing & those things she had. He himself wished to become exactly like that old woman. Then Coyote sat there grinding roots.

— Floosh.

10

Coyote heard the sound of his unmarried granddaughters coming back, hahahahaheee it went, because as they came along now they were laughing. The oldest reached him first.

— My grandmother has been grinding & grinding, she said.

— Ah, granddaughter, Coyote said, I have assuredly been grinding.

Then all the granddaughters came in. It was the youngest granddaughter who surely knew. Yes, she said, this is assuredly not my grandmother, this one is strange & different. Even when the granddaughters had begun to eat the roots, this youngest knew.

Then the oldest one said to her grandmother, They say that tomorrow you are to go. Your nephews want you, they say, & so they say we are to carry you on our backs and bring you with us. Then, they say, you may assuredly handle Coyote's eyes too.

The old woman said, Oh!

Then they slept through the night.

11

The sun rose. Then the oldest one carried him on her back. Ouch, ouch, ouch, he said, ouch, ouch, a little lower!

The next one to the oldest said to her, Well, you are really hurting our grandmother. So they made her packstrap a little longer & placed her lower down. Then they said to her, Well, how is that?

— Why, yes, Coyote said, that assuredly is fine now, granddaughters.

So the granddaughter was packing him along now while Coyote was desiring to fuck her. So he slipped it into the granddaughter.

— Dear, oh dear, said the granddaughter, with what are you doing it to me, grandmother?

— With a protuberance from my body, when you yourself have become an old woman you will certainly also have protuberances from your body.

So they were going along then, while they were doing so he would most certainly be doing it to her. Then she was becoming tired because of the grandmother on her back, she would set him down then.

12

Then another one would be carrying him on her back. As they were going along he would be shoving it into his granddaughter.

— Dear, oh dear, the granddaughter would be saying, with what are you doing it to me, grandmother?

— I am doing it to you with a protuberance from my body. When you yourself have become an old woman you will certainly also have protuberances.

The granddaughter was continuing to be packing him along, as they were going along he would be doing it to her, as they would be going along he was fucking her. She would be becoming tired of it.

13

Soon another one was packing him along, in precisely the same manner he would be shoving it into her as they would be going along.

— I am doing it to you with a protuberance from my body, he would be saying. You yourself will also become an old woman with protuberances from your body.

She would be packing him along, again he would be doing it to her as they were going doing it to her from behind. When she would be tired out then she would set him down.

14

Then another one now carried him on her back. As they would be going along he was doing it to her in the same manner slipping it into her as they would be going along. This was the fourth to be carrying him, while they were carrying their grandmother along he would be doing it.

15

— Yes, yes, he said, now the youngest one must be carrying me.

Then the last one set him down. Then they said to her, Now you must also be carrying our grandmother on your back.

The youngest one had told them, the youngest one was telling her older sisters, You must be carrying this one on your back yourselves, no, no, this one is certainly not my grandmother.

Then the oldest would again be carrying her, they were arriving now where all those people would be gathered.

16

There was a long house, a great many people were there, they were passing & carrying around Coyote's eyes. When they brought the old woman into the house, the nephews said to them, Yes bring her to the center.

— No, nephews, she said. No, I will be sitting over near the door.

17

Then Coyote saw.

— My eyes!

Yes they were passing around those eyes, then they came to the old woman's place, Coyote held his eyes.

— My own eyes, wow! My own eyes, wow!

— What'd she say?

— She said those were her own eyes!

— No, no, certainly not. What she was certainly saying was "I wish those eyes were mine."

They were passing them around & around four times in that way.

— My own eyes, wow!

— But certainly she must be saying these are my own eyes!

— No certainly, what she must be saying was "I wish those eyes were my eyes!"

Yes they were passing them around, they had all of them been handling them, then they gave them to Coyote.

18

The old woman who had seized the eyes inserted one clink! on the first side, she was doing it to both of them, she was getting up, Coyote was running, he was running out, he ran away.

— Yahyahyah yah yah, yahyahyah yah yah!

— He is running away with our valuable thing! so some were saying. But being careful some said those were his own eyes.

When Coyote ran far away he stopped & stood, he was calling out to those women to those certainly who had been carrying him on their backs.

— You will be placing your infants on cradle boards, you will use diapers, you will be putting mine on cradle boards.

Now the youngest who had not been carrying him on her back was saying, Do you hear him? Now you certainly were carrying Coyote on your backs, you certainly were carrying Coyote.

But Coyote had pushed on.

19

Those women who had reached their home there were searching for their grandmother, they found her stuck underneath a log & dead.

Her granddaughters were crying for her there then.

Soon they took their grandmother & were putting her away, they buried her.

20

Coyote had been pushing on. When he had gone very far away he found two women there, these were exceedingly old women.

— Look, Coyote said to them, there are very bad ones who are traveling around here.

While the old women were also going on canes, Coyote was making magic, wishing people would be traveling along there, no not grasshoppers but people.

— You should be grabbing one, he said, you should certainly be making it your slave. Some who are passing by are very bad ones. Now you should be doing it.

One old woman was saying to the other, You should be doing it yourself.

— Now they have face paint on, Coyote said.

They said, This is the way we do it.

Coyote said, These are certainly ones traveling from here to way out there. Well, there they go, he said.

Once they were going farther he also said, Let's strip for action.

When he was saying that she made a leap for him, she ran, Coyote said, Now you should be doing it quickly from behind, you should do it with a *yahyahyah* & with an *ugh*.

That was how he was having her prepare for it, she would be turning on it from behind, now she would do it with a *yahyahyah* & with an *ugh*.

When she would turn her back on it Coyote would be grabbing & hugging her from behind, She has caught the slave he cried. Then he was shoving it into that old woman, when they were finished fucking he was pushing her away.

— Go far away from me, he said. When he had finished doing it to her & fucking her, that old woman went away, she was going back to where she got the face paint. She was letting it get dry, soon she would be going home.

When she was back she said, That one really must have been Coyote.

21

Meanwhile Coyote had been pushing on, while he was pushing on he was coming on an old woman & her granddaughter, this young woman who was the old one's granddaughter was still unmarried.

Soon Coyote was telling her, You are an orphan motherless & fatherless, you should be going looking for a guardian spirit power.

He was saying it to that unmarried girl, her grandmother was also saying, He is telling you the really right thing.

— Yes, Coyote said, you should be going to the mountain top. When you will see a red thing sticking out that thing will be a power. You will assuredly be finding a little hilly place there.

22

Coyote had gone away, he had been running then he had reached that place, he dug a hole there, he had gotten into it, he had been covering himself over. He was himself being that little hilly place there, his own red cock was sticking out of it.

The girl had been going away too, when she was finally arriving at the place she saw it.

— Here is where that thing is, she was thinking. That red one is the sticking-out thing.

She saw it, she was lifting up her dress, she looked around her, Coyote said to her, You should be masturbating on your power!

So the woman was starting to be masturbating on it there, he was raising it up towards her, he was hugging her, now she was taking in the guardian spirit power.

When Coyote had been fucking the unmarried woman & had finished doing it to her there, he said to her, They sent you to your power. He also said, Get out of here, yes you should be getting home!

Then the woman was going away in tears, yes she was crying when she found her grandmother.

— Yes that really must have been Coyote.

23

So how about that.

— *Working by Jerome Rothenberg, after Melville Jacobs*

THE FLIGHT OF QUETZALCOATL

Aztec

•

Then the time came for Quetzalcoatl too, when he felt the darkness
twist in him like a river, as though it meant to weigh him down,
& he thought to go then, to leave the city as he had found it & to
go, forgetting there ever was a Tula

Which was what he later did, as people tell it who still speak about
the Fire: how he first ignited the gold & silver houses, their
walls speckled with red shells, & the other Toltec arts, the
creations of man's hands & the imagination of his heart

& hid the best of them in secret places, deep in the earth, in moun-
tains or down gullies, buried them, took the cacao trees & changed
them into thorned acacias

& the birds he'd brought there years before, that had the richly
colored feathers & whose breasts were like a living fire, he sent
ahead of him to trace the highway he would follow towards the
seacoast

When that was over he started down the road

•

A whole day's journey, reached

THE JUNCTURE OF THE TREE
(so-called)

   fat prominence of bark
   sky branches

I sat beneath it
saw my face / cracked
mirror

An old man

        & named it
        TREE OF OLD AGE

thus to name
it to raise stones
to wound the bark
with stones

to batter it with
stones the stones to
cut the bark to fester
in the bark
        TREE OF OLD AGE

stone patterns: starting
from the roots they
reach the highest leaves

•

The next day gone with walking
Flutes were sounding in his ears

        Companions' voices

He squatted on a rock to rest
he leaned his hands against the rock

        Tula shining in the distance

: which he saw he
saw it & began to cry
he cried the cold sobs cut his throat

     A double thread of tears, a hailstorm
     beating down his face, the drops
     burn through the rock

     The drops of sorrow fall against the stone
     & pierce its heart

& where his hands had rested
shadows lingered on the rock: as if
his hands had pressed soft clay
As if the rock were clay

The mark too of his buttocks in the rock,
embedded there forever

The hollow of his hands preserved forever

       A place named TEMACPALCO

  •

To Stone Bridge next

water swirling in the riverbed
a spreading turbulence of water

: where he dug a stone up
made a bridge across
       & crossed it

•

: who kept moving until he reached the Lake of Serpents, the elders waiting for him there, to tell him he would have to turn around, he would have to leave their country & go home

: who heard them ask where he was bound for, cut off from all a man remembers, his city's rites long fallen into disregard

: who said it was too late to turn around, his need still driving him, & when they asked again where he was bound, spoke about a country of red daylight & finding wisdom, who had been called there, whom the sun was calling

: who waited then until they told him he could go, could leave his Toltec things & go (& so he left those arts behind, the creations of man's hands & the imagination of his heart: the crafts of gold & silver, of working precious stones, of carpentry & sculpture & mural painting & book illumination & featherweaving)

: who, delivering that knowledge, threw his jeweled necklace in the lake, which vanished in those depths, & from then on that place was called The Lake of Jewels

•

Another stop along the line

This time
THE CITY OF THE SLEEPERS

And runs into a shaman

Says, you bound for somewhere honey

Says, the country of Red Daylight know it? expect to land there probe a little wisdom maybe

Says, no fooling try a bit of pulque brewed it just for you

Says, most kind but awfully sorry scarcely touch a drop you know

Says, perhaps you've got no choice perhaps I might not let you go
   now you didn't drink perhaps I'm forcing you against your will
   might even get you drunk come on honey drink it up

Drinks it with a straw

                    So drunk he falls down fainting
                    on the road & dreams &
                    snores his snoring echoes very far

& when he wakes finds silence
& an empty town, his face
reflected & the hair shaved off

                    Then calls it
                    CITY OF THE SLEEPERS

•

There is a peak between Old Smokey
& The White Woman

Snow is falling
& fell upon him in those days

                    & on his companions
                    who were with him, on
                    his dwarfs, his clowns
                    his gimps

                    It fell

till they were frozen
lost among the dead

The weight oppressed him
& he wept for them

He sang

  The tears are endless
  & the long sighs
  issue from my chest

Further out
THE HILL OF MANY COLORS

which he sought

Portents everywhere, those
dark reminders
of the road he walks

•

It ended on the beach
It ended with a hulk of serpents formed into a boat
& when he'd made it, sat in it & sailed away
A boat that glided on those burning waters, no one knowing when
  he reached the country of Red Daylight
It ended on the rim of some great sea
It ended with his face reflected in the mirror of its waves
The beauty of his face returned to him
& he was dressed in garments like the sun
It ended with a bonfire on the beach where he would hurl himself
& burn, his ashes rising & the cries of birds
It ended with the linnet, with the birds of turquoise color, birds
  the color of wild sunflowers, red & blue birds

It ended with the birds of yellow feathers in a riot of bright gold
Circling till the fire had died out
Circling while his heart rose through the sky
It ended with his heart transformed into a star
It ended with the morning star with dawn & evening
It ended with his journey to Death's Kingdom with seven days of
    darkness
With his body changed to light
A star that burns forever in that sky

— English version by Jerome Rothenberg

A BOOK OF NARRATIVES (II)

THE BOY & THE DEER
Zuni

Performance by Andrew Peynetsa

Total Translation by Dennis Tedlock

AIDS TO READING ALOUD

Line changes indicate brief silences (averaging a little less than one second) and double spaces between lines indicate longer ones (two to three seconds). In the printed version that follows, page breaks always indicate the shorter pause.

Loud words and passages are indicated by CAPITALS and soft ones (in parentheses).

Lengthened vowel sounds are indicated by ————, as in "She worked o————n for some time," in which the o should be held for a full second or so.

When a line is set on different levels, each level indicates a single sustained pitch, almost as controlled as in singing. In the following example, the intervals are roughly fa, mi, do:

> KILLED THE DEER
>   killed the deer
>   killed the deer.

Special manipulations of voice quality (tone of voice) are indicated by italicized instructions in parentheses at the beginnings of affected lines. The same device (italics in parentheses) is also used to indicate interruptions by the audience.

In the Zuni words, the vowels should be given their continental values; double vowels are held a bit longer than single ones. The consonants should be pronounced as in English; ' indicates a glottal stop; double consonants are held a bit longer than single ones (ssh in Tísshomahhá" is a double sh). Stress is on the first syllable except in "Tísshomahhá," which takes not only the initial stress but a final one as well.

THE BOY AND THE DEER

SON'AHCHI.
(*audience*) Ee———so.
SONTI LO———NG AGO.
(*audience*) Ee———so.
THERE WERE VILLAGERS AT HE'SHOKTA
and
up on the Prairie-Dog Hills
the deer
had their home.

The daughter of a priest
was sitting in a room on the fourth story down weaving basket-plaques.
She was always sitting and working in there, and the Sun came up
every day when the Sun came up
the girl would sit working
at the place where he came in.
It seems the Sun made her pregnant.
When he made her pregnant
though she sat in there without knowing any man,
    her belly grew large.
She worked o———n for a time
weaving basket-plaques, and
her belly grew large, very very large.
When her time was near
she had a pain in her belly.
Gathering all her clothes

she went out and
went down to Water's End.

On she went until
she came to the bank
went on down to the river, and washed her clothes.

(Then)
having washed a few things, she had a pain in her belly.

She came out of the river. Having come out she sat down
by a juniper tree and strained her muscles:
(the little baby came out).
She dug a hole, put juniper leaves in it
then laid the baby there.
She went back into the water
gathered all her clothes
and carefully washed the blood off herself.
She bundled
her clothes
put them on her back
(and returned to her home at He'shokta).

And the DEER
who lived on the Prairie-Dog Hills
were going down to DRINK, going down to drink at dusk.
(The Sun had almost set when they went down to drink and the
    little baby was crying.
"Where is the little baby crying?" they said.)
It was two fawns on their way down
with their mother

who heard him.
The crying was coming from the direction of a tree.
They were going into the water

(and there)
they came upon the crying.
Where a juniper tree stood, the child
(was crying).

The deer
the two fawns and their mother went to him.
"Well, why shouldn't we
save him?
Why don't you two hold my nipples
so
so he can nurse?" that's what the mother said to her fawns.

The two fawns helped the baby
suck their mother's nipple and get some milk.
(Now the little boy

was nursed, the little boy was nursed by the deer)
o———n until he was full.
Their mother lay down cuddling him the way deer sleep
with her two fawns
together
lying beside her
and they SLEPT WITH THEIR FUR AROUND HIM.
They would nurse him, and so they lived on, lived on.
As he grew
he was without clothing, NAKED.
His elder brother and sister had fur:

they had fur, but he was NAKED and this was not good.

The deer
(the little boy's mother)
spoke to her two fawns: "Tonight
when you sleep, you two will lie on both sides
and he will lie in the middle.
While you're sleeping
(I'll go to Kachina Village, for he is without clothing, naked, and
this is not good.")

That's what she said to her children, and
there
at the village of He'shokta

were young men
who went out hunting, and the young men who went out hunting
    looked for deer.
When they went hunting they made their kills around the Prairie-
    Dog Hills.
And their mother went to Kachina Village, she went o———n until
    she reached Kachina Village.
It was filled with dancing kachinas.

"My fathers, my children, how have you been passing the days?"
    "Happily, our child, so you've come, sit down," they said.
"Wait, stop your dancing, our child has come and must have some-
    thing to say," then the kachinas stopped.
The deer sat down, (the old lady deer sat down.
A kachina priest spoke to her):
"Now speak.
You must've come because you have something to say." "YES, in
    TRUTH

I have come because I have something to SAY.
(There in the village of He'shokta is a priest's daughter)
who abandoned her child.
We found him
we have been raising him.
But he is poor, without clothing, naked, and this
is not good.
So I've come to ask for clothes for him," that's what she said.
"Indeed." "Yes, that's why I've come, to ask for clothes for him."
"Well, there is always a way," they said.
Kyaklo
laid out his shirt.
Long Horn put in his kilt and his moccasins.

And Huututu put in his buckskin leggings
he laid out his bandoleer.

And Pawtiwa laid out his macaw headdress.

Also they put in the BELLS he would wear on his legs.

Also they laid out

strands of turquoise beads
moccasins.
So they laid it all out, hanks of yarn for his wrists and ankles
they gathered all his clothing.
(When they had gathered it his mother put it on her back): "Well,
    I must GO
but when he has grown larger I will return to ask for clothing again."
That's what she said. "Very well indeed."
(Now the deer went her way.

When she got back to her children they were all sleeping.
When she got there they were sleeping and she
lay down beside them.
The little boy, waking up
began to nurse, his deer mother nursed him
and he went back to sleep.) So they spent the night and then
(*with pleasure*) the little boy was clothed by his mother.
His mother clothed him.

When he was clothed he was no longer cold.
He went around playing with his elder brother and sister, they
    would run after each other, playing.
They lived on this way until he was grown.
And THEN
they went back up to their old home on the Prairie-Dog Hills.
    Having gone up
they remained there and would come down only to drink, in the
    evening.
There they lived o————n for a long time

until
from the village
(his uncle
went out hunting. Going out hunting
he came along
down around
Worm Spring, and from there he went on toward

the Prairie-Dog Hills and came up near the edge of a valley there.
When he came to the woods on the Prairie-Dog Hills he looked
    down and)
THERE IN THE VALLEY was the herd of deer. In the herd of deer

there was a little boy going around among them
dressed in white.
He had bells on his legs and he wore a macaw headdress.
(He wore a macaw headdress, he was handsome), surely it was a
    boy
(a male
a person among them.
While he was looking) the deer mothers spotted him.
(When they spotted the young man they ran off.
There the little boy outdistanced the others.)

"Haa————, who could that be?"
That's what his uncle said. ("Who
could you be? Perhaps you are a daylight person.")
That's what his UNCLE thought and he didn't do ANYTHING to
    the deer.
(He returned to his house in the evening.)

It was evening
dinner was ready, (and when they sat down to eat
the young man spoke):
"Today, while I was out hunting
when I reached the top
(of the Prairie-Dog Hills, where the woods are, when I reached the
    top), THERE in the VALLEY was a HERD OF DEER.
There was a herd of deer

and with them was a LITTLE BOY:
whose child could it be?
When the deer spotted me they ran off and he outdistanced them.
(He wore bells on his legs, he wore a macaw headdress, he was
    dressed in white.")

That's what the young man was saying
telling his father.
It was one of the boy's OWN ELDERS
his OWN UNCLE had found him. (*audience*) Ee————so.
His uncle had found him.

Then
he said, "If
the herd is to be chased, then tell your Bow Priest."
That's what the young man said. "Whose child could this be?
PERHAPS WE'LL CATCH HIM."
That's what he was saying.
(A girl
a daughter of the priest said), "Well, I'll go ask the Bow Priest."
She got up and went to the Bow Priest's house.
(Arriving at the Bow Priest's house
she entered):
"My fathers, my mothers, how have you been passing the days?"
      "Happily, our child
so you've come, sit down," they said. "Yes.
Well, I'm
asking you to come.
Father asked that you come, that's what my father said," that's what
      she told the Bow Priest.
"Very well, I'll come," he said.
(The girl went out and went home), and after a while the Bow
      Priest came over.
He came to their house
while they were still eating.

"My children, how are you

this evening?" "Happy
sit down and eat," he was told.
He sat down and ate with them.
(When they were finished eating), "Thank you," he said. "Eat plenty,"
    he was told.
(He moved to another seat)

and after a while
the Bow Priest questioned them:
"NOW, for what reason have you
summoned ME?
Perhaps it is because of a WORD of some importance that you have
summoned me. You must make this known to me
so that I may think about it as I pass the days," that's what he said.
"YES, in truth
today, this very day
my child here
went out to hunt.
(Up on the Prairie-Dog Hills, there)
HE SAW A HERD OF DEER.
But a LITTLE BOY WAS AMONG THEM.
Perhaps he is a daylight person.
Who could it be?
He was dressed in white and he wore a macaw headdress.
When the deer ran off he OUTDISTANCED them:
he must be very fast.
That's why my child here said, 'Perhaps
they should be CHASED, the deer should be chased.'
He wants to see him caught, that's what he's thinking.
Because he said this
I summoned you," he said. "Indeed."

"Indeed, well

perhaps he's a daylight person, what else can he be?
It is said he was dressed in white, what else can he be?"
That's what they were saying.
"WHEN would you want to do this?" that's what he said.
The young man who had gone out hunting said, "Well, in four days
so we can prepare our weapons."
That's what he said.
"So you should tell your people that in FOUR DAYS there will be a
     deer chase."
That's what
he said. "Very well."

(*sharply*) Because of the little boy the word was given out for the
     deer chase.
The Bow Priest went out and shouted it.
When he shouted the VILLAGERS
heard him.
(*slowly*) "In four days there will be a deer chase.
A little boy is among the deer, who could it be? With luck
you might CATCH him.
We don't know who it will be.
You will find a child, then," that's what he SAID as he shouted.

Then they went to sleep and lived on with anticipation.
Now when it was the THIRD night, the eve of the chase

the deer
spoke to her son
when the deer had gathered:
("My son." "What is it?" he said.)

"Tomorrow we'll be chased, the one who found us is your uncle.
When he found us he saw you, and that's why

we'll be chased.
They'll come out after you:
your uncles.

(*excited*) The uncle who saw you will ride a spotted horse, and
    HE'LL BE THE ONE who
WON'T LET YOU GO, and
your elder brothers, your mothers
no
he won't think of killing them, it'll be you alone
he'll think of, he'll chase.
You won't be the one to get tired, but we'll get tired.
It'll be you alone
WHEN THEY HAVE KILLED US ALL
and you will go on alone.
Your first uncle
will ride a spotted horse and a second uncle will ride a white horse.
THESE TWO WILL FOLLOW YOU.
You must pretend you are tired but keep on going
and they will catch you.
But WE
MYSELF, your elder SISTER, your elder BROTHER
ALL OF US

will go with you.
Wherever they take you we will go along with you."
That's what his deer mother told him, (that's what she said).
THEN HIS DEER MOTHER TOLD HIM EVERYTHING:
    "AND NOW

I will tell you everything.
From here

from this place
where we're living now, we went down to drink. When we went down
    to drink
it was one of your ELDERS, one of your OWN ELDERS
your mother who sits in a room on the fourth story down making
    basket-plaques:
IT WAS SHE
whom the Sun had made pregnant.
When her time was near
she went down to Water's End to the bank
to wash clothes
and when you were about to come out
she had pains, got out of the water
went to a TREE and there she just DROPPED you.
THAT is your MOTHER.
She's in a room on the fourth story down making basket-plaques,
    that's what you'll tell them.

THAT'S WHAT SHE DID TO YOU, SHE JUST DROPPED
    YOU.
When we went down to drink
we found you, and because you have grown up
on my milk
and because of the thoughts of your Sun Father, you have grown
    fast.
Well, you
have looked at us
at your elder sister and your elder brother
and they have fur. 'Why don't I have fur like them?' you have asked.

But that is proper, for you are a daylight person.
That's why I went to Kachina Village to get clothes for you
the ones you were wearing.
You began wearing those when you were small
before you were GROWN.
Yesterday I went to get the clothes you're wearing now
the ones you will wear when they chase us. When you've been caught
you must tell these things to your elders.

When they bring you in
when they've caught you and bring you in
you
you will go inside. When you go inside
your grandfather
a priest
will be sitting by the fire. 'My grandfather, how have you been passing
    the days?'
'Happily. As old as I am, I could be a grandfather to anyone, for we
    have many children,' he will say.
'Yes, but truly you are my real grandfather,' you will say.
When you come to where your grandmother is sitting, 'Grandmother
    of mine, how have you been passing the days?' you will say.
'Happily, our child, surely I could be a grandmother to anyone, for we
    have the whole village as our children,' she will say.
Then, with the uncles who brought you in and
with your three aunts, you will shake hands.
'WHERE IS MY MOTHER?' you will say.
'Who is your mother?' they will say. 'She's in a room on the fourth
    story down making basket-plaques, tell her to come in,' you will
    say.

Your youngest aunt will go in to get her.

When she enters:

(*sharply*) 'There's a little boy who wants you, he says you are his mother.'

(*tight*) 'How could that be? I don't know any man, how could I have an offspring?'

'Yes, but he wants you,' she will say

and she will force her to come out.

THEN THE ONE WE TOLD YOU ABOUT WILL COME OUT:

you will shake hands with her, call her mother. 'Surely we could be mothers to anyone, for we have the whole village as our CHILDREN,' she will say to you.

'YES, BUT TRULY YOU ARE MY REAL MOTHER.

There, in a room on the fourth story down

you sit and work.

My Sun Father, where you sit in the light

my Sun Father

made you pregnant.

When you were about to deliver

it was to Water's End

that you went down to wash. You washed at the bank

and when I was about to come out

when it hurt you

you went to a tree and just dropped me there.

you gathered your clothes, put them on your back, and returned to your house.

But my MOTHERS

HERE

found me. When they found me

because it was on their milk

that I grew, and because of the thoughts of my Sun Father

I grew fast.

I had no clothing
so my mother went to Kachina Village to ask for clothing.'
THAT'S WHAT YOU MUST SAY."

(That's what he was told), that's what his mother told him. "And
tonight
(*aside*) we'll go up on the Ruin Hills."
That's what the deer mother told her son. "We'll go to the Ruin
    Hills
we won't live here any more.
(*sharply*) We'll go over there where the land is rough
for TOMORROW they will CHASE us.
Your uncles won't think of US, surely they will think of YOU
ALONE. They have GOOD HORSES," that's what
his mother told him. It was on the night before
that the boy
was told by his deer mother.
(The boy became
so unhappy.)
They slept through the night
(and before dawn the deer
went to the Ruin Hills).

They went there and remained, and the VILLAGERS AWOKE.
It was the day of the chase, as had been announced, and the people
    were coming out.
They were coming out, some carrying bows, some on foot and
some on horseback, they kept on this way
o———n they went on
past Stone Chief, along the trees, until they got to the Prairie-Dog
    Hills and there were no deer.
Their tracks led straight and they followed them.

(Having found the trail they went on until
when they reached the Ruin Hills, there in the valley
beyond the thickets there
was the herd, and the
young man and two of his elder sisters were chasing each other)
by the edge of the valley, playing together. (Playing
they were spotted.)
The deer saw the people.
(They fled.)
Many were the people who came out after them
(now they chased the deer).
Now and again they dropped them, killed them.
Sure enough the boy outdistanced the others, while his mother
        and his elder sister and brother
still followed their child. As they followed him
he was far in the lead, but they followed on, they were on the
        run
and sure enough his uncles weren't thinking about killing deer,
        it was the boy they were after.
And ALL THE PEOPLE WHO HAD COME
        KILLED THE DEER
                        killed the deer
                                killed the deer.
Wherever they made their kills they gutted them, put them on
        their backs, and went home.
Two of the uncles

(then)
went ahead of the group, and a third uncle
(*voice breaking*) (dropped his elder sister
his elder brother
his mother.

He gutted them there) while the other two uncles went on. As
   they went ON
the boy pretended to be tired. The first uncle pleaded:
   "Tísshomahhá!
STOP," he said, "Let's stop this contest now."
That's what he was saying as
the little boy kept on running.
As he kept on his bells went telele.
O———n, he went on this way
on until
(the little boy stopped and his uncle, dismounting, caught him.

Having caught him):
(*gently*) "Now come with me, get up," he said.
His uncle
(helped his nephew get up, then his uncle got on the horse).
They went back. They went on
(until they came to where his mother and his elder sister and brother
   were lying
and the third uncle was there. The third uncle was there.)
"So you've come." "Yes."
(The little boy spoke): "This is my mother, this is my
elder sister, this is my elder brother.
They will accompany me to my house.
(They will accompany me," that's what the boy said.
"Very well."
His uncles put the deer on their horses' backs.)
On they went, while the people were coming in, (coming in, and
   still the uncles didn't arrive, until at nightfall
the little boy was brought in, sitting up on the horse.
It was night and the people, a crowd of people, came out to see the
   boy as he was brought in on the horse through the plaza

and his mother and his elder sister and brother

came along also

as he was brought in.

His grandfather came out. When he came out the little boy and
his uncle dismounted.

His grandfather took the lead with the little boy following, and they
went up.

When they reached the roof his grandfather

made a corn-meal road

and they entered.

His grandfather entered

with the little boy following

while his

uncles brought in the deer. When everyone was inside

the little boy's grandfather spoke: "Sit down," and the little boy
spoke to his grandfather as he came to where he was sitting):

"Grandfather of mine, how have you been passing the days?" (that's
what he said).

"Happily, (our child

surely I could be a grandfather to anyone, for we have the whole
village as our children." "Yes, but you are my real grandfather,"
he said.)

When he came to where his grandmother was sitting (he said the
same thing.

"Yes, but surely I could be a grandmother to anyone, for we have
many children." "Yes, but you are my real grandmother," he said.)

He looked the way

his uncle had described him, he wore a macaw headdress and his
clothes were white.

He had new moccasins, new buckskin leggings.

He wore a bandoleer and a macaw headdress.

He was a stranger.

He shook hands with his uncles and shook hands with his aunts.

"WHERE IS MY MOTHER?" he said.

"She's in a room on the fourth story down weaving basket-plaques,"
(he said.
"Tell her to come out."
Their younger sister went in.)
"Hurry and come now:
(some little boy has come and says you are his mother)."
(*tight*) "How could that be?
(I've never known any man, how could I have an offspring?" she
said.)
"Yes, but come on, he wants you, he wants you to come out."
(Finally she was forced to come out.)
The moment she entered the little boy
(went up to his mother).
"Mother of mine, how have you been passing the days?"
"Happily, but surely I could be anyone's
mother, for we have many children," that's what his mother said.
(That's what she said.)

"YES INDEED
but you are certainly my REAL MOTHER.
YOU GAVE BIRTH TO ME," he said.

Then, just as his deer mother had told him to do
(he told his mother everything):

"You really are my mother.
In a room on the fourth story down
you sit and work.

As you sit and work
the light comes through your window.
My Sun Father
made you pregnant.
When he made you pregnant you
sat in there and your belly began to grow large.
Your belly grew large
you
you were about to deliver, you had pains in your belly, you were
    about to give birth to me, you had pains in your belly
you gathered your clothes
and you went down to the bank to wash.
When you got there you
washed your clothes in the river.
When I was about to COME OUT and caused you pain
you got out of the water
you went to a juniper tree.
There I made you strain your muscles
and there you just dropped me.
When you dropped me
you made a little hole and placed me there.
You gathered your clothes
bundled them together
washed all the blood off carefully, and came back here.
When you had gone
my elders here
came down to DRINK
and found me.
They found me

I cried

and they heard me.
Because of the milk
of my deer mother here
my elder sister and brother here
because of
their milk
I grew.
I had no clothing, I was poor.
My mother here went to Kachina Village to ask for my clothing.

That's where
she got my clothing.
That's why I'm clothed. Truly, that's why I was among them
that's why one of you
who went out hunting discovered me.
You talked about it and that's why these things happened today."
        (*audience*) Ee———so.
That's what the little boy said.

"THAT'S WHAT YOU DID AND YOU ARE MY REAL
        MOTHER," that's what he told his mother. At that moment
        his mother
embraced him (embraced him).
His uncle got angry (his uncle got angry).
He beat
his kinswoman
(he beat his kinswoman).
That's how it happened.
The boy's deer elders were on the floor.
(His grandfather then)
spread some covers

(on the floor, laid them there, and put strands of turquoise beads on
them.
After a while they skinned them.)
With this done and dinner ready they ate with their son.

They slept through the night, and the next day
the little boy spoke: "Grandfather." "What is it?"
"Where is your quiver?" he said. "Well, it must be hanging in the
other room," he said.

He went out, having been given the quiver, and wandered around.
He wandered around, he wasn't thinking of killing deer, he just
wandered around.
(In the evening he came home empty-handed.
They lived on

and slept through the night.
After the second night he was wandering around again.
The third one came)
and on the fourth night, just after sunset, his mother
spoke to him: "I need
the center blades of the yucca plant," she said.
"Which kind of yucca?"
"Well, the large yucca, the center blades," (that's what his mother
said. "Indeed.)
Tomorrow I'll try to find it for you," he said.
(aside) She was finishing her basket-plaque and this was for the
outer part. (audience) Ee————so.
That's what she said.
The next morning, when he had eaten
(he put the quiver on and went out).

He went up on Big Mountain and looked around until he found a
    large yucca
with very long blades.

("Well, this must be the kind you talked about," he said.) It was
    the center blades she wanted.
(He put down his bow and his quiver), got hold of the center blades,
    and began to pull.
(*with strain*) He pulled

it came loose suddenly
(and he pulled it straight into his heart.
There he died.)

He died (and they waited for him but he didn't come).

When the Sun went down
(and he still hadn't come, his uncles began to worry.
They looked for him.
They found his tracks, made torches, and followed him)
until they found him with the center blades of the yucca in his
    heart.

(Their
nephew
was found and they brought him home.
The next day

he was buried.)
Now he entered upon the roads
of his elders.
THIS WAS LIVED LONG AGO. LEE———SEMKONIKYA.

A SECOND SERVICE

> *Directions:* Thank someone for being that one.
> Then, while singing a song, walk with that one
> to the center of a room & back again. Burn
> something.
>
> *Seneca*

WOLF SONGS & OTHERS OF THE TLINGIT

•

I keep dreaming I'm dead
keep feeling like I'm home

•

SHAMAN SONG

I don't have any place to come up through
think I'll go to Chillkat, come up there
I'll come up over there, & cry

•

Throw him into the river
let him float down
Crow can fish him out
downstream

•

HOW TO GET GRIZZLY SPIRIT

Come out of your body among us & we're all one
(we drop grease into the fire, before the grizzly's head
Whu Whu Whu is what we all say)

CRADLE SONGS

1.

I'm gonna marry my brother's wife
after he dies

2.

I like to crawl around the house after my brother's wife
I thought he might get up out of his grave & I was worried
I always follow her around town

3.

If I don't take anything to the party I'll feel bad
Little girls have to take something to a party or they'll feel bad
All you little girls better listen

4.

I'll shoot a little bird for little brother
I'll spear a little trout for little sister

FUNERAL SONG

You're like a drifting log with iron nails in it
I built my house from that log
I hope you float in like that log did
on a good sandy beach
The sun goes into the clouds
like you go into our great mother
That's why the world is so dark

•

That's a rich man coming
keep your feelings to yourself

•

We've all been invited up to Killisnoo
all us high bred people are going to eat together

•

How is it all gonna turn out
people on crow's river going up to wolf's town
I don't have any bad feelings about the crow people
never said anything at all about the wolf's children
if they'd come by I'd shake all their hands

•

I wonder what eagle did to him
all those crows around him
it only took one crow to make the world

•

I think about you & it's like having spirits come down on me
where is it that we were going to die together
don't you think you ought to do like you say

•

I know how people get treated when they die
I'm gonna have a good time, a lot to drink

•

You surprise me, crow
whenever you see wolf people
you get way up on some branch

•

I'm gonna die & won't see you all any more
it doesn't matter that I'll lose lots of property
it's only what's gonna happen to me that I'm crying about

•

SONG ON THE WAY TO JAIL

They sound like howling wolves from here
everybody just beginning to get drunk
& I have to go away

•

SONG FOR THE RICHEST WOMAN IN WRANGELL

I used to make fun of you when you were a little girl & poor
where do you get all your whiskey & why aren't you ashamed

•

I don't know why you tell me I'm drunk
it's you been giving me all that whiskey

•

It's only whiskey that makes you pity me
what would it take to make you love me

•

My wife went away, left me
& like somebody who needs a good drink
I can't sleep

•

If you'd died I would've cut off my hair
I love you so much I would've blackened my face

•

Before he died
I saw his ghost

•

It would be very pleasant to die with a wolf woman
it would be very pleasant

•

He followed his own mind
got himself killed
can't blame anybody else

— *James Koller's workings, after John Swanton*

Travel Song

Leaving the white bear behind in his realm of sea-ice
we set off for our winter hunting grounds on the inland bays.
This is the route we took:
First we made our way across dangerous Dead-man's Gulch
and then crossed High-in-the-sky Mountain.
Circling Crooked Lake
we followed the course of the river over the flatlands beyond
where the sleds sank in deep snow up to the cross slats.
It was sweaty work, I tell you,
helping the dogs.

You think I even had a small fish
or a piece of musk-ox meat to chew on?
Don't make me laugh: I didn't have a shred on me.
The journey went on and on.
It was exhausting, pushing the sled along the lakes
around one island and over another,
mushing, mushing.
When we passed the island called Big Pot
we spit at it
just to do something different for a change.

Then after Stony Island
we crossed over Water Sound at the narrows,
touching on the two islands like crooked eyes
that we call, naturally, Cross-Eyed Islands,
and arrived at Seal Bay, where we camped,
and settled down to a winter season

of hunting at the breathing holes
for the delicious small blubber beasts.

Such is our life,
the life of hunters
migrating with the season.

— English working by Edward Field

song of the old woman

    all these heads these ears these eyes
    around me
    how long will the ears hear me?
    and those eyes how long
    will they look at me?
    when these ears won't hear me any more
    when these eyes turn aside from my eyes
    I'll eat no more raw liver with fat
    and those eyes won't see me any more
    and my hair my hair will have disappeared

— English version by Armand Schwerner

spring fjord

I was out in my kayak
I was out at sea in it
I was paddling
very gently in the fjord Ammassivik
there was ice in the water
and on the water a petrel
turned his head this way that way
didn't see me paddling
Suddenly nothing but his tail
then nothing
He plunged but not for me:
huge head upon the water
great hairy seal
giant head with giant eyes, moustache
all shining and dripping
and the seal came gently toward me
Why didn't I harpoon him?
was I sorry for him?
was it the day, the spring day, the seal
playing in the sun
like me?

— *English version by Armand Schwerner*

the old man's song, about his wife

husband and wife we loved each other then
we do now
there was a time
each found the other
beautiful

but a few days ago maybe yesterday
she saw in the black lake water
a sickening face
a wracked old woman face
wrinkled full of spots

I saw it she says
that shape in the water
the spirit of the water
wrinkled and spotted

and who'd seen that face before
wrinkled full of spots?
wasn't it me
and isn't it me now
when I look at you?

— *English version by Armand Schwerner*

dream

> I dreamt about you last night
> you were walking on the pebbles of the beach
> with me
> I dreamt about you
> as if I had awakened
> I followed you
> beautiful
> as a young seal
> I wanted you like a hunter
> lusting after a very young seal
> who plunges in, feeling pursued.
> That's how it was
> for me

— *English version by Armand Schwerner*

a man's song, about his daughter

> *That's*
>
> your son? the brother
> of your first-born boy?
> That's what they say to me
> well I've got some work to do again
> a little better this time
> if it's a boy I want
> I need a sharp prick
> well I'll sharpen it up and do the job again
> and then if they say that I messed up
> it'll be just the one time that's what

— *English version by Armand Schwerner*

first I lowered my head
and for a start I stared at the ground
for a second I couldn't say anything
but now that they're gone
I raise my head I look straight ahead I can answer
They say I stole a man
the husband of one of my aunts
they say I took him for a husband of my own
lies
fairy tales
slander
It was him, he
lay down next to me
But they're men
which is why they lie
that's the reason
and it's my hard luck.

— *English version by Armand Schwerner*

LULLABY

Tsimshian

The little girl will pick wild roses.
That is why she was born.

The little girl will dig wild rice with her fingers.
That is why she was born.

She will gather sap of pitch pine trees in the spring.
She will pick strawberries and blueberries.
That is why she was born.

She will pick soapberries and elderberries.
She will pick wild roses.
That is why she was born.

—Working by Carl Cary, after Marius Barbeau

Tsimshian mourning song

and now the words
       I'm grieving all by myself
       would rather be dead, what's the meaning
       of what I'm saying?
       I'll force the river to run upstream
       me sick at heart
       to do what I can't;
       little man at the corner of the sky
       boasting for nothing
       I'm way down like you
       why talk?
       this costly lament
       this song of moaning
       this one

— English working by Armand Schwerner, after Marius Barbeau

TWO DIVORCE SONGS

Tsimshian

1.

Now you love me;
Now you admire me,
but you threw me away
like something that tasted bad.
You treated me as if I were a rotten fish.
Now my old grandmother takes her dry
blackberries and puts them under her blanket.

2.

I thought you were good.
I thought you were like silver;
You are lead.

You see me high up on the mountain.
I walk through the sun;
I am sunlight myself.

— *Translations by Carl Cary*

insult before gift-giving

Tsimshian

man you
              are
                    a liar
what you say
                  it's all
lies
              Now the words!
who's afraid of you snow-on-the-leaves,
melting away
I mean Where's your gun your money big mouth
                Now. Louder!
man what
you say it's all a crock of shit

— *English working by Armand Schwerner, after Marius Barbeau*

SPYGLASS CONVERSATIONS

Tule/Cuna

(*A girl looking through a spyglass says*)
You cannot see mountains & valleys in the clouds,
I see the clouds as big as trees,
when I look far away I see the clouds like cliffs of high, gray rocks.
I see a cloud that looks like a coconut tree.
The clouds come up & come up in different shapes.
There are clouds that look like breakers,
you don't see the colors & shapes of the clouds,
I see them like people moving & bending, they come up just like
    people.
There are clouds like many people walking.
I see them every time I look out to sea with the glass.
Sometimes a cloud comes up like a ghost, & sometimes like a ship.
I look far off through the glass & see everything.
I see a cloud that looks like a sea horse, a wild sea horse that
    lives in the water
I see a cloud like a deer with branching horns.

(*The boy beside her says*)
You don't see that at all.

(*But the girl says*)
From the time I was a child I didn't think I would see such things
    as these.
If I don't look through the glass I can't see them.
Now I find out the different things the clouds make.
Do you want to see them too?

(*The boy says*)
All right. I want to see them too. (*He looks through the glass.*)
Now *I* see funny things.

(*The girl says*)
Now you see all those funny things.

(*Then the boy says to a younger girl*)
You want to see them too?

(*But she says*)
I'm too young.

(*The boy says to the older girl*)
Look down into the water with the glass.

(*The older girl says*)
Now I see strange things under the water.
I see things moving around as though they were live animals.
I see things there that look like little bugs—many strange animals
under the sea.

— *Translation by Frances Densmore*

NAVAJO ANIMAL SONGS

1.

Chipmunk can't drag it along
can't drag it along
Chipmunk holds back his ears

2.

Chipmunk was standing
jerking his feet
with stripes
he's a very short chipmunk

3.

Mole makes his pole redhot
Says: I'll shove it up your ass
Says: feel how it shakes your belly

4.

Wildcat was walking
He ran down here
He got his feet in the water
He farted
Wow, wow! says Wildcat

5.

A turkey is dancing near the rocks
shoves out his pelvis
woops-a-daisy we all go crazy

6.

Big Rabbit goes to see his baby
pisses
pissing all around him

7.

Pinionjay shits pebbles
now he's empty

—Workings by Jerome Rothenberg, after David McAllester

MORE ESKIMO SONGS ABOUT PEOPLE & ANIMALS

1.

Name of a man name of a man
who kills bear
                    the spearhole
here I am trying to drink blood
he pushed him down by the head
                              and the front of his inner coat
                              and the back of his inner coat
then girl
she isn't sorry
man who sleeps with her

2.

I'm crying I'm able to eat
I'm working well
                    when she desires
her husband or when he isn't angry
he comes off
it is enough he has another one
but not big it is enough he is old it is right
snow snow hoop of seal skin mouth spear
knife knife teeth mouth clothes
                              a woman's hip muscles

3.

Let the man turn to me
this is a woman's song
                    probably
                              he's sleeping outside
I'm trying to stop freezing
he's getting up early
thanks
let the man turn to me
let him turn let you and I go
but your animals
                    your one time wife
they are leaving
                    she is pregnant

4.

And his kayak
he's looking at something big
name of man do you think I am dark
                                        and his kayak
name of man thank you thank you
my big wife
            I follow her around
                              only one
it's a five dog team
a little behind us
a tiny bird
            I used to catch it

5.

Give it to me name of the baby
some deer fat
                they are coming
some deer marrow
                  they are coming
only his big mouth
this one fat from the stomach of the animal
                            frozen land
now it's cold weather now he is shiny
I'm near the camp I'll warm you shall I carry it
he's showing me
            sound
Wonderful!

6.

they hunt the square flippered seal and the whale
not quite night and lonely and his daughter
many young inhabitants of a place called
                        he is eating me
                        his sleeping boy
                        he's an old man
he is not afraid we are afraid
the young woman because she sleeps slept with a man

7.

Sounding
she cuts it
now he wishes
I would like to fill her

                        now
I have nothing to do
I can't feel anything
he hooks it
              in his hole
now
sounding
          now
I have nothing to do

— Workings by Stephen Berg, after Franz Boas

ORPINGALIK'S SONG: IN A TIME OF SICKNESS

Eskimo

My biggest worry is this:
that the whole winter long
I have been sick and helpless as a child.
   Ay me.

As long as I'm in this sorry condition
I really think it would be better
if my wife walked out on me
for I'm not much of a husband any more.
I should be taking care of her and getting food.
What good am I
now that I can't get up on my two feet?

Have you forgotten what a man you were? I ask myself.
Try to remember the beasts you hunted.
Remember and be strong again.

Yes, I remember once coming on a great white bear
who thought he alone was a fighter.
What a battle we had!
He came straight at me across the ice
rising high on his hind legs.
We grappled, and again and again
he threw me down,
but I didn't let go until he was dead.
When the bear came out of the water that day
and lay down calmly on the ice
he thought he was the only male around
but I came along and showed him!

I also remember a seal I once got
in a time when we were all weak with hunger.
Everyone was still asleep
when I went out on the ice that morning
and luckily found the breathing hole of a seal.
That blubbery beast was in there all right
about to come up for a breath of air
but he heard me, the sly one,
and waited to one side under the thick ice
where I could not spear him through the hole.
But just as I was ready to give up
he made a false move and I got my harpoon into him,
and we had his blubber and blood for breakfast that day!

Now with me sick
there is no blubber in the house
to fill the lamp with.
Spring has come
and the good days for hunting
are passing by, one by one.
When shall I get well?
My wife has to go begging skins for clothes and meat to eat
that I can't provide —
O when shall I be well again?

I can't understand it:
I was once a hunter
but now I've come to this.
I remember a fat caribou cow
swimming out in the open water,
and I went after her in my kayak
hardly believing I could ever catch up.
I chased hard
— I almost feel strong again remembering it —

and other kayaks were chasing too
thinking they would get the caribou first.
They were already shouting cries of victory
but I put everything I had into my paddle,
— O I remember now how it feels to be a real man again —
and I won the race:
It was my caribou, all mine,
and the others got nothing at all!

— *English version by Edward Field, after Knud Rasmussen*

A BOOK OF EVENTS (I)

DREAM EVENT (I)

Iroquois

After having a dream, let someone else guess what it was. Then have everyone act it out together.

DREAM EVENT (II)

Iroquois

Have participants run around the center of a village, acting out their dreams & demanding that others guess & satisfy them.

A MASKED EVENT FOR COMEDIAN & AUDIENCE

Lummi (Salish)

1. A comedian's mask is painted red on one side, black on the other; the mouth is twisted, the hair in disarray. For a costume he wears a blanket or a strip of fur which leaves his right hand free. He dances along with the other performers, often dances out-of-time to attract attention, & repeatedly annoys the dancers by quizzically scrutinizing their masks, poking at their eyes, looking at their noses, picking their teeth, etc. Sometimes the dancers whip the comedian vigorously with cedar boughs to drive him away, keeping time with the drums as they do so. When not annoying the dancers, the comedian goes around the room pretending to take lice from the singers' hair. He sometimes goes to a very old woman or a very pretty girl to do this, using it as a pretext to carress her.

2. The audience refrains from laughing.

BUTTERFLY SONG EVENT

Maricopa

A circular, roofless enclosure of willow poles is built, walled in with leafy branches. Across the top runs a series of parallel strings along which many yellow butterflies, cut out of mountain-sheep skin, are hanging. A singer sits at the center of the enclosure. As he sings he beats on an inverted basket with one hand, scraping a stick a foot long on it with the other. This makes the butterflies look as though they were fluttering, dancing in time to his tune.

AUTUMN EVENTS

Eskimo

A man & a woman both wear masks of seal skins, that of the woman being tattooed. The man's hair is arranged in a bunch protruding from the forehead, the woman's in a pigtail on each side & a large bunch at the back of the head. Their left legs are tied up by a thong running around the neck & the knee, compelling them to hobble as they walk.

1. *Threshold Event.* With their legs bound the man & woman must try to enter a hut while the occupants hold a long sealskin thong before them to keep them off. If they fall down in an attempt to cross the threshold, they are thoroughly beaten with a short whip or with sticks. After they succeed in entering a hut they blow out all the fires.

2. *Snow Event.* The organizers of the Autumn Events wake everybody up by climbing on their roofs & screaming & shouting. When all have assembled outside, the man & woman from the previous event sit down in the snow. The man holds a knife in his hand & sings:

> Oangaja jaja jajaja aja
> Pissiungmipadlo panginejernago
> Qodlungutaokpan panginejerlugping
> Pissiungmipadlo panginejernago.

To this song the woman keeps time by moving her body & her arms, at the same time flinging snow on the bystanders. Then everybody goes into a singing house & joins in dancing & singing. The men are first to leave & stand outside while the masked man & woman guard the entrance. With the men outside the women continue to sing, until the original couple leads them one by one to the waiting men. Each newly formed couple now re-enters the singing house & walks around the central lamp, all the men & women crying "hrr! hrr!" from both corners of their mouths. Each pair goes to the woman's hut & spends the night together.

TAMALE EVENT

Aztec

"For seven days all fasted. Only water tamales, soaked in water, were eaten, without chili, without salt, with neither saltpeter nor lime. And they were eaten only at midday. And he who fasted not at this time, if he were noted, he was punished. And much was this, the eating of water tamales, hallowed. And he who did not this, if he were not seen or noted, it was said—he was visited with the itch.

"And when the feast arrived, it was said: 'Ashes are put on faces,' & 'They are adorned with sea shells.' And it was when indeed all the gods danced. Thus it was named the dance of the gods.

"And all came forth as humming birds, butterflies, honeybees, flies, birds, giant horned beetles, black beetles—those forms men took; in these guises they came dancing. And still others were in the guise of sleep. Some had garlands of fruit tamales; birds' flesh tamales formed yet others' garlands. And before them was the maize bin, filled with fruit tamales.

"And soon also all these appeared—those who played the roles of the poor, those who sold vegetables, those who sold wood. Also appeared one in the guise of a leper. And still more took the forms of birds, large owls, screech owls. And even other birds they counterfeited."

MUD EVENTS

Navajo

1. The organizers of the event strip down & smear themselves & each other with mud & water from head to foot. They dip their headbands in mud before tying back their hair.

2. The participants run & dance about, then ask others to join them, lifting the newcomers high in the air, tossing them up & catching them again, or throwing them up & down in a blanket.

3. A small piece of sheepskin with a red blotch in the center (of fresh menstrual blood, excretion from the sore of a horse, etc.) is rubbed on the heads & backs of participants; some are made to sit on it.

4. Participants run into the audience & pull horsemen off their horses: then they oblige them to undress & join the mud event. The horsemen are smeared from foot to head, especially the back, face & hair. The original participants blow upon them, spit on them & put mud into their mouths. Horses are also caught & bathed with mud.

5. At the end of the event the organizers lie down flat on their stomachs one in line behind the other & so close that the head of each one touches the feet of the one in front of him. The last one gets up, walks along the trail of bodies & lies down; the next one does the same in leapfrog style until each participant has walked the length of the entire line. Some actually step on the prostrate bodies, while others place their feet on the ground close by the men. When this is over, all the participants stand up, form a snake-line & run over to a spring of water, where they sprinkle cornmeal on themselves & wash.

(1) Hot Water Event

Participants jump into a kettle of hot water & then run & dance where they please.

(2) Fish Event

Four or five men lie down & imitate a fish out of water.

(3) Half-Man Event

They paint one-half their bodies with white clay & the other half black to represent a man split in two front & rear.

(4) Moon Event

A man & woman cut themselves & cry & dance for five days fasting. They cut through the skin of the breast & tie in a string. They tie the string to the top of the lodge, the man facing the woman.

(5) Horse Event

Putting boughs on the head. Men & women cut willows or boughs & trim their horses' heads & their own. They tie up the horses in one place & then the men dance around them.

GIFT EVENT II

Kwakiutl

Start by giving away different colored glass bowls.

Have everyone give everyone else a glass bowl.

Give away handkerchiefs & soap & things like that

Give away a sack of clams & a roll of toilet paper.

Give away teddybear candies, apples, suckers & oranges.

Give away pigs & geese & chickens, or pretend to do so.

Pretend to be different things.

Have the women pretend to be crows, have the men pretend to be something else.

Talk Chinese or something.

Make a narrow place at the entrance of a house & put a line at the end of it that you have to stoop under to get in.

Hang the line with all sorts of pots & pans to make a big noise.

Give away frying pans while saying things like "Here is this frying pan worth $100 & this one worth $200."

Give everyone a new name.

Give a name to a grandchild or think of something & go & get everything.

GIFT EVENT IV

Winnebago

1. Have someone make a dummy out of grass & dress it with whatever objects he wishes to receive as gifts. If he wants a horse have him put a bridle crosswise around the body of the dummy; if he wants clothes, have him dress the dummy up in Indian clothes.

2. The maker of the dummy then places it near a gathering of people or where he expects such a gathering to take place. He sits down near his dummy.

3. When a second participant sees the dummy he goes over & either kicks or strikes the man who made it, at the same time giving him one of the objects he desires. Others may join in upon the same conditions.

4. The participants only stop kicking the dummy-maker when someone, preferably a warrior who at some time or other had cut up an enemy in war, cuts up the dummy.

5. As soon as his bruises permit him, the man who made the dummy gets up, gathers all his gifts together, & goes home.

LANGUAGE EVENT I

Eskimo

Use the language of shamans.

Say		& mean	
Say	the leash	& mean	the father
"	a road	"	the wind
"	someone with a something sticking out	"	a man
"	where things get soft	"	the guts
"	soup	"	a seal
"	Big Louse	"	a caribou
"	what makes me dive in headfirst	"	a dream
"	what cracks your ears	"	a gun
"	what looks like piss	"	your beads
"	a piece of frozen meat	"	a child
"	a piece of almost frozen meat	"	a grandchild
"	a jumping thing	"	a trout
"	what keeps me standing straight	"	your clothes
"	the person with a belly	"	the weather
"	the person with a belly getting up	"	it's morning
"	the person with a belly goes to bed	"	it's nightfall
"	little walker	"	a fox
"	walker with his head down	"	a dog
"	the bag it lies in	"	a mother
"	the bag it almost lies in	"	a stepmother
"	a person smoke surrounds	"	a live one
"	a floating one	"	an island
"	a neighbor	"	a wife

" a flat one	" a wolf
" a shadow	" a white man
" another kind of shadow	" a person
" the dark one	" the liver
" making shadows	" a seance
" the shadow-maker	" the shaman
" he turned my mind around	" he told me something

LANGUAGE EVENT II

Navajo

Hold a conversation in which everything refers to water.

If somebody comes in the room, say: "Someone's floating in."

If somebody sits down, say: "It looks like someone just stopped floating."

PICTURE EVENT, FOR DOCTOR & PATIENT
(to be performed after making a sandpainting
of male & female dancing figures with yellow legs
from dancing knee-deep in pollen)

Navajo

1. Meal applied to divine figures.
2. Plumed wands erected.
3. Cup placed on the rainbow's hands.
4. Cold infusion made, sprinkler placed on cup.
5. Pollen applied to figures.
6. Doctor departs, unmasked.
7. Patient enters, song begins.
8. Patient sprinkles picture.
9. Patient sits, southeast, & disrobes.
10. Doctor, masked, returns as god.
11. Doctor sprinkles picture.
12. Assistant takes up meal from picture.
13. Doctor touches moistened sprinkler to figures.
14. Patient sits on picture.
15. Infusion offered to gods & given to patient.
16. Assistant moistens doctor's hands.
17. Sacred dust applied to patient.
18. Doctor yells into patient's ear.
19. Doctor departs, masked.
20. Patient leaves picture.
21. Patient fumigated.
22. Doctor returns, unmasked.
23. Plumed wands pulled out.
24. Picture despoiled.
25. Picture erased.
26. Material from picture taken out & discarded.

NAMING EVENTS

Papago

1. A shaman has a dream & names a child for what he dreams in it. Among such names are Circling Light, Rushing Light Beams, Daylight Comes, Wind Rainbow, Wind Leaves, Rainbow Shaman, Feather Leaves, A-Rainbow-as-a-Bow, Shining Beetle, Singing Dawn, Hawk-Flying-over-Water-Holes, Flowers Trembling, Chief-of-Jackrabbits, Water-Drops-on-Leaves, Short Wings, Leaf Blossoms, Foamy Water.

2. A person receives a name describing something odd about him, always on the bad side. Such names include: Grasshopper-Ate-His-Arrow, Gambler, Ass-Side-to-the-Fire, Pants-Fall-Down, Blisters, Fish-Smell-Mouth, Bed Wetter, Rat Ear, Yellow Legs.

3. A person receives a name describing something odd & sexual about the namer. Here the namer is a woman or a transvestite, who makes the name public by shouting it after the man named when others are present. The man invariably accepts it & is regularly called by it, even by his wife & family. Such names include: Down-Dangling-Pussy-Hairs, Big Cunt, Long Asshole.

4. A group of namers gathers around a dead enemy & shouts abusive names at the body. These names are then given to the shouters. They include: Long Bones, Full-of-Dirt, Back-of-a-Wildcat, Yellow Face, & Gold Breasts, the latter spoken of a girl.

5. A person buys a name or trades names with another person. For example, Devil-Old-Man exchanges names with Contrary, or Looking-for-Girls-at-a-Dance changes with Big Crazy, but has to give him four pints of whiskey in addition because of the desirability of the name.

PEBBLE EVENT

Omaha

Part One: The Painting. Those present at the pebble event sit along the sides of the room where the event is taking place. Four men leave their seats & go one by one to a place on the south side of the room, where a board with powdered charcoal has been set up for them. As each man reaches the board, he stoops & touches his hands to the earth, then passes them over his arms & body, down to his feet. Then he dips the fingers of his right hand into the charcoal & draws a black line from his mouth down the length of one arm, & a similar line down the other. After that he makes black lines on his body with his blackened fingertips. Taking some powder in the palm of his hand he goes back to the side of the room he came from, where he puts black lines down the arms of all those near him. When all four men have finished painting themselves & the others, they go to the rear of the room, where a pile of calico cloth has been placed, & stand there facing the east.

Part Two: The Shooting. The four men leading the pebble event bend over & make movements as though retching. After doing this for a while they begin to spit out pebbles. Then they circle the room, & as they do so, they "shoot" four other participants with their hands, shielding their shooting hands with an eagle wing held in the other. Each person "shot" immediately presses his hand on the "wound," assumes a tragic attitude, falls to the ground, & lays there rigid. The four leaders now circle the room again, with the other four joining them. Then these four "shoot" another four, who after circling the room shoot another four, and so on by fours until everybody has been "shot" & is circling the room. At that point a drum song begins & goes on for a while. Just before the event ends, each participant sings a song of his own choice—all these songs being sung simultaneously.

CRAZY DOG EVENTS

Crow

1. Act like a crazy dog. Wear sashes & other fine clothes, carry a rattle, & dance along the roads singing crazy dog songs after everybody else has gone to bed.

2. Talk crosswise: say the opposite of what you mean & make others say the opposite of what they mean in return.

3. Fight like a fool by rushing up to an enemy & offering to be killed. Dig a hole near an enemy, & when the enemy surrounds it, leap out at them & drive them back.

4. Paint yourself white, mount a white horse, cover its eyes & make it jump down a steep & rocky bank, until both of you are crushed.

ANIMAL SPIRIT EVENT

Lummi (*Salish*)

Imitate the spirit of the animal or thing inside you.

Let the one who imitates the wolf, dance squatting. Let him draw his arms up at the beginning of each measure bringing his bent wrists up below his chin with fingers pointing directly downwards. If he can, have him crack his knuckles & spurt blood.

Let the spirit of the sea, which appears half-bear & half-human & whose home is surrounded by hovering flies because there is so much food there, sing a song that goes: "O the flies in the home of the awful beast."

Let the spirit of the whistle imitate a whistle.

Let the spirit of the west wind sing: "Hey look out the west wind's going to blow."

Let the person who imitates a cedar be accompanied by five to ten other dancers. Have him warm up some cedar poles with mops of shredded cedar bark or twilled goat wool fastened at the ends, as he describes the approach of his spirit in a canoe. Let him sing the phrase, "Now the spirit is walking," then hand the poles to the other dancers who hold them vibrating from the waist. Then let him dance around the house with his own pole outstretched, the others joining him. Let him try to find food hidden in the house by prodding any bundles he sees with his pole, then toss what he finds into the center of the room, to be burnt as an offering to the dead or served to the assembled guests. Let the dance end with a great shout.

Let the spirit of the locomotive go through the locomotive's motions in his dance.

Let the man who imitates a fire swallow burning cedar bark.

VISION EVENT (I)

Eskimo

Go to a lonely place & rub a stone in a circle on a rock for hours & days on end.

VISION EVENT (II)

Eskimo

Let the person who wants a vision hang himself by his neck. When his face turns purple, take him down & have him describe what he's seen.

VISION EVENT (III)

Sioux

Go to a mountain-top & cry for a vision.

A BOOK OF EVENTS (II)

THEATER & RITUAL-THEATER

SIXTY-SIX POEMS FOR A BLACKFOOT BUNDLE
with scenario for an accompanying bundle-event

Give a bundle of turnip leaves & other things to a woman.

Have the woman & her husband follow the actions of another man & wife who are experts in transferring a bundle.

Call the transferrers "mother" & "father," & the receivers "son" & "daughter."

Seat any men who are watching on the north side & any women on the south. Seat the transferrers & receivers at the rear.

Begin the event by singing a smudge song.

1

I was looking for the powerful spring grass, how powerful
I was finding it I was lifting it up, how powerful

2

Oldman was coming in telling us he would like to have a sweat
Oldman says I want a damn fast fisher I want a damn white
  buffalo robe

3

Oldwoman was coming in
she was saying ditto ditto ditto

4

Morningstar was coming in saying he would like to have a sweat
Morningstar says I want a damn fast fisher I want some fine tailfeathers

5

Man was coming in saying let's go have a sweat
Man was giving all of us a real sense of security

6

Oldman says I want some black & white buffalo robes
Let's go have a sweat

7

Oldwoman says I want some black & white wolfhides
Let's go have a sweat

8

Oldman was coming in says hurry & fix me up a sweathouse
He was coming in & happy: now he wants another sweathouse

Now begin to make a smudge.

9

Now she wants another sweathouse
Man came in   He'd like to have a sweat

10

Morningstar shows up with lots of things

Begin to bring in robes & clothes
& tailfeathers & other things.

11

Oldman says this man's got to want some tailfeathers

12

Oldman wants some tailfeathers

13

Oldman says I want a hundred tailfeathers

14

Oldwoman says I want all different kinds of tailfeathers

15

Oldman says you better hurry up with my tailfeathers
Oldwoman says be sure & get me some other kinds of tailfeathers

16

Oldman says better not forget my white buffalo robe

17

Oldwoman says better not forget my different kind of elkrobe

18

Somebody up there sees me, how powerful
Oldwoman sings, I was just looking at the ground, how powerful

> *Have one of the "transferrers" level
> out the smudge place with the toe of a
> new moccasin.*
>
> *Touch moccasin to smudge place, then
> smoothe the loose earth over.*

19

I have lifted up the buffalo, how very powerful

> *Have the "transferrer" pick up the
> tailfeathers.*

20

Oldman says better hurry up & smudge me
Oldwoman says you better smudge me in a different place
Morningstar says smudge me in an even different place
Oldman says better paint me now
Oldwoman says you better paint me with a different paint
Morningstar says paint me even different

> *Smudge & bodypaint are applied as per
> instructions.*
>
> *The order of the paint is first yellow,
> then black, then with sundog symbols.*

21

A Song for the Rawhide on Which the Rattles Are Beaten

Man says I'm standing powerfully upon these mountains, how powerful
I powerfully am coming down
I come down powerfully in summer
I'm standing powerfully upon the earth

22

A Song for the Rattles

I'm in a hurry

> *Spread out the rawhide in front of the men.*
>
> *Have the men pick up rattles.*

23

Raven says I'm on the ground looking for something to eat
Now I found it, how powerful

24

Raven says I'm looking for some buffalo
Now I've got them

25

Oldman says don't I look good with rattles?
Now I'm shaking them

> *Begin to beat the rattles.*

26

Oldman says I'm looking for some timber, now I found it I've taken it

> *Have the "father" pick up the smudgestick & make a new smudge.*

27

The Sun Dance Shelter

Let's put my sunhouse up & no one knock it over

28

The Turnip Bundle

It's been a long time now, Man
You'd best get up

29

Oldman comes in & squats, says I'm looking for my bundle
Now I found it, how powerful

30

Oldwoman just comes in, says I'm looking for my bundle
Ditto ditto

31

Oldman says I'm picking up my bundle
Now I'm getting full of power

32

Oldwoman says I'm carrying my bundle on my back now I'm getting
  full of power
How powerful

33

I'm picking up my bundle
Now it's starting up now it's stopping
Now it wants to sit down someplace powerful

> *Have the "father" lay the bundle
> down. He exposes the inner
> wrapping of badger-skin.*

34

The Badger's Song

The earth's my home, how powerful
I'm looking for my home, how very powerful

35

Oldwoman says why can't I see my bundle which is so damn
  powerful?

36

Song for the Bundle-Event Women

Oldman says those women looking at me must be pretty smart

> *Take turnip leaves from the badger-skin*
> *wrapping.*
> *Hold them up & shake them.*

37

My bundle wants to do some shaking

38

Man says I want some fine tailfeathers
My bundle says I want to sit down someplace powerful
Oldwoman says why can't I see my bundle?

39

Blacktail deer was running all around, how powerful

> *Remove cloth wrappings from*
> *the turnip leaves.*

40

Another Skin Song

Weasel's my headdress he was running all around, how powerful

41

The Doll / The Dwarf*

Boys are running all around, how powerful

42

The Teal Duck Is the Water Ouzel

Duck says this water is my medicine, how very powerful

43

Man says I want a buffalo tail

44

Lizard says hey man I'm getting angry

45

Song for a Scalplock Necklace

I'm picking up my necklace, how powerful
Man says I want to have that string of scalphair

46

A Woman's Dress

Elk were running all around, how powerful

---

* *Names for doll-shaped tobacco-seed containers.*

47

Song for an Elkrobe

I've given you my elkrobe

48

A Song for White Paint

The earth's my medicine, how powerful

49

I'm looking for some timber, now I found it I've taken it
How powerful

> *Have an assistant bring in a small cottonwood tree.*
>
> *The "transferrer" hands him an ax, & he stands holding tree & ax, while someone tells a war story.*
>
> *Then he cuts a point onto the tree butt.*

50

Timber's looking for someplace powerful to sit

> *Stick the tree in the ground on the south side of the performance area.*
>
> *Let the "mother" take up the headdress, followed by the "daughter."*
>
> *Have both women make dancing movements with their bodies, while hanging the headdress on the tree & singing.*

51

I'm looking for some timber I can sit on

52

A Song Without Words

Wow! Wow! Wow! Wow! Wow!

> *During the song-without-words, the "mother" takes the headdress from the tree, puts it on her head, her body swaying with the rhythm of the singing, makes hooking motions at the tree, rubs her head up and down the limbs, & then places the headdress upon her daughter. She also makes the whistling sound of the elk.*

53

Song for a Digging Stick

I was looking for my medicine I've taken it, how powerful

54

I landed some buffalo they're looking for someplace powerful to sit

> *Tie dewclaws to the end of the stick.*

55

I'm digging up this powerful turnip

> *Have someone imitate a crane's call.*
> *Have the "mother" hold the stick*
> *on her back, then make four passes*

> *toward the smudge place before pull-*
> *ing the stick into position on the*
> *"daughter's" back.*

> *Now prepare the "son" by taking off*
> *his robe & having the "transferrer"*
> *paint him while both sing.*

56

I'm taking off this young man's robe

> *Paint the "son's" entire body*
> *& face with charcoal.*

57

Oldman says to take some black paint
I'm powerfully going to paint him up, how powerful

58

I want to paint the sun & dogs on him

> *Have the "transferrer" mark a*
> *half moon on the "son's" breast with*
> *his fingertip.*

> *Mark a circle on his back for the*
> *sun; a bar on each cheek, the chin*
> *and the forehead, for the sundogs.*

59

A Painting Song Without Words

WOOOOₒₒOOOOOW!

> *Draw a line across the "son's" face*
> *at the bridge of the nose, while*
> *singing #60.*

60

Buffalo trail, how powerful
Hey I'm going for a trip on it

> *Have the "transferrer" draw a circle*
> *around each wrist & ankle, then hand*
> *the "son" his robe again, while both*
> *are singing.*

61

Hey I'm giving you your robe, Man

62

This man says I want some feathers

> *Tie tailfeathers in the "son's" hair.*

63

Man wants a string of scalphair

> *Put on his necklace.*

64

I'm looking for my whistle now I found it
It's whistling how powerful it sounds

65

I want a bow

66

I want an arrow

> Place four bunches of sage grass
> about two feet apart at the north
> end of the performance area. At this
> point the four participants are
> standing up.

> The "father" takes hold of the "son's"
> right leg & makes four passes toward
> the first bunch of sage. The "mother"
> does likewise with the "daughter."
> Then the pair are made to step from
> one bunch to the other.

> Now the "father" takes the lead, the
> "son" next, then the "daughter," then
> the "mother," & all file out in pro-
> cession.

— Adaptation & scenario by Jerome Rothenberg, after Clark Wissler

THE TEXT OF THE RAINGOD DRAMA

San Juan Pueblo

From the Prologue (the Winter Cacique passing out Holy Water to those who will be kachina, saying):

> This sacred water
> of O·yi·ke
> Mother of Us All
> you take it   your body
> will grow stronger with it
> & we're praying
> that you be loved & liked
> have your dream of life come true

(& those who receive the holy water, taking a drink out of the pottery vessel, swallowing some of the water, spitting the rest in their hands, rubbing it over their bodies, & saying):

& I pray too
my body growing stronger
going on in being
loved & liked
a life of all good things
I wish for

Part One   The Sacred Clowns

> Inside the Large Kiva, small fires are burning in the fireplace. Candlelight flickers from the posts supporting the ceiling. Two ushers stand near the entrance & scrutinize the people as they enter, to verify their identity & make sure that no strangers enter the kiva. One by one, the

Children of the Great Ones—the people: men, women & children—climb down the ladder, file into the kiva silently, & sit down on their sheepskins spread out on the floor. Two guards take their seats on the top steps, while the Governor sits down on the lower step of the adobe, fireplacelike, step-shaped structure near the entrance.

The Caciques & Priestesses arrive & silently seat themselves on their sheepskins. The men roll ceremonial cigarettes &, in low voices, begin to say *The Smoke Prayer:*

O raingodmen
O raingodwomen
O raingodyoungmen
O raingodyoungwomen
we ask you to sip up this holy moisture
to make your clothing from this sacred fog
O raingods who are here & there
raingods who are red & blue & yellow
& who are grey & waterclear
we ask you to be happy without tears
& to be calm without sadness
& easy without loneliness
but continue to be above us
to do what you've done for us
in love & kindness
to bring us
best things of life
to let us go on in being
loved & liked
catching up with what
has always drawn us

The people are waiting & talking to each other, when suddenly a thunderous noise is heard. It is the Clowns, at the top of the kiva, who are making thunder by stomping their feet. The people laugh in anticipation of the fun they will have. The clowns enter through a circular hole in the ceiling & lower themselves onto the step-shaped structure. Each clown carries his sheepskin pack tied to his back. The people take sacred cornmeal in their right hands & sprinkle it on the floor toward the Clowns. Mothers pass out cornmeal to their children, who likewise perform the Feeding Rite. Each clown then sits down on one of the top steps at opposite sides of the structure, watching the people & looking curiously & searchingly around.

FIRST CLOWN. Hey little twin brother hey wonder where we be at little twin brother?

SECOND CLOWN. In Hell must be hey just lookit all them devilheads around us.

FIRST CLOWN (*pointing at a woman*). Yaas that one's got her sights on me.

SECOND CLOWN. Think she's hot for you?

The people laugh as the Clowns descend slowly from the steps & walk toward the kiva, scrutinizing the people. The First Clown walks over to the side where the men are seated & peeks at them. They hide under their blankets, to avoid embarrassment from the Clowns' comments. The Second Clown walks over to the women, who are also hiding under their shawls. But some of the children who aren't covered look curiously around.

FIRST CLOWN (*pointing to a child*). Hey will you just look here little brother. That kid looks like me, yus think it's mine?

Again the people laugh, but the Clowns have now turned their attention to the Governor seated on the lowest of the steps.

SECOND CLOWN. Hey hey just-a-little-older-than-me-little-brother, yus see who's sitting here? Why it's the Governor himself I do believe. They tell me he's been making it with the War Chief's wife.

(WOMAN IN AUDIENCE). I do wish these clowns wouldn't talk like that. With all the children here.

> The two Clowns change places from the women's to the men's side, respectively, & continue their jokes for a while, walking & looking around leisurely.

FIRST CLOWN. Know sumpin brudder? people traveling like this they got to stop & eat I do believe.

SECOND CLOWN. Yaas indeed just-a-little-older-than-me-younger-brother. People do & I do too so let's sit down & try some.

> The Clowns, taking their sheepskin packs off their backs, unwrap meat & bread, & sit down on their sheepskins near the Caciques. They break off small bits of bread, throw them to the ground, & mumble the following food offering prayer.

CLOWNS. *A Prayer to the Dear Dead*

> Eat some of this food hey
> Body gets a little stronger.

> The clowns begin to eat a little.

FIRST CLOWN. Hey when people eat chomp chomp yus know waal that's the time for telling stories.

SECOND CLOWN. Waal whynchoo start wif one then little-older-mmm-me-lil-brudder?

FIRST CLOWN. Okay sure hmmm t'other day whilst I was walking past the Garbage Gardens who should I see but Flower Mountain (chomp) & she was going out ter gather cowchips. And who would yus think was coming out ter help her?

SECOND CLOWN. Could be Bear Mountain maybe?

FIRST CLOWN. Yaas indeed little-older-than-me-little-brother & was he ever helping her hot shit!

SECOND CLOWN. Waal preety good yaas but yus know what I saw whilst I was down by the riverside last week?

FIRST CLOWN. Nix no couldn't even start to guess.

SECOND CLOWN. Waal I saw Big Mountain running after Cactus Blossom.

FIRST CLOWN. Did he git her?

> The clowns continue for about twenty minutes to eat & tell jokes, mostly about lovemaking. When they have finished their meal they begin to hand out bits of meat & bread to the people, saying "Here, throw this away." They then roll up their sheepskins, tie them carefully, & lay them by the Caciques, whom they address: "Please, don't take care of this for me."

Part Two   *The Bringing of the Raingods*

SECOND CLOWN. Hey now let's git down to business.

> The First Clown steps carefully over some of the women & children seated to his right, walks to one of the fireplaces along the north wall, picks up some ashes & carries them to the center of the kiva.

FIRST CLOWN. Let's try our luck!

> He claps his hands as if brushing off the ashes which form an ash cloud. He looks upward toward this ash cloud called *the heavens,* shading his eyes with one hand to indicate that he's trying to see something in the distance. (This gesture is always repeated just before a Clown speaks about what he "sees.")

FIRST CLOWN. Waal I don't see a solitary thing. Maybe you try it little-older-than-me-little-brother.

SECOND CLOWN. Hmmm you say you didn't see a solitary thing little-older-than-me-little-brother & izzat so?

FIRST CLOWN. So tis I didn't see a solitary thing you betcha.

SECOND CLOWN (*clapping his hands, throwing the ashes downward & looking toward the ash cloud*): Waal I can't see a solitary thing either!

> The clowns repeat these actions by looking in the other four directions: north, west, south & east. Each Clown pretends to throw his ashes in one direction, then with a quick movement turns around & actually throws them the opposite way; then he tries again to "see," but always with the same result: "I can't see a solitary thing."

FIRST CLOWN (*clapping his hands then shading his eyes with his left hand*). Soooo yus say you didn't see a thing either little twin brother. Hee hee waal I see Thundercloud feeling up Blue Corn soo lovely. (*The people laugh.*) And and wowWW I see a lake now muddy waters yass it's far away sooo very far—

SECOND CLOWN. Yass & I see water moving hey it's churning & it's bubbling hey yus just hear them troubled waters splashing. (*He imitates the sound & motion of the water.*) Sumpin must be happening in that lake is all I know. Come on you try it now, see what you can see.

FIRST CLOWN. Waal you say yus saw that muddy water lake with the water a-churning & a-splashing izzat so? Waal I see jist a little of that bubbling: yahrss it's bubbling & yass I see a head come sticking out of it. One poor old lonely head. Hey little-older-than-me-little-brother now you try it.

SECOND CLOWN. Hmmm yus say yus saw one poor old lonely head came sticking out?

FIRST CLOWN. Yaas.

SECOND CLOWN. Waal this one lonely one whose head came sticking out is coming out himself now & there's another one's jist coming & another & another. And now he's coming out yass & there's another one that's coming out & there's another & they keep coming out & coming out & coming out & yaaas they're lifting the Sacred Cornflower out of that lake & they're carrying it in their outstretched hands. And more & more of them are coming out bringing the Sacred Cornflower with them & bringing the power (yaas) to make rain & the power to raise watermelons & the power to raise muskmelons & the power to raise squashes & wheat & corn & the power to hunt deer & hunt buffalo & they just keep a-coming out with all that power & with the power to hunt rabbits & the power yaas to kill skunks. (*The people laugh.*) And yaas they're a-coming out now with the power to bring lots of crops & to make more animals & children, & wow they're coming here, they're coming, here they come. Come on little-older-than-me-little-brother hurry on up & see what you can see.

FIRST CLOWN. Yass hmmm yus say you saw them coming out from that old Muddy Water Lake & there was lots of them. Waal let's see now. Yaaaas they're rising from that lake & lifting their fog rainbow & their Cloudflower they're rising with their thunder & their lightning with their bird songs & their cricket chirps & with their power to bring the rain & lots of Everything. And hey they're moving on to Stone Man Lake & now they're laying down their fog rainbow & they're taking their Cloudflower with them & disappearing in the water. But yass yass there are lots more of them in that lake too & it's deeper there yass it's deeper & they're coming out they keep on & keep on coming out. And now you try it little-older-than-me-little-brother.

SECOND CLOWN. Yass waaal yus said yus saw them coming out of Stone Man Lake & izzat so? And now they're coming on they still keep on a-coming & yass they're lifting up the Cloudflower & coming along with their fertilities yass with all their powers to raise corn & raise muskmelons & wheat & with their powers to kill deer & buffalos & rabbits yass & with all these goodnesses they're moving on to Stone Man Mountain & way up & over the top of it & traveling past of it yass with their thunders & their lightnings & their bird songs & their cricket chirps. There they are too & they're a-coming to Thunder Lake & submerging into it & coming out of it again & lots of others in emergence with them now & more & more are keeping on in coming & are coming on & keeping coming. But now you try it little brother.

The Clowns continue to "see" the Raingods coming on a cloud, from lake to lake, coming closer & closer, bringing the Cloudflower & all their powers, goodnesses & blessings with them. But where more & more Raingods were emerging from every lake during the first part of their voyage, the number of emerging gods begins to decrease as they approach the pueblo.

FIRST CLOWN. Yass & yass yus said some of them was staying on in Willow Leaf Lake yus said fewer of them was coming out of it & izzat so? Yus said it & now I see some few of them 're coming closer yass some with their deer killing & their buffalo killing powers & with their powers to raise corns & watermelons & squashes & beans, & now I see them yaaas they're a-coming to Clearwater Lake & yass they're going into & submerging into it. They're coming out of it & coming out & coming out of it, & there are some now that are coming out of it & they're coming with their thunders & their lightnings & their rainbringings yass & all the goodnesses of raising beans & raising squashes & raising corns & raising melons & killing deer & killing foxes & killing rabbits. But there aren't so many emerging from out of Clearwater Lake as had entered into it yass some must just have stayed inside that lake but such few as were coming out are moving toward San Juan now coming closer yass & closer & waaal little-older-than-me-little-brother maybe you should just try it now.

SECOND CLOWN (clapping hands, holding his left hand on his forehead as before). Waal yus did say that some were coming closer to San Juan & izzat so? Yaass now I see them coming up to Garbage Gardens they're coming up to it now with all their powers for bringing rain & growth & their fertilities & yass you better give a try now little-older-than-me-little-brother see what you can see.

Three Priestesses, who have been sitting in front of the audience in their ceremonial mantas, arise. Each has a ceremonial feather hanging down over her forehead. While the Clowns report the progress of the Raingods, the Priestesses walk slowly along the lighted posts to the step-shaped structure. From the ladder behind this structure, they start walking solemnly in an elongated circuit to the Caciques & back to the ladder, performing the Sanctifying Rite by taking cornmeal out of their baskets, blowing their breath over it, & then sprinkling the cornmeal. They recite a slow prayer for making a path for the Raingods.

PRIESTESSES. *A Prayer Making a Path for the Raingods*

> O you Great Ones
> who have come
> to visit us
> we small ones
> make
> this sacred path
> for you   the Great Ones
> who will walk along
> this sacred path
> we small ones
> make for you.

When the cornmeal path is completed near the ladder behind the stepped structure, the Priestesses start to their seats, reaching there at about the same time that the Raingods arrive at the bottom of the outside ladder.

FIRST CLOWN (*clapping his hands & shading his eyes*). Yus said they had come to Garbage Gardens, waaal izzat so?

SECOND CLOWN. Yass.

FIRST CLOWN. Waal from Garbage Gardens they are going right on with their Cornflower & with their thunders & their lightnings yass & 're bringing their bird songs & cricket chirps & their powers yass to be bringing rain & their fertilities & growings. Yass yass they're coming right into the pueblo with all their packs of goodnesses. Getting closer now & YAAASSS I see them yass they're getting to the middle of San Juan & now, & now they're at Earth's Navel at the Sacred Stone Shrine yasss they're waiting at Earth's Navel Sacred

Stone Shrine laying their fog rainbow down depositing their Cloud-flower & breathing easy. But now you try it little-older-than-me-little-brother.

> While the Clowns are bringing in the Raingods, the Winter Men who, wrapped in their blankets, had lined up near the entrance to the kiva, have slowly turned their backs on the audience & with outstretched arms spread the blankets so as to form a screen concealing the kiva entrance & partitioning off the part of the kiva closest to the entrance. (This back stage is called the "fire shadow" since it is separated from the lights & fires of the kiva by the blanket screen.) In the meantime the Assistants have led the masked Kachinas from the Small Kiva, where they had been preparing themselves over the past few hours, to the Large Kiva. They go silently down the ladder, still invisible to the people, lining up in the shadow of the blanket screen. Now the Attendants take out the silencing cornhusks from the belts of the Kachinas & give each Raingod his paraphernalia: yucca whips, melons, rabbits, evergreen tree, etc.

SECOND CLOWN. Sooo yus say they've jist gotten to Earth's Navel & izzat so?

FIRST CLOWN. Yass Little Twin Brudder that is jist what I did say.

SECOND CLOWN (*clapping & lifting his left hand above his eyes*). Waal I do now & rrreally see them a-coming from Earth's Navel & a-coming closer & a-coming & a-coming closer & yaaasss they really are a-coming here & here they come: they're coming to the foot of this old ladder & they're a-bringing their thunders & their winds & their bird songs & their cricket chirps. And yass & here they are here at the foot of this old ladder & with all their powers to bring rain & growth & lots of everything yass & their powers to raise corns & squashes & beans & muskmelons & to kill rabbits yass & deer & buffalos they're here yass & at the foot of this old ladder. So now you try it little-older-than-me-little-brother & see what you kin do.

FIRST CLOWN. Yus said that yus had seen them right there at the foot of that old ladder & izzat so?

SECOND CLOWN. Yass yass.

FIRST CLOWN. Waal from the foot of that old ladder they are just starting & 're a-climbing up the steps yass they just keep climbing up & climbing & climbing up & yass yass here they are right here at that old kiva top above us.

SECOND CLOWN. Waal yass they're here & with their thunders their winds their lightnings their bird songs & yass their cricket chirps.

FIRST CLOWN. Yass yass & they're here with their powers to raise corn & to raise squashes & watermelons & 're here with their powers for killing deer & buffalos & for killing foxes yass & their powers to bring rain & thunders & lightnings & to bring fertilities & growth yass & lots of everything right here yass at that old kiva top above us.

Part Three   *The Solemn Entrance of the Raingods*

Unnoticed by the people, the Raingods have lined up silently behind the blanket screen. They have been helped by their Assistants who, as long as the Kachinas are invisible to the audience, make their noises for them. During the preceding scene the Clowns have stirred up everybody's feelings to the utmost. Now people get cornmeal ready & say prayers to themselves; everybody straightens out to get a better view.

Suddenly a deafening noise breaks loose from behind the blanket screen; the closely packed, dimly lit kiva is astir with joyful anticipation. There is a wild roar from the top of the kiva opening, & the gods seem to have dropped suddenly, bringing with them frightening thunder, lovely bird songs & cricket chirps, & the rhythmic jingling of a hundred tiny bells attached to their writhing waists & swiftly moving feet. The shrill hoots, the resounding whooping, & the weird piercing sounds which identify each individual Raingod intermingle. All these sounds continue for the duration of the scene.

In the midst of this, a long, bony, white painted hand, representing a spirit, suddenly reaches down through the circular opening in the center of the kiva ceiling, to throw blessed corn & piñons to the people who reach out for them. The Clowns, shivering with fright, cry "Yigh yigh yigh" & rush to the sheepskin rolls which they had left with the Caciques. They unroll the sheepskins, fasten them with ropes around their waists &, pretending to be fear-stricken & jittery, draw closer together. In this posture they rush toward the entrance to welcome the Great Ones.

THE CLOWNS.   To have it & to have
                these Great Ones
                wise gods   goddesses we love
                come here
                & find a warm spot
                in our hearts
                by making us feel great
                to be your children
                who you come & see
                & see us happy seeing you
                our Great Ones
                come here   feeling happy
                & at home with us

The first one to make his appearance from behind the blanket screen is the Chief Raingod. He stomps his feet heavily, first bending over to one side, then shifting his weight & pounding the floor with his other foot. The tiny bells around his waist & ankles jingle, & the loose ends of the colored yarn around his knees flutter as he moves. The feather headdress topping his mask trembles; the big, blue turquoise earrings swing on their cotton strings, while the threatening yucca whips in his hands—like all other Raingods he carries two of these, which he holds at the root ends, pointed downward—quiver, & the evergreen collars around his neck, waist & arms seem to be vibrating with life. From under his mask comes a long, guttural, mumbled roar, rising at intervals to a fortissimo. Simultaneously the noises of other—still invisible—Raingods are heard, & there are high-pitched hoots from behind the blanket screen. Slowly & majestically the Chief Raingod advances toward the Caciques, preceded by the First Clown, who welcomes & leads him without touching him.

FIRST CLOWN. Yass yass Great One yass yass jist this way Great One.

The people are performing the Feeding Rite by taking corn-meal in their hands, exhaling their breath on it, & then throwing the cornmeal to "feed" the gods, all the while praying:

THE PEOPLE. O Great Ones
          who come & see us
          happy seeing you
          at home with us.

The Chief Raingod hands his watermelon to the First Clown, who carries it to the Caciques & lays it down. Gradu-ally the thunder, wind & bird noises are fading away, until by the end of the scene only the sounds of the Raingods will be heard.

In the meantime the Sun Raingod has entered from the enclosure. The Second Clown welcomes him &, by simple gestures without touching him & still walking back-wards, leads him in front of the Cacique. In the meantime the First Clown has returned to the entrance where he welcomes the Third Raingod. Now both Clowns take turns welcoming the Raingods, leading them to the Caciques, presenting their watermelons, etc. until about eight or ten of the gods have made their grand entrance. Each of them holds his yucca whip, & one of them carries a whole evergreen tree.

During their entrance & throughout this scene, the Raingods continue their individual noises & move counterclockwise around the kiva in an oblong circle. The Chief Raingod continues his characteristic stamping. When all the Raingods have entered, the thunder, wind & bird noises stop; the blanket screen is folded up & disappears as the "makers of the blanket screen," who had been standing behind it, drop their blankets so that they too may join in the scene that follows.

Part Four   The Reception of the Raingods

FIRST CLOWN (*approaching the Raingods with wide, outstretched arms*). Hey Great Ones hey come on let's be friends.

The Chief Raingod strikes the Clown with his yucca whips.

FIRST CLOWN (*although somewhat protected by his sheepskin, he has gotten a good switch across his back*). Ouch goddamn that hurts. (*He jumps to the side. Then, with outstretched arms, he again approaches the same Raingod who still continues to move around.*) Aw come on let's be friends already.

The Chief Raingod now extends his slightly bent arms alternately to the right & left in a gesture of welcome. These motions—of rejection & later of welcome—are repeated between each Raingod & each Clown. All this time, & until their final exit, the Raingods, except the Chief while he is "talking," continue to move around in an elongated circle repeating their specific vocal sounds. The Chief Raingod approaches the Caciques.

SECOND CLOWN (*to the Chief Raingod*). Yass yass Mister Great One I do believe yus must have sumpin on your mind yass sumpin yus would like to say I betcha.

The Chief Raingod nods with his whole body & continues his grunting & stomping. He points at himself, indicating "we," then motions with his arms in a roundabout gesture—"have come"—then points to a place before himself—"here"

—then points from his masked head toward the Caciques, thus expressing his desire to talk to them. A young man, motioned to by one of the Clowns, stands up.

FIRST CLOWN (*pointing at the young man*). Waal here he is yass.

The Chief Raingod shakes his head violently. The Second Clown motions both Caciques to stand up. They move from their seats & stand directly in front of the Chief Raingod who is facing them. The Chief Raingod "talks" to the Caciques, & the Winter Cacique interprets these gestures to the People: "We—have come—from afar—as we—were concerned—about you—& wanted—to see—how our Children—are getting along.—It has reached my ear—that you people —have not listened—to your gods—& we—came—to punish —you."

WINTER CACIQUE (*speaking for the people now*). No, Great Ones, no we have certainly not been so bad but trying to get along with one another, have lived in peace & harmony with one another. We have been good people, yes & is that so O Children of the Great Ones?

THE PEOPLE (*having stopped the ceremonial feeding, they are just watching & listening*). Yes, yes, yes!

WINTER CACIQUE. So glad & thankful all of us are that all of you Great Ones have come here & honored all of us poor people with your being here & being so thoughtful of your Children all of us poor people who will go on in being good & trying to get on in peace & harmony with one another. We were happy in your coming & now are hoping for your safe return to those you love.

The Makers of the Blanket Screen line up again & during the rest of the scene gradually unfold their blankets & once more set up the blanket screen separating the backstage.

FIRST CLOWN (*to the Chief Raingod*). Yass that's so yer see we're glad & thankful yus could visit us.

SECOND CLOWN. Yass but the climate's jist a little too warm for you here so yus could really be getting back to your own kind I do believe. Yus know: your dear beloveds & all of that.

The Raingods still move around in a counterclockwise, elongated circle, continuing their individual noises. One by one they are led out by the Clowns to the blanket screen. However, each Raingod, before leaving, stops near the exit & performs his Blessing Rite. Still holding his yucca whips, he joins his closed fists & with slightly bent arms he reaches out, first upward, then downward, then toward the east, south, west, & north—to take in the Great Goodness, that is, the powers of rainmaking & fertility described by the Clowns. He then passes his hands over his body &, with outstretched arms, offers the Great Goodness to the People who are watching in devout silence. With a catching movement of their arms the People reach out & with deep breaths, take in the Great Goodness extended to them, mumbling "Yes yes oh yes." The Clowns, who have watched attentively & also "breathed in" the Goodness, repeat "Yass yass oh yaaass."

As solemnly as they entered, the Raingods leave, each one led to the blanket screen, from behind which an unmasked Assistant will lead him up the ladder to the Small Kiva. After the last Raingod has left, a Clown exclaims:

FIRST CLOWN. Hot damn they're gone that bunch of rascals!

Part Five   The Man Ceremony

While the People are still under the spell of the preceding scene, the Silent One enters from behind the blanket screen. He is alone & hasn't been seen before. A kind of clownish Raingod, he wears a funny mask with a crooked mouth & does not utter a sound. Everything in the kiva is quiet now, & nothing can be heard but the feet of the Silent One tapping heavily on the kiva floor as he slowly advances. He walks like an old man, carrying a bow & arrow, taking a few steps, then pausing to give his body a good shake. In what follows it's only the Clowns who speak; the Silent One uses gestures.

FIRST CLOWN (*looking around, observing the Raingod & staring at him*). Hey who is zis one anyway?

SECOND CLOWN. Some kind of tramp yus think?

> The Silent One continues his shaking motions while the Clowns scrutinize him.

FIRST CLOWN. Saaay I betcha it's our Great One. Izzat what yus are huh a Great One?

> The Silent One nods his head affirmatively.

SECOND CLOWN. I think yer onto sumpin.

> The Silent One puts his hands—with outstretched fingers— to his head, thus gesturing "deer."

FIRST CLOWN. Ooooh yus mean yer looking for a deer?

SECOND CLOWN. Which waydit go?

> The Silent One gestures: that way, over there.

FIRST CLOWN. We didn't see no deer yus know.

SECOND CLOWN. How come yus looking fer a deer?

> The Silent One indicates: here are its tracks.

FIRST CLOWN. Waal if yus find a deer what will yer do with it?

> The Silent One answers by lifting up his bow & arrow to shooting position.

SECOND CLOWN. Zatso? Waal where will yus shoot it?

> The Silent One points to his breast. He continues to move around without a sound, as if searching for something.

SECOND CLOWN. What 're yus looking for? Did yus lose sumpin maybe?

> The Silent One shakes his head.

FIRST CLOWN. I guess yus got sumpin on yer mind & izzat so?

> The Silent One nods affirmatively.

SECOND CLOWN. Waal whut is it already?

> The Silent One holds both hands before his chest in a gesture indicating small firm breasts & thus expressing his desire for a virgin.

FIRST CLOWN (*asking a young boy to stand up*). Is zis what you was wanting?

> The People laugh, & the Silent One shakes his head vigorously.

SECOND CLOWN (*suddenly enlightened*). Oh yaaaas! (*Calling.*) Corn Blossom! Corn Blossom where are yer?

> A young girl about ten years old, dressed in shawl & manta & sitting with her family, is taken from the crowd & escorted by the Clown to the Silent One, who now stands in front of the two Caciques.

FIRST CLOWN (*to the Silent One*). What're yus wanting to give her?

> From his waist the Silent One unties one of several freshly killed rabbits wrapped in evergreen, & gives it to the Clown who passes it on to the girl. Corn Blossom accepts the evergreen bundle containing the rabbit & holds it in front of her on her slightly bent arms.

SECOND CLOWN (*to Corn Blossom*). Now give us yer shawl here.

> The girl, standing motionless, takes off her shawl & passes it to the Clown. The Silent One indicates that no, she should lie down.

FIRST CLOWN (*arranging the girl's shawl on the floor directly in front of her in the shape of a woman lying down for her husband*). Waal yass & she will too. So you jist take a shot at it.

> The Silent One shakes his head & gestures that she should spread her legs more. The People laugh. The Second Clown stretches the ends of the shawl, but again the Silent One indicates that the legs should be spread farther. The Clown

complies as the People laugh again. The Silent One lays down his bow & arrow, then goes through the Blessing Rite. He reaches out with his hands into space to catch the breath & goodness from the air. He catches the goodness from above, he catches the goodness from below, he catches the goodness from the north, the west, the south, & the east. He passes his hands over his body, as if trying to get the goodness & strength from within himself; then he takes all this goodness & strength & blessing &, by clapping his hands, shoots it at the girl who stands silent & embarrassed.

FIRST CLOWN. I'd say he's finished.
SECOND CLOWN. Did it hurt yer?

The People laugh.

FIRST CLOWN (*to the Silent One*). And now yus have consummated yer Man Ceremony!

The Silent One calls by motions for three other young girls & goes through the above scene of the spread of the shawl & the Blessing Rite with each of them. Then he gives the Blessing Rite to everybody present & eventually walks out behind the blanket screen. From there, unseen by the people, he leaves the kiva. The people utter: "Yes yes oh yes" after the departing Raingod. Both Clowns walk out behind the enclosure but come back a few moments later imitating the sounds & gestures of the Raingods to everybody's laughter. Then they advance toward the Caciques & pick up the sacred melons which the Raingods have brought. With their hands they break the melons into small pieces which they pass out, especially to the women & children. Everybody eats the pieces of blessed melon, while some of the older women pick little bits of melon &, by throwing them on the ground, "feed" them to the departed ones, mumbling:

WOMEN. *A Prayer to the Dear Dead*

Eat some of this food hey hey
Body gets a little bit stronger.

SECOND CLOWN. Yass let's git outer here!

> Both Clowns roll up their sheepskin packs, sling them over their shoulders, & give the Blessing Rite to everybody present. They take the goodness from the six directions, pass their hands over their bodies, & throw the goodness at the people, saying:

CLOWNS. May thou be loved & liked through the great goodnesses of You-Know-Who & may thou drop dead on the spot!

> The People again exclaim: "Yes yes oh yes." Both Clowns then remove their hide & cornhusk headgear & disappear behind the blanket screen, which gradually folds up, thus transforming the Large Kiva again into one large room without a backstage. The men who had spread their blankets to make the enclosure go up the ladder & join the other offstage performers in the inner sanctum.

(*The Thanksgiving Prayer*). While the people are still sitting on the floor, the two Caciques stand up & speak to them. The Summer Cacique speaks first:

> Evil of the people
> but the Great Ones being good
> were good to us
> though they came among us
> to punish us
> in their goodness & kindness
> they granted us forgiveness
> Now this night
> made sacred by the Great Ones
> being among us
> can remind us
> to give each other kindness
> & helpfulness
> to be going on in harmony & peace
> as Children of the Great Ones

gathered in this place
in our desire to go on living
& being loved & liked
receiving goodness
from these spiritual beings
growing tired
in our arms & legs
but more than tiredness
& soreness
have come to us

THE PEOPLE (*mumbling*).

Hard work   yes
& tiredness
& our muscles growing sore
but we have done it
ALL   to go on in being
rich in children
& being loved & liked
having our dreams of life come true

WINTER CACIQUE.

Growing tired
in our arms & legs
but more than tiredness
& soreness
have come to us
now we have won
a life of all good things
& pray
that you be loved & liked
take in the goodness
of O·yi·ke
Mother of Us All
& of myself
a poor man only

that you be loved & liked
catching up with what
has always drawn you

The Winter Cacique gives his blessing to the people by inconspicuously bringing the goodness out of himself & throwing it to them with both open hands.

THE PEOPLE (*reaching out with catching movements of their arms & with deep breaths, taking in the Great Goodness bestowed upon them*).

& we pray too
to go on being loved & liked
taking in the goodness
of O·yi·ke
Mother of Us All
& catching up with what
has always drawn us
to win
a life of all good things
we wish for

WINTER CACIQUE.

Everything is open
now go home
& leave your worries
& your tears
& sadnesses

THE PEOPLE (*mumbling as they leave silently*). Yes oh yes yes yes.

—*Workings by Jerome Rothenberg after scenario arranged by Vera Laski*

RABINAL-ACHÍ: ACT IV

Maya

Quiché-Achí, speaks for the Tenth time, coming before Hobtoh Rabinal-Rahaual, Chief Five-Rains:

Cala-Achí!   Ha! Aha! Yeha! Ahau! Wow! Achí!   I: Quiché-Achí   Balam-Achí   Balam-Quiché   Rahaual-Quiché-Vinak iiiiiiiiiiiiiiiiiiiiiii kiiiiiiiii kikikikikikikikikikikiki   Quiché-Vinak
to you: Hobtoh Rabinal-Rahaual

Great Chief Five-Rains.

Oyeu Achí!   Hail Valiant!   Hail Warlike!

O.K. I'm here   O.K. I've just arrived
to the great walls' entrance
to the great fortress
over which you throw
your hands
over which you throw
your shadow.
You've heard about my presence
in your teeth
in your face.

I'm valiant   I'm warlike   because your valiant   your war-
like   Galel-Achí
eminent among the warlike   vanguard of valiants   valiant of
Rabinal
came to throw his challenge
his war-cry
to my teeth
to my face.

"O.K. I've told my Man about you
Hobtoh Rabinal-Rahaual   Great Chief Five-Rains
            in the great walls.
And he said right back:
Bring in this motherfucking valiant   this vinak
                        to my teeth
                        to my face
and let me see
                        his teeth
                        his face
how valiant he is   how warlike he is.
But tell him from me   this valiant   this warrior
to keep his mouth shut
I don't want any trouble   I don't wan't any noise.
Let him touch his toes
let him bend down his face
when he gets to the doors
            of the great walls
            of the great fortress."

That's what your valiant said   your warrior
                        to my teeth
                        to my face.
Goddamn it I am a valiant   a warrior
and if I've got to bend down
                        bend down my face
here's what I'll bend with
what'll bend my knee.
This is my arrow
this is my shield

with which I'll break your destiny
your day of birth

> your lower mouth
> your upper mouth

and you'll swallow it
Great Chief Five-Rains!

Ixok-mun, a Servant-girl, speaks for the Second time, as Quiché-Achí menaces Five-Rains with his truncheon:

Valiant!   Warlike!   Rahaual Cavek Quiché Vinak!
Don't kill my Man   my Governor   my Chief   Great Chief
    Five-Rains
          in the heart of his great fortress!

Quiché-Achí, speaks for the Eleventh time:

O.K. go get my bench then   go get my seat
the way it was in my mountains   the way it was in my valleys
with my destiny shining   my day of birth.
Some bench that was!   Some seat that was!
Are you going to freeze me in this place
freeze me with ice   freeze me with cold?
I'm speaking

> to the sky-face here
> to the earth-face here.
> May sky
> and earth
> be with you
> Chief Five-Rains!

Hobtoh Rabinal-Rahaual, Chief Five-Rains, speaks for the Fourth time:

Valiant!   Warlike!   Cavek Quiché Vinak!   iiikiiiiiiiikikikiki
Quiché Vinak!

                              thanks to sky
                              thanks to earth
you've just arrived
                    at the great walls
                    at the great fortress
over which I throw
                              my hands
over which I throw
                              my shadow.
I   the grandfather   Great Chief Five-Rains.

O.K.   Tell us   open your mouth   let's hear
why you make like coyote   weasel   fox
                    through the great walls
                    through the great fortress
to call   to attract
my white children
my white sons
to call   to attract
                    to the great walls
                    to the great fortress
                    in the corn-city   Iximche
to ferret out
to get your fingers on
THE YELLOW HONEY
the green honey of bees
my food for me   the grandfather
Great Chief Five-Rains?
You were the one who got the nine   the ten white children
and it's a miracle they weren't dragged off
to the Quiché mountains
to the Quiché valleys
                    if my valiance   if my bravura
                    v'oyeualal   v'achihilal
                    Galel-Achí   Rabinal-Achí
hadn't been there on guard

you'd have cut the vine there   cut the trunk
cut the lineage
of the white children
of the white sons!
And damn near got me at the baths as well!
Damn near got hooked out there
by the son of your arrow
the son of your shield!
You shut me in there
inside the stones
inside the chalk
of the Quiché mountains
of the Quiché valleys
and you'd have cut my vine there   cut my trunk
cut my lineage

                if my valiance   if my bravura
                v'oyeualal   v'achihilal
                Galel-Achí   Rabinal-Achí

hadn't freed me from there
hadn't dragged me from there
with the son of his arrow
with the son of his shield
and brought me back
                to the great walls
                to the great fortress.
And you also destroyed
                two   three   great cities
                cities with moats
In Hidden-Buzzard   Balanvac
where feet stamp the ground with great noise
in Calcaraxah   Cunu   Gozibal-Tagah-Tulul
as the names go.

Well how long are you going to be hung up
by the lust of your heart   your valiance   your bravura?
how long are they going to block you

and keep you rampaging here?
This arrogance   this bravura
weren't they buried once and for all
in Qotom   in Tikiram   in Belehe Mokoh   in Belehe Chu-
    may?
This arrogance this bravura
didn't we beat them out of you   we Governors   we Men
                Men of the walls
                Men of the fortress?

But you'll pay for this here

                            under the sky
                            on the earth.
You've said goodbye
                to your mountains
                to your valleys
because you're going to die in this place
to disappear in this place

                            under the sky
                            and on the earth.
                            May sky
                            and earth
                            be with you
                            Cavek Quiché Vinak!

Quiché-Achí, speaks for the Twelfth time:

Cala-Achí!   Ha! Aha! Yeha! Ahau! Wow! Achí!   I: Quiché-
Achí   Balam-Achí   Balam-Quiché   Rahaual-Quiché-Vinak
iiiiiiiiiiiiiiiiiiiiiiiii kiiiiiiiii kikikikikikikikikikikiki   Quiché-Vinak
                        to you: Hobtoh Rabinal-Rahaual
Great Chief Five-Rains
                    Now hear this
                        to the sky-face here
                        to the earth-face here

Sure
   these are the words
   these are the opinions
   you've gone on and on about
                              to the sky-face here
                              to the earth-face.

Sure
   I've done wrong.
You also said:
   "Didn't you call   attract
   the white children
   the white sons
   to ferret out   to get your fingers on
   THE YELLOW HONEY
   the green honey of bees
   my food for me   the grandfather
   Great Chief Five-Rains
              in the great walls
              in the great fortress?"

Sure
    I've done wrong
   because of the hang-ups of my heart
   because I couldn't grab
   these beautiful mountains   these beautiful valleys
                         here   under sky
                         here on the earth
You also said:
   "and you destroyed
              two   three   great cities
              cities with moats
   in Hidden-Buzzard   Balanvac
   where feet stamp the ground with great noise
   in Calcaraxah   Cunu   Gozibal-Tagah-Tulul."

Sure
    I've done wrong
    because of the hang-ups of my heart
    because I couldn't grab
    these beautiful mountains   these beautiful valleys
                here   under sky
                here on the earth
You also said:
    "Kiss your mountains goodbye
    and your valleys
    because you're going to die in this place
    to disappear in this place
    we'll cut your vine here   your trunk
    we'll cut your lineage here

                here under sky
                here on the earth."
Look:
    I don't give a damn for your words
    you go to hell with your orders
                to the sky-face here
                to the earth-face
    because of what I want in my heart.
And if I have to die here
if I really have to disappear in this place
then this is what I've got for you
                in your teeth
                in your face:
Since you're so rich here
since you don't know what do do with all you've got
        in the great walls
        in the great fortress
I'll borrow your food
I'll have a go at your drinks
those cool drinks called Ixtatzunin
those twelve drinks

those twelve stoning liquors
sweet   fresh   jubilant   lip-smacking
    you drink before sleep
                    in the great walls
                    in the great fortress
and also
the marvels of my Mother
the marvels of my Lady.
I'll try them out just once
as a sort of signal of my death
to mark my disappearance under sky   and on the earth.
                    May sky
                    and earth
                    be with you
                    Hobtoh Rabinal-Rahaual!

Hobtoh Rabinal-Rahaual, Chief Five-Rains, speaks for the Fifth time:

Valiant!   Warlike!   Cavek iiiiiiiiiiiii kiiiiiiiiiiii kikikikikikikikiki
    Quiché-Vinak:
This is what you came up with
                    to the sky-face
                    to the earth-face:
"Give me your food
your drinks
I'll try them out"   is what you said.
"As a sort of signal of my death
to mark my disappearance"   is what you said.

O.K. Fine.
Here they are take them
here they are I'm lending them.
Men   Girls   Get my food and drink!
Give them to this Valiant   this Achí   Cavek-Quiché-Vinak
as a supreme signal of his death
and of his disappearance

                    here   under sky
                    here on the earth.

A Servant: (bringing a low table with food and drinks)

Yessir! My Chief   My Governor!
I'm giving them to this Valiant   this Achí   Cavek-Quiché-Vinak.
Try a little of the food   of the drink
of my Chief   my Governor   grandfather   Chief Five-Rains
                    in the great walls
                    in the great fortress
                    in which he lives enclosed.

*Quiché-Achí eats and drinks disdainfully, then dances in the midst
of the court, then returns and speaks for the Thirteenth time:*

Ha!   Aha!   Yeha!   Ahau!   Wow!   Achí!   I: Quiché-
     Achí   to you
Hobtoh Rabinal-Rahaual
Great Chief Five-Rains:

Hey   call this food?
call this drink?
you crazy or something?
Comments?   Forget it!
                                        to my mouth
                                        to my face!
Look if you ever tried just once
                    in *my* mountains
                    in *my* valleys
what *I* call drink
sweet   fresh   jubilant   lip-smacking
drinks *I* drink
                    in my mountains
                    in my valleys
Man   you wouldn't ask

                    the sky-face here
                    the earth-face here!

Are *these* your groaning dishes
your overflow of drinks?
Hey but this skull right here
is my grandfather's skull!
this skull right here
is my father's skull!
Right?   Couldn't you do the same
with my head's bones?
with my skull's bones?
chisel my mouth?
engrave my face?
Then   when they quit my mountains
then   when they quit my valleys
to push five loads of cacao-coin
to push five loads of cacao-liquor
                    from my mountains
                    from my valleys

my sons
my children can say
Hey   this is grandpappy's skull!
hey   this is our old man's skull!
and sing all day long!

And here's my arm-bone
for a silver gourd's handle
to sound and thunder
                    in the great walls
                    in the great fortress
And here's my leg-bone
hey   that's a great drumstick
for the big drum
for the little drum
the sky can throb to
the earth can throb to

                    in the great walls
                    in the great fortress!

And while I think of it:
how's this for a suggestion?
O.K.   Repeat after me:
    "I'll lend you the great cloth also
    smooth   brilliant   resplendent
    very well woven by God
    my Mother made   my Lady
    so you can wear it
                    in the great walls
                    in the great fortress
                    in the four corners
                    along the four walls
                    as a sort of signal of your death
                    to mark your disappearance
                                    here   under sky
                                    here on the earth."

Hobtoh Rabinal-Rahaual, Chief Five-Rains, speaks for the Sixth time:

Valiant!   Warrior!   Cavek iiiiiiiiiiiii kiiiiiiiiiiii kikikikikikikikiki
Quiché-Vinak:
What the hell are you coming up with?
O.K. nevertheless   here's what I'll do
I'll give you that
as a sort of signal of your death
to mark your disappearance
                                    here   under sky
                                    here on the earth.

Men   girls   go get that cloth
smooth   brilliant   resplendent
well woven here by God
                    in the great walls
                    in the great fortress

Give them to this Valiant   this Achí
as a supreme signal of his dying
and of his disappearance

                              here   under sky
                              here on the earth.

A Servant: (bringing a kind of shawl Quiché-Achí puts around his
shoulders)

Yessir!   My Chief   My Governor!
I'll give this Valiant   this Achí
this cloth he's been begging for.
Man   here's the good-looking cloth
you've been panting for!
Take care not to spoil it now!

Quiché-Achí, speaks for the Fourteenth time:

Ha!   Aha!   Yeha!   Ahau!   Wow!   Achí!   I:
     Quiché-Achi   to you
Masters of the "tun" drum   Masters of the flute!

Hey   You   the flutes!
Hey   You   the drums!
Could you manage to make
like my flute
like my drum?
O.K. now
play the great melody
play the little melody
swing all those tunes!
Play my Toltec flute   play my Toltec drum
my flute from the Quiché   my drum from the Quiché!
the dance of my prisoner
the dance of my captive
                    among my mountains
                    among my valleys!

As if we were going to make the sky throb
as if we were going to make the earth throb
as our foreheads bend down
as our heads bend down
when we make great leaps and turns zapateando
when we dance and rock and beat the ground
with the men and the girls

                   here   under sky
                   here on the earth

That's what I have to say

                   to the sky-face here
                   to the earth-face.
                   May sky
                   and earth
                   be with you
                   O flutes   O drums!

Quiché-Achí dances a round-dance in the midst of the Court and goes to each angle in turn to shout his war-cry.

Hey!   Chief Five-Rains!

               Now hear this
                 to the sky-face
                 to the earth-face

This is what you lent me
This is what you let me have so far
I'm back to let you have it again
I'm taking it off here
             at the great walls
             in the great fortress.
Take good care of it   put it back   bury it
in its bundle   in its box
             in these great walls
             in the great fortress.
You granted my desire
you granted my petition

                                   to the sky-face
                                   to the earth-face
I've made a big thing of it here
                    in the great walls
                    in the great fortress
                    in the four corners
                    along the four walls
                    as a sort of signal of my death
                    to mark my disappearance
                                        under sky here
                                        on the earth
But . . . if it's true you're so rich here
if you don't know what to do with all you've got
                    in the great walls
                    in the great fortress
then just for a minute let me have
                    U Chuch Gug   Mother of Feathers
                    U Chuch Raxon   Mother of Humming-
                                                    birds
                    Yamanim Xtekoh   the Brilliant Emerald
                    come from Tzam-Gam-Carchag
                    whose mouth hasn't ever been touched
                    whose face hasn't ever been seen
so I can graze her mouth
so I can glimpse her face
so I can dance with her
so I can show her off
                    in the great walls
                    in the great fortress
                    in the four corners
                    along the four walls
                    as a supreme signal of my dying
                    and of my disappearance
                                   under the sky here
                                   and on the earth.
                                   May sky

and earth
be with you
Great Chief Five-Rains!

*Hobtoh Rabinal-Rahaual, Chief Five-Rains, speaks for the Seventh
time:*

Valiant!   Warrior!   Cavek iiiiiiiiiiiii kiiiiiiiiiiii kikikikikikikikiki
Quiché-Vinak:
Man   do you know what you're asking?
O.K.   O.K.
O.K. nevertheless   here's what I'll do
Because she's cloistered here
                        Our Feather-Mother
                        Mother of Hummingbirds
                        the Brilliant Emerald
                        come from Tzam-Gam-Carchag
                        whose mouth hasn't been touched
                        whose face hasn't been seen
I'll grant her to you
as a supreme signal of your dying
and of your disappearance

                        under the sky here
                        and on the earth.
Men   girls   bring us that Lady
                        Mother of Feathers
                        Mother of Hummingbirds
Give her to this Valiant   this Achí
since he asked for her
as a supreme signal of his dying
and his disappearance

                        under the sky here
                        and on the earth.

Ixok-mum, a Servant-girl, speaks for the Third time:

Very well my Chief   my Governor
I give her to this Valiant   to this Achí.

They bring the Mother of Feathers and present her to Quiché-Achí.

Here she is   Valiant   Achí   Cavek-Quiché-Vinak
I'm giving you what you wished for   what you asked for
               the Feather-Mother
               Mother of Hummingbirds
Don't offend her
don't wound her
But show her off
merely by dancing with her
              in the great walls
              in the great fortress.

Quiché-Achí salutes the young Lady who keeps her distance, dancing in front of him, turning away her face. He follows her in the same fashion, weaving before her, like a length of cloth—they dance round the Court to the sound of trumpets and then return before Chief Five-Rains.

Quiché-Achí, speaks for the Fifteenth time:

Chief Five-Rains
Listen to me

                          to the sky-face
                          to the earth-face.

Here is the Lady
lent to me   conceded to me
as a companion.
I showed her off   I danced with her
              in the four corners
              along the four walls
              in the great fortress

Take her back now
and cloister her
            in the great walls
            in the great fortress.
Now I'm saying:
Remind yourself   remember   and lend me now
                  the Twelve Golden Eagles
                  the Twelve Golden Jaguars
                  Kablajuh u ganal Cot
                  Kablajuh u ganal Balam
I've met with night and day
arms in hand   spears in hand.
Lend them to me to go and shoot
with the son of my arrow   the son of my shield
            in the four corners
            along the four walls
            in the great walls
            in the great fortress
only . . .   only . . .
as a supreme signal of my dying
and of my disappearance
                        under the sky here
                        and on the earth.
                        May sky
                        and earth
                        be with you
                        Hobtoh Rabinal-Rahaual
                        Great Chief Five-Rains!

*Hobtoh Rabinal-Rahaual, Chief Five-Rains, speaks for the Eighth
time:*

Valiant!   Warrior!   Cavek iiiiiiiiiiiii kiiiiiiiiiiiiii   kikikikikikiki
Quiché-Vinak:
You've said it now

                              to the sky-face
                              to the earth-face
that I should lend you
                    the Twelve Golden Eagles
                    the Twelve Golden Jaguars
O.K.
Here I lend you   here I concede to you
                    the Twelve Golden Eagles
                    the Twelve Golden Jaguars
that you beg of me   that you solicit
                              to my teeth
                              to my face.

Get going then
                    O my Eagles
                    O my Jaguars
and do what's needed
so that this Valiant   this Achí
parades with the son of his arrow
parades with the son of his shield
                    in the four corners
                    along the four walls!

Quiché-Achí, speaks for the Sixteenth time; Quiché-Achí going forward
with the Eagles and the Jaguars and dancing a war-dance with
them around the Court, then returning to the Gallery where Chief
Five-Rains sits with his family:

Ha!   Aha!   Yeha!   Ahau!   Wow!   Achí!   I: Quiché-
      Achí   to you
Hobtoh Rabinal-Rahaual, Great Chief Five-Rains:

Listen to me   Approve of me
                              to the sky-face here
                              to the earth-face here.
You granted me
what I wished for   what I asked for

                    the Golden Eagles
                    the Golden Jaguars
I paraded with them
with the son of my arrow
with the son of my shield.
                    COME ON NOW!
                    Are *these* your Eagles then?
                    Are *these* your Jaguars?
                    HA!
You can't brag about these

                              to my teeth
                              to my face
                    Some of them come on
                    some of them don't come on
                    they don't have any teeth
                    they don't have any talons
HA!   if you could spare a moment
                    in *my* mountains
                    in *my* valleys
                    how powerfully mine come on
                    how powerfully they gaze
                    they combat   they fight
                    with teeth
                    with talons!

*Hobtoh Rabinal-Rahaual, Chief Five-Rains, speaks for the Ninth
time*:

Valiant!   Warrior!   Cavek iiiiiiiiiiiiiii kiiiiiiiiiiii kikikikikikiki
Quiché-Vinak:
We've seen your Eagles' teeth
your Jaguars' teeth
in your mountains
in your valleys
          WELL
What's this sight

Where's this gaze
from your Eagles
from your Jaguars
in your mountains
in your valleys?

Quiché-Achí, speaks for the Seventeenth time:

Cala-Achí   Ha!   Aha!   Yeha!   Ahau!   Wow!   Achí!
I: Quiché-Achí   Balam-Achí   Balam-Quiché   Rahaual-Quiché-
Vinak   iiiiiiiiiiiiiiiiiiiiiii   kiiiiiiiiiiiiiiiiiiiiiiiii   kikikikikikikikikiki-
kikikikikiki Quiché-Vinak

                       to you: Hobtoh Rabinal-Rahaual
Great Chief Five-Rains   OYEU ACHÍ!!!

Listen to me   Approve of me
                       to the sky-face
                       to the earth-face.
This is what I say
                       to your mouth
                       to your face:
Allow me two hundred and sixty days
allow me two hundred and sixty nights
to go salute
           u vach nu huyabal
           u vach nu tagahal
           my mountains' faces
           my valleys' faces
where long   and long ago   I went alone
           to the four corners
           to the four walls
           to look for
           to encounter
           my needs   my food.

No one answers him. Then, dancing away, he disappears for a moment. Without returning to the Gallery where Five-Rains is seated, he approaches the Eagles and Jaguars posted in the middle of the Court around an altar.

                              O Eagles!
                              O Jaguars!
"He's gone" you said
a moment ago.
No   I hadn't gone
No   I hadn't disappeared
I went for a moment
to say goodbye
               to my mountains' faces
               to my valleys' faces
where long   and long ago   I went alone
               to find my food
               to find my meals
               in the four corners
               along the four walls.

                         AAAAH   SKY!
                         AAAAH   EARTH!

my valiance   my bravura
were no use.
I figured out my way

                         below sky
                         below earth

I opened my way
among grasses
among thorns.
My valiance   my bravura
were no use.

                                        AAAAH   SKY!
                                        AAAAH   EARTH!

Do I really have to die
to die in this place?
really disappear
disappear in this place?

                                        O my gold!
                                        O my silver!
                                        O my arrow's sons!
                                        O my shield's sons!
                                        my Toltec war-club!
                                        my Toltec axe!
                                        my wreaths   my sandals!
                        go back to our mountains
                        go back to our valleys!

Take our news
to the teeth of our Man
to the face of our Governor
"It's a long time since
our valiance   our bravura
has looked for our food
has found our meals!"
says the word of our Man
the word of our Governor

He won't say so any more
now all I expect is my death
now all I expect is my disappearance
                                        under sky here
                                        and on the earth.

                                        AAAAH   SKY!
                                        AAAAH   EARTH!
Since I can't do anything else but die
since I can't do anything else but disappear
                                        under sky here
                                        and on the earth

why can't I change fates with this squirrel with this bird dying on
the branch of the tree dying on the bud of the tree dying in their
own little country in which they've found their food   in which
they've found their needs

> chuvach cah
> chuvach uleu?
> under sky here
> and on the earth?

> O Eagles!
> O Jaguars!

Come on then!
Let's get your work done
let's get your duty over with
> sink your teeth
> sink your talons
> get it over with
> in one moment

since I am a Valiant   an Achí
> from our own mountains
> from our own valleys

> May sky
> and earth
> be with you

> O Eagles!
> O Jaguars!

*Eagles and Jaguars surround Quiché-Achí, Balam-Achí, Balam-Quiché,
Rahaual-Quiché-Vinak—lay him on the sacrificial altar and open
his breast. Then all present dance a general dance.*

— *English version by Nathaniel Tarn*

A THIRD SERVICE

Directions: Imitate the spirit of the animal or thing inside you.

Salish

the little random creatures

Fox

found a hole with a light in it, and saying
Whose?
        set a trap
with a bowcord for a noose.
A giant of light, something alive, dazzled the path
on its slow way up, blinding
the little random creatures
o something alive was dying in the bowcord and it said
            Allow me to choke to death
            And you'll have night forever
and they let the Sun go

— Armand Schwerner's English working, after William Jones

POEMS FROM A DEER DANCE CYCLE

Yuma

(1st Set) "The Water Bug"

The Water Bug (i)

The water bug is drawing the shadows of the evening toward him on the water.

The Water Bug (ii)

The water bug is dipping the end of his long body in the water & dancing up & down.

The Water Bug (iii)

The water bug keeps dancing now he's on the mountain that he stands on top of.
Gazing out smelling breezes from the western ocean.

The Water Bug (iv)

While the water bug stands there the ocean seems to be drawing nearer.
He sees the fish in the water moving up & down with the tides.

The Water Bug (v)

Water Bug was standing in a dream.
He came to the ocean stood on top of a fish while thinking he was standing on the ground.
When he found it was moving he said "something here must be alive."

The Water Bug (vi)

The water bug wanders forever beside the sea.
But he becomes black from standing on that fish & catching its
  disease.
So he wanders forever on the shore of the ocean.

(2nd Set) "The Deer"

The Deer (i)

The deer is taking away the daylight.
After taking away the daylight he named it darkness.

The Deer (ii)

The deer is alone in the darkness.
Grazing on a lonely plain.
Near the high mountain.

The Deer (iii)

The deer was a long time in the darkness.
He asked the spider to have a road made for him in the darkness.
Spider made the road & the deer's been traveling it.

— *Jerome Rothenberg's working, after Frances Densmore*

the eagle above us

Cora

he lives in the sky
far above us
the eagle
looks good there
has a good grip on his world

his world wrapt in grey
but a living a humid
a beautiful grey

there he glides in the sky
very far
right above us

waits for what Tetewan
netherworld goddess
has to say

bright
his eye
on his world

bright
his eye
on the water of life
the sea
embracing
the earth

frightful his face
radiant his eye
the sun

his feet a deep red
there he is
right above us

spreading his wings
he remembers
who dwell down below

among whom the gods
let rain fall let dew fall
for life on their earth

there above us he speaks
we can hear him
his words make great sound

deep down they go
where mother Tetewan hears him and answers
we can hear her

here they meet
her words and the eagle's
we hear them together
together they make great sound

eagle words
fading
far above the water of life

mother words
from deep down
sighing away through the vaults of the sky

— *English version by Anselm Hollo*

A SONG OF THE RED & GREEN BUFFALO

Oto

. . . The fourth man to lead me was my nephew. He said, "In the early days there were many buffalos, but there was only one head among the buffalos. This buffalo was called One Rib. He had one red & one green horn. That is why old Indians paint their faces, one side red & the other side green." My nephew said, "I am going to sing a song for this buffalo & take this boy along the road to the end." The people said, "Hau! It is a great thing. It is going to be good."

The Song

All those buffalos have green horns.
Must go on with him towards the north
With the sole of your one green toe.

— *Translation by William Whitman*

THE SONG OF THE ROLLHEAD OWL

Modoc

Man carrying his sister on
his back
got home & sang:

> Back then I went out
> to the pine & now
> I'm heading back from it

> His dog sang
> ARRRF

(Man said to dog):
You sweet dog
O Sandy
come to papa, do
I only   want to tell you
that I threw
my clothes away
I got so bushed

& then he sang:

> Back then I went out
> to the pine & now
> I'm heading back from it

& throws his moccasins away
dog runs to get them & says
ARRRF

(Man says):
You sweet dog
O Sandy
come to papa, do

I only   want to tell you
that I threw
my legs away
I got so bushed

& then he sang:

> Back then I went out
> to the pine & now
> I'm heading back from it

& throws his legs away
dog runs to get them & says
ARRRF

(Man says):
You sweet dog
O Sandy
come to papa, do
I only   want to tell you
that I threw
everything away
I got so bushed

& then he sang:

> Back then I went out
> to the pine & now
> I'm heading back from it

& throws everything away
dog runs to get the rest of it & says
ARRRF
my man is nothing but a head
& he just keeps rolling along

— English working by Jerome Rothenberg, after Albert Gatschet

ONE FOR COYOTE

Skagit

One day when Coyote
was walking through Snoqualmie Pass,
he met a young woman.

What do you have in your pack?
she said.

Fish eggs.

Can I have some?

If you close your eyes
and hold up your dress.

The woman did as she was told.

Higher.
Hold your dress over your head.

Then Coyote stepped out of his trousers
and walked up to the woman.

Stand still
so I can reach the place.

I can't.
There's something crawling between my legs.

Keep your dress up.
It's a bumble bee. I'll get it.

The woman dropped her dress.

You weren't fast enough.
It stung me.

— *English version by Carl Cary*

THE GREAT FARTER
(by Nakasuk)

Eskimo

The great farter, like they say
        because they couldn't get a
                meat-cache
open
        was called to fart at it.
                The great farter
answered:
        If I farted on it
                the meat no longer
would be good to eat!
        But when they kept on asking him to fart
                he let off a
tremendous fart
        & their blubber bags
                which they had
hammered
        with a stone
                but notwithstanding
no one could get loose
        I tell you
                now they burst
& being burst
        loose on the ground
                so could be used

for food
>   but now they had
>   a wicked smell
were simply
>   thrown away.
>   Not even the dogs
would eat them
>   owing
>   to the smell of fart.

— *English working by Jerome Rothenberg, after Knud Rasmussen*

HOW HER TEETH WERE PULLED

Paiute

In the old time women's cunts had teeth in them.
It was hard to be a man then
Watching your squaw squat down to dinner
Hearing the little rabbit bones crackle.
Whenever fucking was invented it died with the inventor.
If your woman said she felt like biting you didn't take it lightly.
Maybe you just ran away to fight Numuzoho the Cannibal.

Coyote was the one who fixed things,
He fixed those toothy women!
One night he took Numuzoho's lava pestle
To bed with a mean woman
And hammer hammer crunch crunch ayi ayi
All night long:
"Husband, I am glad," she said
And all the rest is history.
To honor him we wear our necklaces of fangs.

— *English version by Jarold Ramsey*

THREE SONGS OF MAD COYOTE

Nez Percé

1.

Ravening Coyote comes,
red hands, red mouth,
necklace of eye-balls!

2.

Mad Coyote
madly sings,
then the west wind roars!

3.

Daybreak finds me,
eastern daybreak finds me
the meaning of that song:
with blood-stained mouth
comes mad Coyote!

— *Translation by Herbert J. Spinden*

THE EVIL SONG OF TAWEAKAME PEYOTE
GOD OF LUSH

Huichol

I'm the air tree you betcha
I can change
into a man or woman
As a man I'm making it
with women
as a woman with men
I'm the lush
the madman
maddest man there is
which is why they call me
maddest-man-there-is

I'm multi-powerful you betcha
not just evil
I come on good as well
I dress in different flowers
say! I'll teach you how to play the violin
but better not put me down because
I likewise am
the lush   the madman

Don't pay attention to my shouting
or what I have to tell you
I like walking on high rocks you betcha
running in the mountains
& you'll do better on the fiddle
the less you hear from me

Hell no you won't go mad
from looking at me
don't be so scared of me
I've got something here besides you betcha
something made of rainbows
flower garlands
redhot serpents
yellow shining powder
say! I'll teach you how to play the violin

— *English version by Jerome Rothenberg*

THE INVISIBLE MEN
(by Nakasuk)

Eskimo

There is a tribe of invisible men
who move around us like shadows—have you felt them?
They have bodies like ours and live just like us,
using the same kind of weapons and tools.
You can see their tracks in the snow sometimes
and even their igloos
but never the invisible men themselves.
They cannot be seen except when they die
for then they become visible.

It once happened that a human woman
married one of the invisible men.
He was a good husband in every way:
He went out hunting and brought her food,
and they could talk together like any other couple.
But the wife could not bear the thought
that she did not know what the man she married looked like.
One day when they were both at home
she was so overcome with curiosity to see him
that she stabbed with a knife where she knew he was sitting.
And her desire was fulfilled:
Before her eyes a handsome young man fell to the floor.
But he was cold and dead, and too late
she realized what she had done,
and sobbed her heart out.

When the invisible men heard about this murder
they came out of their igloos to take revenge.
Their bows were seen moving through the air

and the bow strings stretching as they aimed their arrows.
The humans stood there helplessly
for they had no idea what to do or how to fight
because they could not see their assailants.
But the invisible men had a code of honor
that forbade them to attack opponents
who could not defend themselves,
so they did not let their arrows fly,
and nothing happened; there was no battle after all
and everyone went back to their ordinary lives.

— *English version by Edward Field, after Knud Rasmussen*

SWEAT-HOUSE RITUAL NO. 1

Omaha

listen   old man   listen
you rock   listen
old man   listen
listen   didn't i teach all their children
to follow me   listen
listen
listen   unmoving time-without-end   listen
you old man sitting there   listen
on the roads where all the winds come rushing
at the heart of the winds where you're sitting   listen
old man   listen
listen   there's short grasses growing all over you   listen
you're sitting there living inside them   listen
listen   i mean you're sitting there covered with birdshit   listen
head's rimmed with soft feathers of birds   listen
old man   listen
you standing there next in command   listen
listen   you water   listen
you water that keeps on flowing
from time out of mind   listen
listen   the children have fed off you
no one's come on your secret
the children go mad for your touch   listen
listen   you standing like somebody's house   listen
just like somewhere to live   listen
you great animals   listen
listen   you making a covering over us   listen
saying   let the thoughts of those children live with me & let them
     love me   listen
listen   you tent-frame   listen

you standing with back bent   you over us
stooping your shoulders   you bending over us
you really standing
you saying   thus shall my little ones speak of me
you brushing the hair back from your forehead   listen
the hair of your head
the grass growing over you
you with your hair turning white   listen
the hair growing over your head   listen
o you roads the children will be walking on   listen
all the ways they'll run to be safe   listen
they'll escape   their shoulders bending with age where they walk
walking where others have walked
their hands shading their brows
while they walk & are old   listen
because they're wanting to share in your stength   listen
the children want to be close by your side   listen
walking   listen
be very old & listen

—*English version by Jerome Rothenberg,
from Alice Fletcher & Francis LaFlesche*

A POEM TO THE MOTHER OF THE GODS

Aztec

Oh, golden flower opened up
                          she is our mother
whose thighs are holy
                      whose face is a dark mask.
She came from Tamoanchan,
                          the first place
where all descended
                    where all was born.
Oh, golden flower flowered
                          she is our mother
whose thighs are holy
                      whose face is a dark mask.
She came from Tamoanchan

Oh, white flower opened up
                          she is our mother
whose thighs are holy
                      whose face is a dark mask.
She came from Tamoanchan,
                          the first place
where all descended
                    where all was born.
Oh, white flower flowered
                          she is our mother
whose thighs are holy
                      whose face is a dark mask.
She came from Tamoanchan.

. . . .

She lights on the round cactus,
                          she is our mother

the dark obsidian butterfly.

                        Oh, we saw her as we wandered
across the Nine Plains,

                she fed herself with deers' hearts.
She is our mother,

             the goddess earth.

                       She is dressed
in plumes

         she is smeared with clay.
In all four directions of wind

                  the arrows are broken.
They saw you as a deer

              in the barren land.
those two men, Xiuhnel and Mimich.

— English version by Edward Kissam

A POEM TO XIPE TOTEC

Aztec

Since you drink night,
                            why are you hiding now?
Put on your golden clothing,
                                  dress yourself in rain.
You are my god,
                      your water is a gift of precious jewels
as it falls down on the aqueducts,
                                        as it feathers
mountain herbs in green.
Sun has already left me,
                              has slithered away like a snake.
I will not die,
                  I am a tender tassle of corn.
My heart is like an emerald,
                                  I must see the gold.
My heart will be refreshed,
                                man will grow ripe,
and the lord of war will be born.
You are my god,
                    let there be an abundance of corn.
The tender tassle of corn
                              is shivering in the wind before you
has fixed its sight on you,
                                toward your mountains,
worships you.
My heart will be refreshed,
                                man will grow ripe
and the lord of war will be born.

— *English version by Edward Kissam*

BEFORE THEY MADE THINGS BE ALIVE THEY SPOKE
(by Lucario Cuevish)

Luiseño

Earth woman lying flat her feet were to the north her head was to the south Sky brother sitting on her right hand side he said Yes sister you must tell me who you are She answered I am Tomaiyowit She asked him Who are you? He answered I am Tukmit. Then she said:

I stretch out flat to the Horizon.
I shake I make a noise like thunder.
I am Earthquake.
I am round & roll around.
I vanish & return.

Then Tukmit said:

I arch above you like a lid.
I deck you like a hat.
I go up high & higher.
I am death I gulp it in one bite.
I grab men from the east & scatter them.
My name is Death.

Then they made things be alive.

— *English working by Jerome Rothenberg, after Constance G. DuBois*

SIOUX METAMORPHOSES

1.

He was an old wolf, no teeth, his tail all but bare. The war party thought he was one of them, singing with a young man's voice, until they saw him. He lay beside their fire, and they cut up their best buffalo meat for him, fed it to him. He taught them this song, and always since they carry their medicine in a wolfskin bag.

With powers you know nothing about
I made them come to life
with powers you cannot understand
I made them walk

Wolf people

With spirit powers
I made them walk
with spirit powers
I made them walk
with spirit powers
I made them walk
with spirit powers
I made them walk

2.

Everybody was there, but they heard somebody singing. One of them climbed the hill and looked over. A wolf was sitting there, looking far off and singing. The war party learned his song.

At daybreak
I go
I gallop
I go

At daybreak
I go
I trot
I go

At daybreak
I go
timidly
I go

At daybreak
I go
cautiously
I go

3.

I dreamed I came to a wolf den. Only the little wolves were there.
They were singing this song.

Father is away somewhere
will come home howling

Mother is away somewhere
will come home howling

Father is away somewhere
a buffalo calf in his belly

Mother is away somewhere
will come home howling

Now she returns
in a sacred manner she returns

4.

I thought I was a wolf
but the owls are hooting
& I'm afraid of the dark

I thought I was a wolf
but I'm so hungry
I'm tired from just standing

I am a wolf
I go to many places
I'm just tired of that one

(2nd Set)

I thought I saw buffalo
& called out
I thought I saw buffalo
& called out
let them be buffalo

They were blackbirds
I walked toward them
& they were blackbirds

I thought I saw buffalo
& called out
I thought I saw buffalo
& called out
let them be buffalo

They were swallows
I walked toward them
& they were swallows

(3rd Set)

1.

In wild flight
I sent the swallows
in wild flight
I made them go
in wild flight
before the clouds were gathered

In wild flight
I sent my horse
in wild flight
a swallow flying running
in wild flight
before the clouds were gathered

2.

My horse flies along
I wear blue earth & brown
I make myself fly along
I make my horse fly along
I make myself fly along
I have done it

3.

When I was courting
they told me
I had no horses
so I'm looking

Crow, Crow
watch your horses
they say I'm a horse thief

Keep your eyes open
I'm wandering around anyway
I might as well look for horses

Night is different
than day
may my horses be many

(4th Set)

1.

He comes from the north
he comes to fight
he comes from the north
see him there

I throw dust on me
it changes me
I am a bear
when I go to meet him

2.

Send word, bear father
send word, bear father
I'm having a hard time
send word, bear father
I'm having a bad time

3.

My paw is holy
herbs are everywhere
my paw
herbs are everywhere

My paw is holy
everything is holy
my paw
everything is holy

— Working by James Koller, from Frances Densmore

A BOOK OF EXTENSIONS (I)

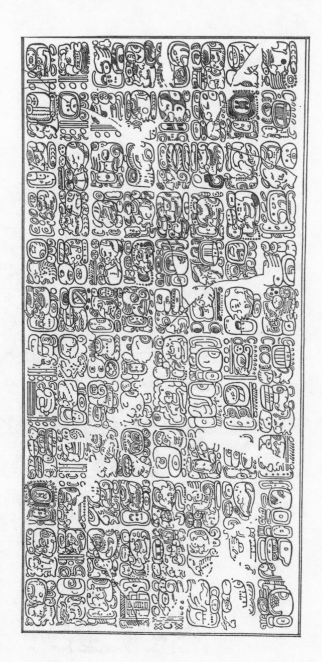

THE TABLET OF THE 96 HIEROGLYPHS
Maya

FROM A BOOK OF THE MAYA
Maya

THE CALENDARS

Ojibwa

1. long moon, spirit moon   2. moon of the suckers   3. moon
of the crust on the snow   4. moon of the breaking of snow-shoes
5. moon of the flowers & blooms   6. moon of strawberries
7. moon of raspberries   8. moon of whortle berries   9. moon
of gathering of wild rice   10. moon of the falling of leaves
11. moon of freezing   12. little moon of the spirit

Mandan

1. moon of the seven cold days   2. pairing moon
3. moon of the weak eyes   4. moon of the wild geese / moon
of the breaking up of the ice   5. moon in which maize is sown /
moon of flowers   6. moon of ripe service berries   7. moon of
ripe cherries   8. moon of ripe wild plums   9. moon of ripe maize
10. moon of the fall of the leaves   11. moon of the freezing
of the rivers   12. moon of the little cold

Netchilli

1. it is cold, the Eskimo is freezing   2. the sun is returning
3. the sun is ascending   4. the seal brings forth her young
5. the young seals are taking to the sea   6. the seals are shedding
their coats   7. reindeer bring forth their young / birds are brooding
8. the young birds are hatched   9. the reindeer is migrating
southward   10. amerairui   11. the Eskimo lay down food depots
12. the sun disappears

Dakota

1. hard moon 2. raccoon moon 3. sore eyes moon 4. moon
in which the geese lay eggs / moon in which the streams are
again navigable 5. planting moon 6. moon in which
the strawberries are red 7. moon in which the chokecherries are
ripe & the geese shed their feathers 8. harvest moon
9. moon in which wild rice is laid up to dry 10. drying rice
moon 11. deer rutting moon 12. moon when deers shed horns

Tlingit

1. goose month 2. black bear month 3. silver salmon month
4. month before everything hatches 5. month everything hatches
6. time of the long days 7. month when the geese can't fly
8. month when all kinds of animal prepare their dens 9. moon
child 10. big moon / formation of ice 11. month when all
creatures go into their dens / the sun disappears
12. ground hog mother's moon

Loucheux

1. moon when dog is cold 2. moon of ice 3. moon of eagles
4. moon in which dog barks 5. moon of the break up of ice /
moon of the sea 6. moon of moulting 7. moon of the long day
8. moon of the rutting reindeer 9. moon of the chase
10. moon of warmth 11. moon of mountain goats 12. moon
in which the sun is dead.

Cree

1. month in which the old fellow spreads the brush / extreme
cold moon   2. month in which the young birds begin to chirp /
old man   3. eagle moon   4. grey goose moon   5. frog moon
6. moon in which birds begin to lay their eggs /
the leaves come out   7. moon in which birds cast their feathers
8. moon in which the young birds begin to fly   9. moon
in which the moose deer cast their horns / snow goose month
10. rutting moon / the birds fly south   11. hoar frost moon /
the rivers begin to freeze   12. moon in which the young fellow
spreads the brush / whirlwind moon

Modoc

1. thumb   2. index finger   3. middle finger   4. ring finger
5. little finger   6. thumb   7. index finger   8. thumb   9. index
finger   10. middle finger   11. ring finger   12. little finger

Kwakiutl

1. spawning season / season of floods   2. elder brother / first
olachen run   3. raspberry sprouting season / no sap in trees
4. raspberry season   5. huckleberry season / oil moon
6. salalberry season / sockeye month   7. southeast wind moon
8. empty boxes   9. wide face   10. right moon   11. sweeping
houses / dog salmon month   12. fish in river moon / cleaned of
leaves   13. split both ways

Tewa

1. ice moon   2. lizard belly cut moon   3. month leaves break
forth   4. leaves open   5. tender leaf month / corn planting
6. dark leaf month   7. horse month / month of ripeness
8. wheat cutting month   9. month when the corn is taken in /
syrup is made   10. harvest month / month of falling leaves
11. month when all is gathered in   12. ashes fire

Eskimo

1. season for top spinning / little sun   2. time of much moon /
the first seals are born / starting out to hunt reindeer   3. time
of taking of hares in nets / time of creeping on game   4. time
of cutting off (from the appearance of sharp lines where the
white of the ptarmigans' bodies is contrasted with the brown of
the new summer neck feathers)   5. geese come / time for going
in kaiaks   6. time of eggs / time of fawn hunting   7. time of
braining salmon / geese get new wing feathers   8. time for
brooding geese to moult   9. swans moult / time for velvet shed-
ding   10. time for seal nets   11. time for bringing in winter
stores   12. time for the drum

Carrier

1. moon of the wind   2. moon of the snow storm   3. moon of
the golden eagle   4. moon of the wild goose   5. moon of the
black bear / moon of the carp   6. moon when they take to the
water   7. the buffalo ruts / moon of the land locked salmon
8. moon of the red salmon   9. moon of the bull trout
10. moon of the white fish   11. during its half they navigate /
the fat of animals disappears   12. what freezes is covered with bare
ice

LEAN WOLF'S COMPLAINT

Hidatsa

Four years ago

the white man

friends

with us

A lie

Done, finished,
"that is all"

ZUNI DERIVATIONS

I.

LIQUID, WATER
water in a shallow container
  honey
collection of water
  in water, floating
water on the surface
  lake, puddle
water on the surface coming out
  spring
  woman
sour water
  beer
  vinegar
water removed from a deep container
  whip
become water
  melt
water with a hot taste
  whiskey
  bilious phlegm
get water with a hot taste
  sick with an upset stomach

II.

GRAINS
grainy pants
    bluejeans
grainy jacket
    bluejean jacket
salty grains
    salt
sweet grains
    sugar
collection of grainy water
    Zuni Salt Lake
toward the collection of grainy water
    south

III.

MOON, MONTH
what belongs to moon
    moonlight
instrument for what belongs to moon
    moon

IV.

DAYLIGHT
instrument for daylight
    sun
    clock

V.

TWO
multiplied with two
   twice
two tens
   twenty
coin of two
   quarter-dollar
two hearts
   witch

VI.

ON TOP
cause to be on top
   put on top
   bewitch
   (placing victim's lock of hair
   piece of clothing
   on top of a tree or bluff)

VII.

ANGULAR PROJECTIONS
(like the corners of a gunnysack)
like a witch
(a witch's hair projects
in two angular bunches
on each side of the head)
good angular projections
   something perfectly square

VIII.

HOLLOW TUBE
hollow tube making rattling sounds
    empty-headed person
become a hollow tube
    faint, forget

IX.

DANCE
cause to dance
    sponsor in a dance
    bounce a child on the lap
    spin a top

X.

WICKERWORK
growing bunch of wickerwork
    pine needles
static wickerwork
    paper
make static wickerwork
    attend school
wickerwork together on the ground
    in single file

XI.

STAND
cause to stand
    stop
cause oneself not to stand
    run
stand together on the ground
    be a village

XII.

OLD
old ones
    parents
terrestrial old one
    dwelling-place of a deity
indeterminate old one
    calm, passive, quiet, shy
    inconspicuous
old person
    man, man of the house, husband

XIII.

BECOME BLUE, BECOME GREEN
one who is black and blue with bruises
one who is blue from the cold
valuable blue, valuable green
    turquoise
    blue corn

XIV.

BECOME LIGHT, BECOME WHITE
terrestrial light
    daylight
    life
cause to be light
    see
    make visible
valuable light
    white corn
    white shell necklace

— Selected & arranged by Dennis Tedlock

NAVAJO CORRESPONDENCES

(First Set)

    1. red willow
       Sun
       yellow

    2. arrow
       Wind
       Cicada
       arrow-crossing
       life

    3. aspen
       white
       summer
       pink

    4. Bat
       Darkness
       wing feather
       Big Fly

    5. Big Fly
       feather
       Wind
       skin at tip of tongue
       speech

(Second Set)

    1. black
       Darkness
       Black Wind
       yellow squash

2. Black God
   Black Star
   Darkness

3. bull-roarer
   lightning
   snakes
   pokers
   danger line
   hoops

4. ambush woods
   emetic frames
   pokers

5. cane
   digging stick
   arrow
   water

(Third Set)

1. cotton
   motion
   clouds

2. Earth
   Yellow Wind
   Pink Thunder
   Reared-in-the-earth
   Pink Snake
   rainbow
   redshell
   sunglow
   Holy Girl

3. feather cloak
   yellow lightning

4. Frog
   hail
   potatoes
   dumplings

5. Old Age
   ax
   Frog

(Fourth Set)

1. cloud water
   fog
   moss

2. smoke
   cloud
   rain
   acceptance
   breathing in

3. spiderweb
   nerves & veins
   marrow
   conveyances

4. red willow
   water
   blue

5. yellow
   Yellow-evening-light
   Yellow Wind
   black squash

MUU'S WAY or PICTURES FROM THE UTERINE WORLD (excerpts)

Cuna

sunrise . . . & toward the sunrise stands the village of the Bow People . . . bowmen move around it

& place a net over the housetop bowmen are coming down from

a bowman sits & aims . . . bent over . . . crouching . . . with bow & arrow . . . arrow point goes whizzing

makes the earth rise in a cloud . . . it darkens the whole place . . . covers Muu's way

bird bowmen going down now

other bowmen too

& other bowmen

but doesn't leave Muu's roads . . . not a single alleyway of hers

he sits defending the sick woman . . . sits protecting her

he calls "O Mountain dweller   dweller on the tops of mountains"

shaman calls the Lords of Animals . . . one like a jaguar . . . tied
    with iron chains . . . the iron chains are rattling

the entrails make a noise . . . the entrails roar . . . an animal comes
    somewhere . . . now the animal comes up . . . it lifts its neck &
    comes with flashing eyes & lifts its iron throat with terrifying eyes

with rattling iron chains . . . noise of its large links under the
    hammock of the sick woman . . . three animals one like a jaguar
    tied with iron chains

while the iron chains are rattling . . . entrails screaming . . . while
    the entrails make a noise & throw Muu's way into a panic . . .
    they defend the sick woman . . . & protect her

"o mountain dweller o dweller on top of the mountain" . . . the Shaman is calling the lords of the Gold Water

the Little Gold Water answers . . . he's coming with lots of gold water

over her hammock he's pouring the strongest gold water

the strongest gold water is steaming . . . gold water is dripping . . . the strong gold waters are gathering . . . making a puddle of gold . . . on the ground

& he's turning them off . . . he's blotting them out on the road in front of the sick woman

"o dweller on mountains dweller on top of the mountain" . . . the Shaman is calling the lord of the Silver Water

the Little Silver Water answers . . . he's coming with lots of silver water

Shaman calls "dweller on mountain o dweller on tops of the mountains" . . . he's calling the lords of the Gold Net

& they come . . . down they come . . . with a gold net like a kerchief they cover her

they come with a gold net . . . to hang it over the treetops . . . to fasten a gold net . . . to make a gold net secure

a gold net starts looking like gold

a gold net is lowered . . . a gold net swells out . . . a gold net hangs down . . . a gold net forms meshes

shamans study a gold net to make sure it's straight . . . they sit down with a gold net . . . they kneel with it

shamans are swinging a gold net

shamans are swinging a gold net

shamans are swinging a gold net

shamans are putting on stockings

shamans are putting on shoes

shamans are polishing shoes

shamans are transforming shoes

shamans are giving each other endless advice

"with a fine piece of cloth you must wipe the child for me"

this medicine man has encouraged them . . . he has given all of them bones . . . has adorned them with *tele*-flutes . . . brought them safely over the Underground road . . . & all underground roads . . . he has put them under the ground "to see if any man will take my castle"

& has put the gold net in front of the sick woman

with iron nails . . . or fastened with iron nails & giving light . . . they put the gold net

& facing the opposite way . . . fastened with iron nails . . . held down with nails of iron . . . they put the silver net

when the time is silent . . . when the time is midnight . . . my lady's essence may try to escape . . . then take a care with it

under the ground . . . beneath its surface & below the earth . . . fastened with iron nails . . . held down with nails of iron & giving light . . . they put the gold net

"o dweller on the mountain o dweller on top of the mountain" the shaman calls to his shaman

his shaman is calling the lords of the animals . . . Drinking Dog is an animal . . . Sucking Dog is an animal . . . tied with an iron chain . . . the iron chain rattles . . . the entrails are roaring . . . the entrails are making a noise

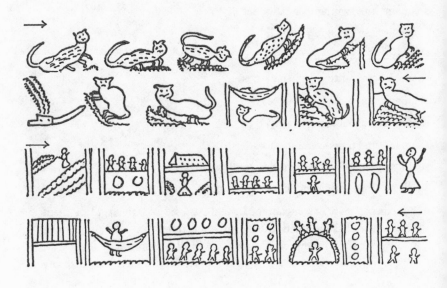

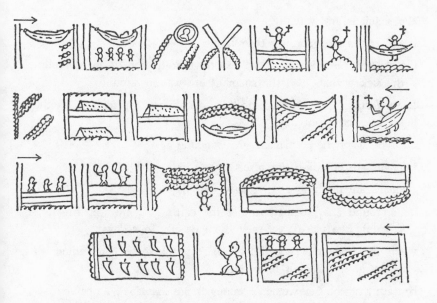

the animal . . . the animal is coming up . . . & comes with flashing
eyes . . . lifts its iron throat & comes . . . with terrifying eyes the
iron chains . . . come rattling . . . entrails roar beneath . . . the
hammock of the sick woman

Drinking Dog is an animal . . . Sucking Dog is an animal . . . tied
with an iron chain . . . the iron chain rattles . . . the entrails are
screaming

& put Muu's way into a panic . . . while they defend her . . . they
protect the sick woman

looking toward the sea . . . the South . . . the shamans are guard-
ing the place . . . the shamans are listening . . . exactly four days

& facing the opposite way not leaving one of Muu's roads I put all
these shamans here . . . dolls . . . to defend the sick woman . . .
being invisible dolls . . . changing to shamans . . . you do things
by seeing

the shamans are watching

the shamans are guarding the place

the shamans are listening . . . exactly four days . . . are defending the sick woman . . . the shamans are waiting around

& are facing . . . are watching . . . guarding the place . . . & they listen exactly four days

all over everywhere shamans are watching

shamans are guarding the place

shamans are listening . . . exactly four days

underground . . . shamans under the earth . . . are watching . . . guarding the place . . . they listen exactly four days

when the woman gets well . . . some people have gone where the plants grow . . . but be careful!

beneath . . . the sick woman's hammock are shamans . . . carved . . . under her hammock the shamans are rising

not stepping foot from her house the lords of the Silver Branch rise

the lords of the Silver Branch talk . . . the lords rise up . . . at the door of the sick woman's house

the lords of the Silver Cross talk to the Silver Cross . . . to the fetus

entangling the road in front of the sick woman

they come to entangle the road in front of the sick woman

come to twist the road in front of the sick woman

pulling the gold net over her hammock . . . when the hour is silent the hour is midnight

if Muu saw that the road through the woman was open . . . the shamans would rise

& strike with their sticks . . . the shamans . . . are holding their sticks in a line

the shamans are swinging a gold net they put a gold net over the housefront they drag a gold net as far as the sky

if Muu saw any road through the sky lying open . . . the shamans
would rise

& would strike with their sticks

& hold their sticks in a line

— Jerome Rothenberg's working, after Nils Holmer & Henry Wassén

THE WINTER REVELATION OF BATTISTE GOOD

Dakota

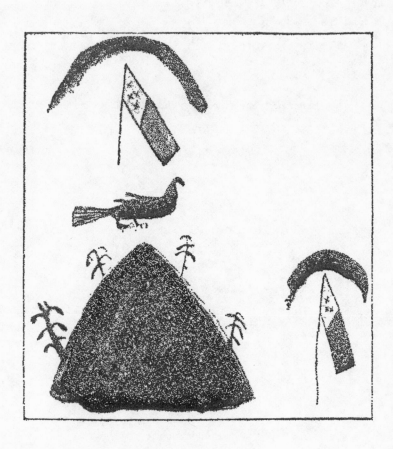

In the year 1856, I went to the Black Hills & cried, & cried, & cried, & suddenly I saw a bird above me, which said: "Stop crying; I am a woman but I will tell you something: My Great-Father, Father God, who made this place, gave it to me for a home & told me to watch over it. He put a blue sky over my head & gave me a blue flag to have with this beautiful green country. My Great-Father, Father God, grew, & his flesh was part earth & part stone & part metal & part wood & part water; he took from them all & placed them here for me, & told me to watch over them. I am the Eagle Woman who tell you this. The whites know that there are four black flags of God: four divisions of the earth. He first made the earth soft by wetting it, then cut it into four parts, one of which, containing the Black Hills, he gave to the Dakotas, &, because I am a woman, I shall not consent to the pouring of blood on this chief house. The time will come when you will remember my words, for after many years you shall grow up one with the white people." She then circled round & round & gradually passed out of my sight. I also saw prints of a man's hands & horse's hoofs on the rocks, & two thousand years, & one hundred millions of dollars. I came away crying, as I had gone. I have told this to many Dakotas, & all agree that it meant that we were to seek & keep peace with the whites.

THE MYTH OF ATOSIS

Abnaki

he was a snake with the power of a young hunter
she would become the mother of all the Black Snakes
he appeared to her on the surface of a lake

STRING GAMES

Bella Bella

1.

Getting Berries

Where you going?
(Getting berries. Think I'll try a little farther.)
Why not go with this canoe?
(Don't guess we can use it. Not enough room for So-&-So's
  mother.)
Can't see how. Canoe's got room enough down in the baling
  hole.
(So-&-So's mother would use it for baling.)
Well I wish you'd go & capsize in the mouth of that river.
(Then they went & capsized in the mouth of that river.)

2.

Ghost & Shaman

Hey let's fight that shaman, let's fight that ghost first &
  then that shaman.
(See them running away. There goes that ghost & that old shaman.)
Well, take along his working box.
(Well, take along his crabapple box.)
Well, take along his viburnum box.
(Well, take along his dry-salmon box.)

3.

Getting Firewood

Where you going?
(Going to get firewood.)
Where's the firewood?
(Down to my house.)
Then you better come & get it.
(Why's your mouth all greasy?)
Been eating some old-woman grease.
(What you using for a grease dish?)
This old-woman clamshell.
(Well what's gonna be your mat then?)
This old-woman mat.
(How about your you-know-what?)
Some old-woman fishmeat.
(And what'll be your backboard?)
Old-woman backboard.
(How about your post?)
That's this old-woman digging stick.
(Then I guess you're the one to go & bring us some soaked salmon.)

4.

Pieces of Snot

Snot goes down.
(Snot goes back up.)
I said snot goes down.
(Now I guess it's dribbling out.)

5.

Lying Down

Don't lie down again.
(When you do lie down maybe hammer a stone.)
Raven & lover on their backs & facing.
(Somebody's asshole.)
Crane's ass is bloody. A lump on his neck.
(Runs out of the house with a mouth of soaked salmon.)

THE STORY OF GLOOSCAP, OR BLACK CAT:
HOW HE SAID GOODBYE TO SABLE, HOW SABLE WAS TRAPPED
IN SNAKE'S TENT & WAS TOLD TO BRING A STRAIGHT STICK FOR HIS
OWN GUTTING, HOW SABLE & BLACK CAT PLANNED SNAKE'S BLINDING
WITH A CROOKED STICK, & HOW BLACK CAT KILLED SNAKE
BESIDE A FALLEN HEMLOCK TREE & CUT HIM INTO SMALL PIECES

Passamaquoddy

OJIBWA LOVE POEM

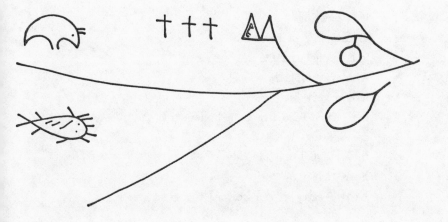

POEMS FOR THE GAME OF SILENCE

1.

Chippewa

it is hanging
in the edge of sunshine
it is a pig   I see
with its double hoofs
it is a very fat pig
the people who live in a hollow tree
are fighting
they are fighting bloodily
he is rich
he will carry a pack toward the great water

2.

Mandan

that
that
whose
track is it like?

grandfather
two-teeth
(he means the beaver!)
if it's like his track
if it is
follow it on
the man came to a wigwam
pounded the wigwam
with worn-out feet
with a wriggled bag
up high
lay a big fat
young buffalo calf
with a soft belly-button
walking
crumbling sticks
crab shells
have a dance
he
knocked his eye out

— *Translations by Frances Densmore*

SONGS & SONG PICTURES

Chippewa

SONG PICTURE NO. 17

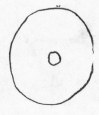

at the center of the earth
is where I'm from

SONG PICTURE NO. 27

when the water's calm
& the fog's just drifting in—
that's when I show up now & then

SONG PICTURE NO. 29

water's flowing
the sound
comes toward my home

SONG PICTURE NO. 30

when I show up
all those seething waters
cast their men up from below

SONG PICTURE NO. 34

sure thing
I'm a spirit!
see me becoming visible?
must be a male beaver

SONG PICTURE NO. 54

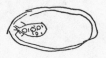

in the middle of the sea
long room of the sea
in which I'm sitting

SONG PICTURE NO. 56

I keep running around
shoot at a man & he falls down
    stoned
try feeling with my hand
see if he's still alive

SONG PICTURE NO. 58

I'm living in a cave
old Grandfather
got arms
with feathers
I must be a cave-man

SONG PICTURE NO. 64

know what I'll promise you?
skies be bright & clear for you
that's what I'll promise you

SONG PICTURE NO. 66

hunting song (i)

there's my war club
booming through the sky—
you animals better come when I
    call you

SONG PICTURE NO. 68

hunting song (ii)

this time I'll show up
everywhere on earth
I'll be dressed in skin of a marten

SONG PICTURE NO. 69

hunting song (iii)

shining like a star—
the animal that looks up's
dazzled by my light

SONG PICTURE NO. 71

the love charm

what's that you're telling me?
I'm dressed up like the roses—
just as beautiful as they are

SONG PICTURE NO. 82

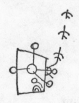

song of the man who succeeded

I'll test my power
on myself

SONG PICTURE NO. 83

song for a scalp dance

some people in the sky
must sure be jealous
me dancing around here
with this scalp

SONG PICTURE NO. 85

song of the crab medicine-bag

I can use it
good as any crab can

SONG PICTURE NO. 86

song of the fire-charm

flames are shooting
far up as my body

SONG PICTURE NO. 87

song of starvation

which of you
is going to take my body?
watch that old lady
making medicine

SONG PICTURE NO. 96

might have known it—
waterbirds come perching
all my body long

SONG PICTURE NO. 106

sound is fading out
it's more like five sounds
FREEDOM
sound is really fading out
it's more like five sounds

—*Workings by Jerome Rothen-
berg, from Frances Densmore*

A BOOK OF EXTENSIONS (I)   335

A BOOK OF EXTENSIONS (II)

SOUNDINGS

SOUND-POEM NO. 1

Navajo

Óhohohó héhehe héya héya

Óhohohó héhehe héya héya

Éo ládo éo ládo éo ládo nasé

Hówani how owów owé

Éo ládo éo ládo éo ládo nasé

Hówani how owów owé

Hówani hówani how héyeyéye yéyeyáhi

Hówowów héya héya héya héya

Hówa héhehe héya héya héya

Óhohohó howé héya héya

Óhohohó héhehe héya héya

Hábi níye hábi níye

Há'huizánaha   síhiwánaha

Há'hayá éaheóo éaheóo

Síhiwánaha   há'huizánaha

Há'hayá éaheóo éaheóo éaheóo éaheóo éaheóo

SOUND-POEM NO. 2
(by Richard Johnny John)

Seneca

gah non   wey yo hey
            yah ney heeyo
                      no heyah heyah
            yah ney heeyo
                            ho wey yah heenay
yah ho ho yo
      o ho wey yo hey
            yah ney heeyo
                      no heyah heyah
           yah ney heeyo
           yah ney heeyo
                            ho wey yah heenay

A POEM FROM *THE SWEATBATH POEMS*

Fox

A gi ya ni a gi yan ni i
A gi ya ni a gi yan ni i
A gi ya ni a gi yan ni i
A gi ya ni agi ya ni
Sky
A gi ya ni i a gi ya ni
A gi ya ni i a gi ya ni
A gi ya ni

From CEREMONY OF SENDING:
A Simultaneity for Twenty Choruses

Osage

The Hidden People & The Star People

THERE, TRULY THEY SAID IN THIS HOUSE
THERE, TRULY THEY SAID IN THIS HOUSE

The Hidden People sitting there said

said'nth'house   *The Water People of Seven Fireplaces*
said'nth'house   O! My Grandfather, they said to him
said'nth'house   *The Water People said*
said'nth'house   we have no suitable totem, My Grandfather
said'nth'house   *to The Star People sitting there*
said'nth'house   O! My Little Ones, he began
said'nth'house   *O! My Grandfather, they said to him*
said'nth'house   you say you have no suitable totem
said'nth'house   *we have no suitable totem, My Grandfather*
said'nth'house   I am a suitable totem
said'nth'house   *THERE, TRULY THEY SAID IN THIS HOUSE*

THERE, TRULY THEY SAID IN THIS HOUSE
You say you have no suitable totem

said'nth'house   He built a small house
said'nth'house   *I am a suitable totem*
said'nth'house   I have not built this house without purpose
said'nth'house   *the female cedar over there*
said'nth'house   I have built it as a place to break animal heads
said'nth'house   *truly I live in that body*
said'nth'house   I have not built this house without purpose
said'nth'house   *when the young take on my body*
said'nth'house   it is a symbol of the spider
said'nth'house   *they'll live to see old age as they walk*
said'nth'house   Indeed, I have built it as a trap
said'nth'house   *The male cedar right there*
said'nth'house   all small animals, whoever they may be
said'nth'house   *they'll walk with that totem*

said'nth'house will ensnare themselves as they walk
said'nth'house   *the male cedar*
said'nth'house and when the young use it, animals will appear
said'nth'house   *when they walk with that totem*
said'nth'house Even before dawn
said'nth'house   *they'll live to see old age as they walk*
said'nth'house animals will appear for them as they walk
said'nth'house   *THERE, TRULY THEY SAID IN THIS*
                     HOUSE
       and also at dusk
said'nth'house   *And these waters*
said'nth'house animals will appear for them as they walk
said'nth'house   *we'll unite with the two cedars as we walk*
said'nth'house This bull buffalo right here
said'nth'house   *and these waters*
said'nth'house this one
said'nth'house   *when they use them for old age*
said'nth'house will make animals appear for them as they walk
said'nth'house   *they'll live to see old age as they walk*
said'nth'house and this animal's blood
said'nth'house   *These grasses right here that never die*
said'nth'house Even before dawn
said'nth'house   *when they use them also for old age*
said'nth'house they'll drink his blood
said'nth'house   *they'll live to see old age as they walk*
said'nth'house also at dusk
said'nth'house   *I stand here approaching old age*
said'nth'house they'll drink this animal's blood
said'nth'house   *between these stooping shoulders*
said'nth'house THERE, TRULY THEY SAID IN THIS HOUSE
       I stand here approaching old age

said'nth'house These shall stand as suitable totems:
said'nth'house *among these topmost white blossoms*
said'nth'house The short-snake
said'nth'house *I stand here approaching old age*
said'nth'house the young will use as they walk
said'nth'house *as the young stalks grow*
said'nth'house there amongst the grass clumps
said'nth'house *they'll live to see white hair as they walk*
said'nth'house he suddenly lifted his head
said'nth'house

Even though the young become spirits

said'nth'house

they'll regain consciousness as they walk

said'nth'house

When the young take on my body

said'nth'house

the four parts of their days

said'nth'house

they'll reach and enter as they walk

said'nth'house

And what totems shall they use?

said'nth'house

The long bull-snake

said'nth'house

the young will use as they walk

said'nth'house

there amongst the grasses

said'nth'house

he suddenly lifted his head

said'nth'house

the long bull-snake

said'nth'house

they'll use as they walk

said'nth'house

And even though the young become spirits

said'nth'house

they'll regain consciousness as they walk

said'nth'house

and the four parts of their days

said'nth'house

they'll reach and enter as they walk

said'nth'house

And what totems shall they use?

said'nth'house

The black-snake

said'nth'house

they'll use as they walk

said'nth'house

there amongst the grasses

said'nth'house

he suddenly lifted his head

said'nth'house

the black-snake

said'nth'house

Even though the young become spirits

said'nth'house

they'll regain consciousness as they walk

said'nth'house

and the four parts of their days

said'nth'house

they'll reach and enter as they walk

said'nth'house

And what totems will they use?

said'nth'house

The rattlesnake

said'nth'house

there amongst the grasses

said'nth'house

he lies buzzing nearby

said'nth'house

the rattler

said'nth'house

Even though the young become spirits

said'nth'house

they'll regain consciousness as they walk

said'nth'house

The rattlesnake

said'nth'house

hissing and hissing

said'nth'house

Beneath their feet

said'nth'house

he stands rattling and rattling

said'nth'house

Toward their necks

said'nth'house

he stands rattling and rattling

said'nth'house

Toward the east wind

said'nth'house

he stands rattling and rattling

said'nth'house

Toward the west wind

said'nth'house

he stands rattling and rattling

said'nth'house

Toward the north wind

said'nth'house

he stands rattling and rattling

said'nth'house

Even though the young become spirits

said'nth'house

they'll regain consciousness as they walk

said'nth'house

When the young take on my body

said'nth'house

the four parts of their days

said'nth'house

they'll reach and enter as they walk

said'nth'house

Those beautiful days

said'nth'house

they'll reach and enter as they walk

said'nth'house

— Barbara Tedlock's working, after Francis La Flesche

TEPEHUA THOUGHT-SONGS

(1–3)

Thought-Song One

Knowing that the music knows

what those will give to Thought,
for whom it's needed

or where it will be entering & who
will ask for pardon

just as the music knows what will be played there.

Where it was going to be present
is where someone was going to a poor friend's home to visit

because he wants them to be looking out for him
because he wants them giving what he needs for living

that's what they did when giving us this light
when they were giving us commandments in this world

For way out there he'll use the thought they gave him
with which he'll enter in the place where he's arriving

& with it he will then begin his doings
& do it where he first went for a visit.

Thought-Song Two

Thought was

& though it had been
still remains

or it was hardly born when
boys & girls were.

Though they weren't Old Ones
they found their way with it—

so Thought was given them
so life was by their fathers.

When the music starts

it tells about the time Thought entered
it wants to speak about its happiness

to grasp the music way out there
knowing where it is

& knowing where to enter now
once it had gotten where its fathers were
it greeted them.

Thought-Song Three

When they play like that where everyone is
everyone is

& everyone is seeing what is being done there
& what these ones are doing moving.

In that place some are coming in between
& moving things   asking favor for it.

This song is how the midwives & curers used to sing
this is how they did it

& the reason for their being there
& being asked for favor & forgiveness.

The asking of it from those there
is the same as what is played there

& what is spoken there
& done there

& the only reason that they play this music.

— *Translation by Charles Boilès, with working by Jerome Rothenberg*

THE 12TH HORSE-SONG OF FRANK MITCHELL

Navajo

Key: wnn N nnnn N gahn   hawuNnawu   nngobaheegwing

Some are & are going to my howinouse baheegwing hawuNnawu N
    nngahn baheegwing

Some are & are going to my howinouse baheegwing hawuNnawu N
    nngahn baheegwing

Some are & some are gone to my howinouse nnaht bahyee nahtgwing
    buhtzzm bahyee noohwinnnGUUH

Because I was (N gahn) I was the boy raised Ng the dawn(n)(n)
    but some are & are gowing to my howinouse baheegwing

& by going from the house the bluestone hoganome but some are & are
    gone to my howinow baheegwing

& by going from the house the shahyNshining hoganome but some
    are & are gone to my howinow baheeGWING

& by going from the swollenouse my breath has blown but some are &
    are going to my howinouse baheegwing

& by going from the house the hohly honganome but some are
    & are gone to my howinow baheegwing ginng ginnng

& from the place of precious cloth we walk (p)pon (N gahn) but
    some are gone to my howinow baheegwing hawunawwing

with those prayersticks that are blu(u)(u) but some are & are
    (wnn N) gahn to my howinouse baheegwing

with my feathers that are b(lu)u but some are & are going to my
    howinouse baheegwing

with my spirit horses that are b(lu)u but some are & are going to my
    howinouse baheegwing

with my spirit horses that are blue & dawn but some are & are gone
    to my howinow baheegwing nngnnng

with those spirit (hawuN) horses that are bluestone (nawu) but some
    are & are gone to my howinow baheegwing

with those hoganorses that are bluestone but some are & are going to
my howinouse baheegwing
with cloth of ever(ee)ee kind tgaahn & draw them on nahhtnnn
but some are & are gone to my howinow baheegwing
with jewels of ever(ee)ee kind tgaahn & draw them on nahhtnnn
but some are & are going to my howinouse habeegwing
with hoganorses of ever(ee)ee kind to go & draw them on nahhtnnn
but some are & are going to my howinouse baheegwing
with sheep of evree(ee)(ee) kind tgaahn & draw them on nahhtnnn
but some are & are going to my howinouse baheegwing
with cattle of every kind (N gahn) to go & draw them on nahhtnnnn
but some are & are going to my howinouse baheegwing
with men of evree(ee)(ee) kind tgaahn & draw them on nahhtnnn
but some are & are going to my howinouse baheegwing
now to my howinome of precious cloth in my backroom Ngahhnn
where Nnnn but some are & are going to my howinouse baheegwing
in my house of precious cloth we walk (p)pon (N gahn) where
Nnnn but some are & are going to my howinouse baheegwing
& everything that's gone before (mmmm) more we walk (p)pon but
some are & are going to my howinouse baheegwing
& everything that's more & won't be (be!) be poor but some are
& some are gone to my howinow baheegwing
& everything that's (nawuN) living to be old & blesst (bhawuN)
some are & are going to my howinouse baheegwing
because I am the boy who goes & blesses/blisses to be old but some are
& are going to my howinouse baheegwing hawuNnawu N nngahn
baheegwinnng

Zzmmmm are & are gone to my howinow baheegwing hawuNnawu N
nngahn baheegwing
Zzmmmm are & are going to my howinouse baheegwing hawuNnawu
N nngahn baheegwing
Some are & some are gone to my house now naht bahyeee naht-
nwinnng buht nawuNNN baheegwinnng

— *Total translation by Jerome Rothenberg*

THE 13TH HORSE-SONG OF FRANK MITCHELL

Navajo

Key: nnnn N N gahn

Some 're lovely N nawu nnnn but some 're & are at my hawuz
nawu wnn N wnn baheegwing
Some 're lovely N hawu nnnn but some 're & are at my howinow
N wnn baheegwing
Some 're lovely N nawu nnnn but some are & are at my howzes
nawu nahht bahyeenwing but bahyeesum nahtgwing

NNNOOOOW because I was (N gahn) I was the boy ingside the
dawn but some 're at my house now wnn N wnn baheegwing
& by going from the house the wwwideshell howanome but some 're
at my howinow N wnnn baheegwing
& by going from the house the darkned hoganome but some 're at
my house N wnn baheegwing
& by going from the swollen hoganouse my breath has blown but
some 're at my house N wnn baheegwing
& by going from the house the hloly hoganome but some 're at my
house N wnn N wnn baheegwingnnng
& from the plays of jewels we walk (naht gahn) (p)pon but some 're
at my howinow N wnn baheegwing
with prayersticks that are white (nnuhgohn) but some 're at my
house N wnn baheegwing
with my feathers that are white (mmm gahn) but some 're at my
house N wnn baheegwing
with my spirit horses that are white (nuhgohn) but some 're at my
house N wnn baheegwing
with my spirit horses that are white & dawn (nuhgohn) but some 're
at my house N wnnn baheegwing
with those spirit horses that are whiteshell nawuNgnnnn but some
're at my house N wnn baheegwing

with those howanorses that are whiteshell nawu but some 're at my
    howinouse wnnn baheegwingnnng
wiiiingth jewels of every kind d(go)nN draw them on nahtnnn but
    some 're at my howinow N wnn baheegwing
with cloth of every kind d(go)nN draw them on nahtnnn but some
    're at my howinow N wnn baheegwing
with sheep of every kind d(go)nN draw them on nahtnnn but some
    're at my house N wnn baheegwing
with horses of evree(ee)(ee) kind d(go)nN draw them on nahtnnn
    but some 're at my howinow N wnn baheegwing
with cattle of every kind d(go)nN draw them on nahtnnn but some
    're at my howinow N wnn baheegwing
with men of every kind d(go)nN draw them on nahtnnn but some
    're at my house N wnn baheegwing
in my house of precious jewels in my back(acka)room (N gahn)
    where nnnn but some 're at my howinow N wnn baheegwing
in this house of precious jewels we walk (p)pon (N gahn) where
    nnnn but some 're at my house N wnn baheegwing
& everything that's g(h)one before mmmmore we walk (p)pon but
    some 're at my howinow N wnn baheegwing
& everything that's more ( ) won't be (be!) be poor but some 're
    at my house N wnn baheegwing
& everything that's now & living to be old & blesst nhawu but some
    're at my howinow N wnnn baheegwing
because I am the boy who blesses/blisses to be old but some 're at my
    house N wnn baheegwing

Zzmmmm 're lovely N nawu nnnn but some 're & are at my
    howinouse N wnn baheegwing
Zzmmmm 're lovely nawu N nnnn but some 're & are at my house
    N wnn baheegwing
Zzmmmm 're lovely N nawu nnnn but some are & are at my howzes
    nahht bahyeenahtnwing but nawu nohwun baheegwing

    — *Total translation by Jerome Rothenberg*

A FOURTH SERVICE

Directions: Go to a mountaintop & cry for a vision.

Sioux

THE NET OF MOON: A Pawnee Hand Game Vision

Full moonlit night   people
playing the Hand Game in a tent
everyone goes outside to dance
One man gets shakey
then starts crying   hands up
to the moon   (he says):   I felt it
something in my mind
when we went out   it seemed
I would be seeing something
it was coming
we went out   when we were dancing
I suddenly looked up
at the moon   Old Moon looks down
& sees me   & laughs at me
that's when I cried

— English working by Jerome Rothenberg

PEYOTE VISIONS

Winnebago

1

tried drinking coffee
        i would spill it
  sleeping
would see great snakes
       would cry out & get up
       raise my cover & look around
       had someone called me?
when the wind blew
        i heard singing
  people were spitting
  loudly   i couldn't sleep
would see things happening in a distant country
ghosts on horseback   drunk
five or six of them were on one horse
the song they sang was
"even i
     gotta die
          bye & bye
  so what's the use of anything
       i think"
later we used to sing it as a drinking song
lots of times

2

        was looking at the button i saw
an eagle
                with outspread wings
                each feather
                had a mark   it looked
        at me but i was looking
                all around me
                wondered
                if it would disappear
then
                when i looked another way
        it did

3

        the lion vanished
   i thought

   the others know this i'm
   only starting to find out

a small man in a blue
soldier's uniform
his brimmed cap shining

was sitting on the drummer's
arm & looked
 at everyone   then
i had lost sight of him

    i thought

   the others had all seen it i'm
   only starting to find out myself

4

& saw a flag, the house
was full of flags
the flags were beautiful with markings
in the middle of the room
a very large flag
was a live one   it was moving
in the doorway was a flag
i couldn't get to
"had never seen anything
so beautiful
in my whole life"

5

i was my thought

— *Jerome Rothenberg's working, after Paul Radin*

FOR THE GOD OF PEYOTE

Huichol

First Peyote Song

Wirikota Wirikota
>>> Where the roses are born
>>> Where they flower
>>> Garlands of flowers & wind
>>>>> Wirikota
At the foot of Eternal Mountain
>>> Roses are breathing: breath of the gods
>>> The mother's moist love: the dew
>>> & from the peyote's heart fog emerges
>>> Blue Stag emerges
>>> Rain comes down
>>> Blue Stag comes down

>>> Maize takes root   the rose lies open
>>> & the Rose sings: "I am the Stag"
>>> & the Stag: "I am the Rose"

And there on the Earth of the Gods they hear singing
>>> The gods are singing
>>> The mountains the hills are singing
>>> & the roses are singing
The song of life in Wirikota   only heard in Wirikota
>>> Eternal song of Life
>>> Only there
>>> Only there & heard in Wirikota

Second Peyote Song

Highway of roses
Peyote Highway
                    Stretches from here
                    to Wirikota
                    From here to Wirikota
They say you were just passing thru here
                    I'm coming to look for you
                    Coming to look for life
                    Coming to look for more life
& if I'm not your kind of pure
                    (meaning "sinless")
I'm passing thru here myself I'm coming for you

Song of an Initiate

climbed the blue staircase up to sky
climbed where the roses were opening
            where roses were speaking

heard nothing   nothing to hear
            heard silence

i climbed where the roses were singing
            where the gods were waiting
            blue staircase up in the sky

but heard nothing   nothing to hear
            heard silence   silence

Third Peyote Song

Armara passed by. The Sea passed by.
Behind it the gods passed by.
Like flowers the gods trailed behind the Sea.
From where the gods came the placenta spewed forth.
       Gods were born here.
       From the placenta gods were flowing like clouds.
With the clouds the Sacred Place appeared.
       And the Stag appeared in it.
       Then the Stag became cloud.
       The Stag became maize.
Then the Sea spoke.
       Spoke to Southwater Lady.
       Spoke to Northwater Lady.
       Spoke to the Sunset.
       Spoke to the gods of Peyote Country.
And the Blue Stag rose from the Sea.
       And Mhari the Small Stag appeared.
       And the Arrow appeared in the Sea.
       The gods saw it & knew it.
And right next to the Arrow the face & horns of the Stag.
       He had changed into clouds & was raining.
And the Bed of the gods appeared called Ittari.
       And the gods brought the Arrow to Coamil
       & the face & horns of the Stag.
Later the gods stopped to see what was born.
       And Tall Grass was born
       & from it burst a yellow tassel.
The gods came near   loosening the yellow tassel.
       The gods became three yellow rays.
Anointed they would be looking like the maizeland
       this was the pollen of the maize.
The gods said: Tall Grass will be the Stag's cradle.
       And Marra Yuavi the Blue Stag appeared.
And in the five regions of the Earth Blue Stags were appearing.

How the Violin Was Born: A Peyote Account

CEDAR CEDAR was born.
Born among stones & rocks.
                BIG STAG made him.
                BIG BRAIN worked him.
But CEDAR CEDAR didn't have a soul.
Heavy was his heart. His heart was silent.

Then Tahomatz the BIG BRAIN
                sent Aimari the BIRD pure & fuckless
Aimari came singing: entered the tree
                & became its pith.
                And the tree's heart filled with music.
& CEDAR CEDAR sang. Quivered to caresses from the Wind.

— *English versions by Jerome Rothenberg*

THE FLOWERING WAR

Aztec

A Song of Chalco

> In the sedge beyond Chalco
> the god raised stones for his house
>
> Green thrushes sang in the fire,
> glowing, changing to roses
> Over these ruins, these diamonds
> the quetzal-bird
> measured its voice into song
>
> The river trembled with flowers, it
> circled through flowers of jade,
> deep perfumes
>
> Lost among flowers
> the tzinitzcan waited,
> making their colors
> its own
>
> & the quetzal-bird
> sang a new measure
> The quetzal-bird ruled them
>
> Being a poet
> I sing: my song
> grafts buds to these branches
> Forests of flowers
> rise, deep
> fragrant perfumes

The flowers are dancing:
the deep perfume
moves to the beat of a drum

Dew globules
thicken with life
& run down the stems

The father stiffens
with lust
   A green sun
moves through the sky
In a jade urn
beautifully clothed
he sinks down

Throat bound by a
necklace of turquoise
While the flowers
rain shadows of color

Oh chieftains who sing
with me, chieftains
bringing him joy:
a new song to rise
from these flowers

The full flowers
tremble, the
flowers grow heavy
with Spring
bathed in sunlight

The sun's heart
throbs in the cup
His flesh
is the darkness of flowers

Who would not cry for
such flowers, oh
giver of life? who
would not rest in your hands
that hold death?
Opening buds & corollas
an endless thirst in the sun

I have gone from your house, I
sing in a dark heavy flower
My song fills rivers with petals

Oh day of libations, oh
flowers blown through the land
Oh deep perfumes

The god has opened his flowers:
flowers born in his house
are alive in this soil

A Song in Praise of the Chiefs

Here death is born among flowers:
the men of Tlapalla
our fathers
return to the earth

For this the song rises
with weeping
The dead take root in the sky
& the music
sticks in my throat, seeing
them lost in that city of shadows

As if a god spoke
the ordinance fell from the sky
You fulfilled it
dying, leaving
us orphaned & sad

Something inhuman
the way things fell out

The mind gets tired of asking:
who knows
if the life-giver
thinks of us now

Oh day of tears
& silence
when even the heart of our mother
is sad
Where have they taken the chiefs

Only a memory now:
the sadness breaks through my heart
when I think of Itzcoatl

No
I don't want to remember him
tired or weary
his face like a god's

Thinking
maybe he lives
in the life-giver's house
No one
braver than him
left
to grow old on this earth

Where can we go
Ah
the sadness breaks through my heart

They were carried away
hidden awhile in the earth
Warriors rulers & chiefs
vanished
leaving us orphaned

For this
the chieftains are sad

Where will my heart go

In search of Axayacatl
who left us here

Chanting the dirge
for Tezozomoctli

The chiefs who ruled here before us
handed this town
to the dogs

What sadness:
who knows if it ever will end
or grow less

Who knows if the grief
I squeeze through my lips
can be borne

A Song for the Eagles & Jaguars

I'd have these eagles & jaguars
embrace
till it sets their shields rattling

The rulers
plot at the banquet
They plan
to take prisoners

Scattering flowers
raining flowers of battle
over our heads
to placate the gods

This is the place of turmoil:
the place where we march
in disorder, place
of hot war, hunting
glory in back of our shields

This is the city of dangers
lost in the dust

The flowering war
will not end
We endure here, trapped
on the banks
of this river
The jaguars' flowers
show their corollas

This is the city of dangers:
dust from
the jaguars' garden
heavy with perfumes

Flowers drop on our heads
from the battlefield, raining
their fragrances on us

Oh soldiers
hunting glory & fame
Terrible flowers, oh
flowers alive in the heart

Flowers
torn from the battlefield
under the cries of war
& the chieftains
murdered for glory & fame

The eagles' shields
twist in the flags
of jaguars: armor
covered with feathers
Waves of plumed helmets
color of gold

The men of Chalcas
fell in the waves
They lie in mud
while the others
move in a line
through the turmoil
of war

The arrow snaps
with a cry
The obsidian point
turns to dust, staining
our shields
The water above us

The Eagle & the Jaguar

No one so strong, no one
so lovely
in all the things of this world

As the eagle
  ready for flight
& the jaguar
  whose heart
is a mountain

See how they carry
my shield now
These slaves

—*English versions by Jerome Rothenberg*

what happened to a young man
in a place where he turned to water

White Mountain Apache

1

no sleep for twelve days

then found himself in a circle of water girls

"come dance with us"

water people
they say
were dancing with him

ahead of the water they came
they were water
the water's soft feathers were theirs

closer they came
and to the very end of the water
closer and closer
their hands were electric

fog people
danced with him they say
where the fog was a wall
they came
they were fog
the fog's soft feathers
were theirs

closer they came
to the very end of the fog
closer and closer
their hands were electric

the moon before him they say
high as a woman's head
or no higher

the sun before him they say
no higher than a man's head
or as high

"come dance with us"

again no sleep for twelve days

2

he woke up and saw
only one had stayed
(remembered stumbling
over her foot in the dance)

they say those two
went away
to where the country is great with maize
there they sat down

they went
where the country grows beautiful pumpkins
there they lay down

great maize
                strong roots
                                big stalks
big pumpkin
                long tendrils
                                wide leaves

where the sun rises
as soon as it sets

yellow-top pumpkin
                    big-bellied
strong maize
            with a bushy tassel

pollen
      and
          dew
              .

3

he came back here
where people were living
his mother was angry but she forgave him
he went and hunted the deer with his brother

— *English working by Anselm Hollo, after Pliny Earle Goddard*

poem to be recited every 8 years
while eating unleavened tamales

Aztec

1

the flower
  my heart
        it opened
at midnight
  that lordly hour

she has arrived
        Tlaçolteotl
         our mother
           goddess desire

2

in the birth house
in the flower place
on the day called 'one flower'
  the maize god is born

in the vapor and rain place
  where we go angling for jewel-fish

  where we too make our young

3

soon day   red sky
quechol-birds in the flowers

4

down here on earth
   you rise in the market place and say

I am the lord Quetzalcoatl

let there be gladness among the flowering trees
   and the quechol-bird tribes
who are the souls of the brave

may they rejoice
   hear the word of our lord
the quechol-bird's word

'your brother whom we mourn
   will never be killed again
never again will the poison dart strike him'

5

maize flowers
   white and yellow
I have brought from the flower place

see there is the lord of the jewel land
   playing ball in his holy field

   there he is the old dog god
                   Xolotl

6

now go look if Piltzintecutli
   lord fertility himself
has yet lain down in the dark house
               in the house where it grows dark

o Piltzintli Piltzintli
   yellow feathers
you glue all over yourself

on the ball-playing field you lie down
   and in the dark house where it grows dark

7

here comes a merchant

a vassal of Xochiquetzal
   mistress of Cholula

(heart o heart
   I fear the maize god is still on his way)

a merchant a man from Chacalla
   sells turquoise spikes for your ears
and turquoise bands for your arms

8

the sleeper the sleeper he sleeps

with my hand I have rolled him to sleep

9

here
      the woman
here
      am I
here

                 asleep

— English version by Anselm Hollo

HEAVEN AND HELL
(by Nalungiaq)

Eskimo

And when we die at last,
we really know very little about what happens then.
But people who dream
have often seen the dead appear to them
just as they were in life.
Therefore we believe life does not end here on earth.

We have heard of three places where men go after death:
There is the Land of the Sky, a good place
where there is no sorrow and fear.
There have been wise men who went there
and came back to tell us about it:
They saw people playing ball, happy people
who did nothing but laugh and amuse themselves.
What we see from down here in the form of stars
are the lighted windows of the villages of the dead
in the Land of the Sky.

Then there are other worlds of the dead underground:
Way down deep is a place just like here
except on earth you starve
and down there they live in plenty.
The caribou graze in great herds

and there are endless plains
with juicy berries that are nice to eat.
Down there too, everything
is happiness and fun for the dead.

But there is another place, the Land of the Miserable,
right under the surface of the earth we walk on.
There go all the lazy men who were poor hunters,
and all women who refused to be tattooed,
not caring to suffer a little to become beautiful.
They had no life in them when they lived
so now after death they must squat on their haunches
with hanging heads, bad-tempered and silent,
and live in hunger and idleness
because they wasted their lives.
Only when a butterfly comes flying by
do they lift their heads
(as young birds open pink mouths uselessly after a gnat)
and when they snap at it, a puff of dust
comes out of their dry throats.

— *Working by Edward Field, after Knud Rasmussen*

From THE BOOK OF CHILAM BALAM:
"A Chapter of Questions & Answers"

Maya

13 Etznab was the day when the land was established. 13 Cheneb was the day when they measured the cathedral off by paces: the dark house of instruction, the cathedral in heaven. It was also measured off by paces here on earth. . . .

Mani is the base of the land. Campeche is the tip of the wing of the land. Calkini is the base of the wing of the land. Itzmal is the middle of the wing of the land. Zaci is the tip of the wing of the land. Conkal is the head of the land.

In the middle of the town of Tihoo is the cathedral, the fiery house, the mountainous house, the dark house, for the benefit of God the Father, God the Son and God the Holy Spirit.

Who enters into the House of God? Father, it is the one named Ix-Kalem.

What day did the Virgin conceive? Father, 4 Oc was the day when she conceived.

What day did he come forth from her womb? On 3 Oc he came forth.

What day did he die? On 1 Cimi he died. Then he entered the tomb on 1 Cimi.

What entered his tomb? Father, a coffer of stone entered his tomb.

What entered into his thigh? Father, it was the red arrow-stone. It entered into the precious stone of the world, there in heaven.

And his arm? Father, the arrow-stone; and that it might be warmed in the sun, it entered the red living rock in the east. Then it came to the north and entered into the white living rock. After that it entered the black living rock in the west. Also it entered the yellow living rock in the south.

Son, how many deep hollows are there? These are the holes for playing the flute.

Son, where is the cenote? All are drenched with its water. There is no

A FOURTH SERVICE   384

gravel on its bottom; a bow is inserted over its entrance. It is the church.

Son, where are the first marriages? The strength of the King and the strength of the other head-chiefs fail because of them, and my strength because of them also. It is bread.

Son, have you seen the green water-holes in the rock? There are two of them; a cross is raised between them. They are a man's eyes.

Son, where are the first baptized ones? One has no mother, but has a bead collar and little bells. It is the small yellow corn.

Son, where is the food which bursts forth, and the fold of the brain and the lower end of that which is bloated, and the dried fruit? It is the gizzard of a turkey.

Son, bring me that which hooks the sky and the hooked tooth. They are a deer and a gopher.

Son, where is the old woman with buttocks seven palms wide, the woman with a dark complexion? It is a certain kind of squash.

Son, show me the light complexioned woman with her skirt bound up who sells white flints. It is another kind of squash.

Son, bring me two yellow animals, one to be well boiled, and one shall have its throat cut. I shall drink its blood also. It is a yellow deer and a green calabash full of chocolate.

My sons, bring me here a score of those who bear flat stones and two married ones. They are a quail and a dove.

Son, bring me a cord of three strands, I wish to see it. It is an iguana.

Son, bring me that which stops the hole in the sky and the dew, the nine layers of the whole earth. It is a very large maize tortilla.

Son, have you seen the old man who is like an overturned tortilla pan? He has a large double chin which reaches the ground. It is a turkey-cock.

Son, bring me the old farmers, their beards come to their navels, also their wives. It is a muddy arrowroot.

Bring to me here with them the women who guard the fields, white complexioned women. I will remove their skirts and eat them. It is a root like a turnip.

Son, bring me the great gallants that I may view them. Perhaps they will not dance badly when I see them. It is a turkey-cock.

Son, where is the first collector? The answer is to undress, to take off one's shirt, cape, hat and shoes.

Son, where was it that you passed? Did you pass to the high rocky knoll which slopes down to the door of heaven, where there is a gate in the wall? Did you see men in front of you, coming side by side? A god called Ninth Heaven and the first town councillor are there. It is the pupils of the eyes and any pair of eyes.

Son, have you seen the rain of God? It passed beneath the mountains of God; it entered beneath the mountains of God, where there is a cross on the savannah. There will be a ring in the sky where the water of God has passed.

Son, where has the water of God passed when it comes forth from the living rock? Father, from a man's head and all a man's teeth, passes through the opening in his throat and comes forth beneath.

Son, whom did you see on the road just now?

. . . .

Son, what did you do with your companions who were coming close behind you? Here are my companions. I have not left them. I await the judgment of God when I shall come to die. This is a man's shadow.

Son, whom did you see on the road? Did you see some old men accompanied by their boys? Father, here are the old men I saw on the road. They are with me; they do not leave me. This is his great toe with the little toes.

Son, where did you see the old women carrying their step-children and their other boys? Father, here they are. They are still with me so that I can eat. I can not leave them yet. It is my thumb and the other fingers.

Son, where did you pass by a water-gutter? Father, here is the water-gutter; it is right with me. This is my dorsal furrow.

Son, where did you see an old man astride a horse across a water-gutter? Father, here is the old man. He is still with me. My shoulders are the horse on which you say the old man sits astride.

Son, this is the old man with you of which you spoke: it is manifest truth and justice.

Son, go get the heart of the stone and the liver of the earth. I have seen one of them lying on its back, and one lying on its face as though it were going into hell. They are a Mexican Agouti and a Spotted Agouti, also the first local chief and the first Town Councillor. As for the heart of the stone, it is the tips of the teeth; and that which covers the opening of hell is a sweet potato and another kind of root to eat.

Son, go and bring me here the girl with the watery teeth. Her hair is twisted into a tuft; she is very beautiful. Fragrant shall her odor be when I remove her skirt and her other garment. It will give me pleasure to see her. Fragrant is her odor and her hair is twisted into a tuft. It is an ear of green corn cooked in a pit.

Son, then you shall go and get an old man the herb that is by the sea. The old man is the rushes, and the herb is a crab.

Son, then you shall go and get the stones from the bottom of a forest pond. It is a *tzac*-fish.

Son, then you shall bring here the stones of the savannah. It is a quail.

Also bring the first sorcerers, there are four of them. They are the gopher, the Spotted Agouti, the Mexican Agouti and the peccary.

Son, then go and get the thigh of the earth. It is the cassava.

Son, go and bring here the green gallant and the green singer. It is a wild turkey hen and cock.

Son, you shall bring your daughter that I may see her in the sun tomorrow. First the smaller one shall be brought and behind her shall come the larger one. Her hair shall be bound with a feathered band; she shall wear a head-scarf. I will take off her head-scarf. Also the Town Councillor is behind her.

Son, then go and get a cluster of Plumeria flowers widely separated. They should be there where the sun is tomorrow. What is meant is roasted corn and honey.

Here I have rolled something that you have which is flat and round. There are many rolls of it in the cave where you live. Then you shall roll it here that we may see it, when it is time to eat. It is a fried egg.

— *Translation by Ralph L. Roys*

her elegy

Papago

I'd run about
on the desert
me a young girl fierce to see
whatever I could. My heart
was not cool.
              When there was no Coyote
I saw Coyote
              then a spider
on the house-post, the central one,
stopped to look at me, just
ready to speak.
I made a song, about Coyote.
A shaman sang over me, to find out.
And when he spoke Father said —No
one shaman in the house is enough—
my body already sheltered
the divining crystals, growing in my body.
The shaman bent over me he sucked them one by one
out of my breast
                 they were long
like the joint of my pinkie, white and moving like worms
o the shaman said See I've taken them out
before they got big
                     He made a hole in a giant cactus
and put them away, inside

—English working by Armand Schwerner, after Ruth Underhill

dance of the rain gods

Cora

now the thinkers our old ones remember
    the gods known as dancers

let's call the dancers
talking and thinking
                    call them to come
            from their far away sky place
call for the rain gods
                  explain the problem

the dancers receive the message
they put on their garments their crowns
their life-giving feathers
black as night
                white as cloud

veil their faces with beads
    talking
their faces are radiant

they take the great cross the great rattle
far away in their sky place
they concentrate
on the high east

then they rise high in the east
radiant as life in their feathers
they come down to talk to the earth

see the life-giving trees
    stand up
line their road

lovely fig trees and tuka trees
lovely anapa trees by their road

lovely the reed
    rising
full of life the banana tree

life-giving reed
           there it stands

then the dancers appear
    down east
stopping to wait for mother and elder brother

'dance you gods
           bring the rain down
dance you dancers
            come down to your earth'
they wait for the fiddles
    for the fiddles to play
             now they hear them
the sound of their fiddles
    sound known as 'words'

they listen to it
          they start dancing

now it resounds on their earth
    the dance of the 'dancers'
           who call themselves rain gods

and when it is over
they go
talking they go
    west
to see Tsevimoa
the goddess
    who sits on her rainstone
fade in the west
with all their thoughts

and the thinkers our old ones
leave them there
in their thought's power
turn back east to the altar
ending
    a good day's work

— English version by Anselm Hollo

POSTLUDES

A KALAPUYA PROPHECY

In the old time, by the forks of the Santiam,
a Kalapuya man lay down in an alder-grove
and dreamed his farthest dream. When he woke in the night
he told the people, "This earth beneath us
was all black, all black in my dream!"
No man could say what it meant,
that dream of our greening earth.
We forgot. But then the white men came,
those iron farmers, and we saw them plow up the ground,
the camas meadow, the little prairies by the Santiam,
and we knew we would enter their dream
of the earth plowed black forever.

— English version by Jarold Ramsey

HUNGER
(by Samik)

Eskimo

You, stranger, who only see us happy and free of care,
If you knew the horrors we often have to live through
you would understand our love of eating and singing and dancing.
There is not one among us
who hasn't lived through a winter of bad hunting
when many people starved to death.
We are never surprised to hear
that someone has died of starvation — we are used to it.
And they are not to blame: Sickness comes,
or bad weather ruins hunting,
as when a blizzard of snow hides the breathing holes.

I once saw a wise old man hang himself
because he was starving to death
and preferred to die in his own way.
But before he died he filled his mouth with seal bones,
for that way he was sure to get plenty of meat
in the land of the dead.

Once during the winter famine
a woman gave birth to a child
while people lay round about her dying of hunger.

What could the baby want with life here on earth?
And how could it live when its mother herself
was dried up with starvation?
So she strangled it and let it freeze.
And later on ate it to keep alive—
Then a seal was caught and the famine was over,
so the mother survived.
But from that time on she was paralysed
because she had eaten part of herself.

That is what can happen to people.
We have gone through it ourselves
and know what one may come to, so we do not judge them.
And how would anyone who has eaten his fill and is well
be able to understand the madness of hunger?
We only know that we all want so much to live!

— English working by Edward Field, from Knud Rasmussen

THREE GHOST DANCE SONGS

•

My children,
when at first I liked the whites,
I gave them fruits,
I gave them fruits.

•

I'yehe! my children —
my children,
we have rendered them desolate.
The whites are crazy — Ahe'yuhe'yu!

We shall live again.
We shall live again.

— Translations by James Mooney

COMMENTARIES

A BREAKDOWN BY REGION & TRIBE

The following is for the reader's convenience in locating tribes &/or language groups, & making comparisons within a region or tribe. It also indicates (very roughly & mostly by omission) those areas in which new translation, etc. might be worth a try. Any finer breakdown is a question of how far each reader wants to take it.

EASTERN. *Abnaki*: 322. *Cherokee*: 59, 62. *Chippewa*: 327, 328, 330 (see Ojibwa). *Creek*: 66. *Fox*: 263, 341. *Iroquois*: 181 (also Seneca). *Ojibwa*: 327 (see Chippewa). *Passamaquoddy*: 326. *Seneca*: 4, 15, 151, 340 (see Iroquois). *Winnebago*: 189, 358.

ESKIMO. 45, 158, 172, 176, 184, 190, 197, 272, 278, 382, 396.

GREAT PLAINS. *Blackfoot*: 201. *Crow*: 13, 51, 195. *Dakota*: 187, 320. *Hidatsa*: 301. *Mandan*: 328. *Omaha*: 194, 280. *Osage*: 342. *Oto*: 268. *Pawnee*: 357. *Sioux* (general): 197, 280. *Teton Sioux*: 280.

MEXICO & CENTRAL AMERICA. *Aztec*: 12, 50, 70, 117, 185, 282, 284, 366, 378. *Cora*: 266, 389. *Cuna*: 56, 92, 168, 312. *Huichol*: 276, 362. *Maya*: 63, 75, 78, 83, 236, 295, 296, 384. *Tepehua*: 347. *Tule*: see Cuna.

NORTHWEST COAST, OREGON & BASIN-PLATEAU. *Alsea*: 49. *Bella Bella*: 323. *Kalapuya*: 395. *Kwakiutl*: 188. *Lummi*: 182, 196. *Modoc*: 269. *Nez Percé*: 102, 105, 275. *Nootka*: 58. *Okanagon*: 96. *Paiute*: 274. *Skagit*: 89, 271. *Tlingit*: 153. *Tsimshian*: 164, 165, 166, 167.

SOUTHWEST & CALIFORNIA. *Apache*: 375. *Keresan* (Acoma): 3. *Luiseño*: 285. *Maricopa*: 183. *Navajo*: 68, 170, 186, 191, 192, 309, 339, 350, 352. *Papago*: 193, 388. *Pueblo*: 3, 127, 214, 304. *San Juan Pueblo*: 214. *Tewa*: see San Juan Pueblo. *Yokuts*: 67. *Yuma*: 264. *Zuni*: 127, 304.

THE COMMENTARIES

Page 3   WHAT THE INFORMANT SAID TO FRANZ BOAS IN 1920

SOURCE: F. Boas, *Keresan Texts,* Publications of the American Ethnological Society, Volume 8, 1928.

A FURTHER CAUTION. To the reader who imagines that a book like this can really hold the spirit-of-a-people, etc. the editor testifies that in instance after instance the best remains untold or its powers reserved for those who "have ears to hear," etc. But the rest of us have to begin somewhere.

Page 4   THANK YOU: A POEM IN SEVENTEEN PARTS

SOURCE: Written down at Allegany Reservation (Steamburg, New York), summer of 1968, first published in *El Corno Emplumado,* Number 30, Mexico, 1969, pages 125–131, "with a note on the process by Jerome Rothenberg."

J.R.'s note for the original publication reads: ". . . The poems themselves are translations of the traditional thanking formulas that the Seneca 'longhouse people' (followers of the Code of Handsome Lake [the late 18th Century Iroquois prophet]) use for opening of all group functions. The wording is R.J.J.'s, also by & large the pauses; I mostly followed his acute use of periods (he was writing it down as 'prose' alongside me), to mark out what appear as lines in this reading. I also asked questions in the process, but in general learned to leave well enough alone. No matter. Johnny John's a singer & song-maker in his own right, absolutely fluent in Seneca & with a poet's delight in getting the right combinations in whatever language. When he wasn't happy with what we were translating from the taped Seneca, he'd tell me: 'Play back just a little. I want to word it just the way it says there.' Which was how it became a poem in English."

Page 12   THE ARTIST

SOURCE: Denise Levertov, *O Taste & See,* New Directions, 1964. Based on Spanish translation from *Códice Matritense de la Real Academia de la Historia* (Náhuatl texts of the 16th Century informants of Bernardino de Sahagún).

SOURCE: Lewis Henry Morgan, *The Indian Journals, 1859–1862*, University of Michigan Press, 1959, page 190.

Page 15   SHAKING THE PUMPKIN

J.R.'s working of sacred curing songs from the Society of the Mystic Animals (also called: Society of Shamans), taking into account all elements of the original (including the non-verbal) but translating the melody in particular into equivalent visual patterns that hold the page. The twelve opening songs are sung by the *hajaswas* or leader of the event; the others are "individual" songs following the *hajaswas'* directions to "open the bag of songs & sing whichever you want." The pumpkin rattle passes counter-clockwise around the circle, each one taking it in turn & singing a Society song of his choice. Songs can be grouped in sets by coincidence of melody & similarities in content, but on a given occasion they may happen in any order. In these versions R.J.J. provided the basic translations (sometimes the idiom as well), & J.R. worked them into paginal structures. By this process it is our hope that the originals (wherein resides the power) remain with the Senecas, where they in fact belong.

The Seneca name for the ceremony is I'dos (pron. ee-dos); the common term for it in English is "Shaking the Pumpkin."

Addenda. (1) "Seneca poetry, when it uses words at all, works in sets of short songs, minimal realizations colliding with each other in marvelous ways, a very light, very pointed play-of-the-mind, nearly always just a step away from the comic (even as their masks are), the words set out in clear relief against the ground of the ('meaningless') refrain. . . . Given the 'minimal' nature of much of the poetry (one of its *strongest* features, in fact) there's no need for a dense response in English. Instead I can leave myself free to structure the final poem by using the English of my Seneca co-translator as a base: a particular enough form of the language to itself be an extra tool for that 'continuation of journalism by other means' that Walter Lowenfels defined poetry as being in the first place." (J.R., "Total Translation: An Experiment in the Translation of American Indian Poetry," *Stony Brook* 3/4, 1969) The resemblance of Seneca verbal art to concrete & minimal poetry among us was another (if minor) point these translations were making.

(2) Work on this series was carried out under a grant-in-aid from the Wenner-Gren Foundation for Anthropological Research. Other workings begun under their auspices appear on pages 4 & 350 above.

SOURCE: Knud Rasmussen, *The Netsilik Eskimos,* Report of the 5th Thule Expedition, Copenhagen, 1931, *passim.*

In *Magic Words for Hunting Caribou,* Field as final translator fuses poems by Orpingalik (see above, page 176, & Commentary, page 431), Inutuk & Nakasuk; in *Seal Hunting,* parts of poems by Orpingalik & Nakasuk. The fantastic opening statement on "magic words," etc. is fused also, from a longer commentary by Nalungiaq, "just an ordinary woman" (she says) who learned it from an old uncle, Unaraluk the shaman, whose helping spirits—his dead father & mother, the sun, a dog & a sea scorpion—enabled him "to know everything about what was on the earth & under the earth, in the sea & in the sky." As elsewhere (see below, page 432) the Eskimo consciousness is notable in its understanding of basic poetic process. "Mighty magic is a mother," writes poet R. Creeley of where it all comes from: thus towards the same comprehension as the Eskimo. Of their actual practice of "magic words" [=poetry], Rasmussen informs us that the usual thing was not to employ ordinary speech but the special language of the shamans(=seers, or proto-poets), in which language (according to Peter Freuchen) "all things & all beings were called by other than their usual names or by circumlocutions. This immediately put a whole new set of images at their disposal. Also, their trade required that they always have numerous magic formulas ready for use when needed. These formulas would lose their power if used by anyone else. Therefore, within the rules of the polysynthetic language, they would make their own word compositions, not understandable to other people. Since the formulas lost their power after too much use, they had to be constantly renewed, & the angakoks [shamans] thus trained themselves in new & unusual word combinations. As a result they could write many poems." (Freuchen, *Book of the Eskimo,* pages 205–206).

Addenda. (1) CEREMONY BEFORE SEAL-HUNTING, to accompany the "magic words for hunting seal": A handsome lemming skin, flayed off whole like a small bag, is filled with miniature carvings of seals, harpoons & harpoon heads, & then as an offering to Nuliajuk, is sunk in *atuArutit,* the tide-water crack that always runs along a little way out from the shore. (Thus: Rasmussen, *Netsilik,* page 169).

(2) Nuliajuk the sea goddess—the story of whose origins the words for seal-hunting get down clearly enough—lives in terrifying presence in a house at sea-bottom. Many of the great shaman spirit journeys recorded here & elsewhere are directed toward confronting her & her surrounding retinue of monsters in times of famine or danger, or to win abundance of seals, who by the story are manifestations of her own being. Another shaman practice is to attempt to draw her to the surface of the land

by "making a hook fast to the end of a long seal thong & throwing it out of the entrance passage: the spirits set the hook fast in her, & the shaman hauls her up into the passage. There everybody can hear her speaking. But the entrance from the passage into the living room must be closed with a block of snow, & this block of snow Nuliajuk keeps on trying to break into pieces in order to get into the house & frighten everybody to death. And there is great fear in the house. But the shaman watches the block, & so Nuliajuk never gets into the house. Only when she has promised the shaman to release all the seals into the sea again does he take her off the hook & allow her to go back down into the depths."

(3) While the coaxing sound in some of the "magic words" is self-explanatory as a strategy, the reader should also note the Eskimo belief that a seal is possessed of a perishable body but an immortal soul, & that a man may catch a seal many times if he only once wins its soul over.

(4) Of the words themselves & his own relation to them, Rasmussen writes further: "Translating magic words is a most difficult matter, because they often consist of untranslatable compounds of words, or fragments that are supposed to have their strength in their mysteriousness"—*coefficient of weirdness* in Malinowski's good term for it—"or in the manner in which the words are coupled together." Obviously comprehension by others isn't the issue here "as long as the spirits know what it is that one wants"—although the level of articulation would seem to have varied from shaman to shaman. For example, the poet Orpingalik (see page 431, below) "uttered (his magic words) in a whisper, but most distinctly & with emphasis on every word. His speech was slow, often with short pauses between the words. I have endeavored to show the pauses by means of a new line of verse" (*Netsilik*, page 14)—that last a clear insight on Rasmussen's part of poetry's origins in other-than-song.

(5) For more on shamans-as-poets, etc. see *Technicians of the Sacred*, pages 423 ff.

Page 49   MOON ECLIPSE EXORCISM

SOURCE: Prose texts in Leo J. Frachtenberg, *Alsea Texts & Myths*, Bureau of American Ethnology, Bulletin 67, 1920, pages 227–229.

The image of the bloody-yellow water is from a parallel sun eclipse exorcism, while the rich man whose death the event prefigures measures his wealth in dentalia shells.

SOURCE: Eduard Seler, *Gesammelte Abhandlungen*, Volume 2, 1902–1915, page 1045.

The lady-who-sits-on-the-tortoise is Mayuel, goddess of pulque, who came to it from observations of a mouse nibbling on maguey cactus & surely acting like no mouse she'd ever seen, so that she looked up closer at the "strangely clouded sap" collecting on the maguey stem, got an idea & fed it to her husband, it acting like a damn strong aphrodisiac with the result that she had lots of children & became not only goddess of pulque but patroness of childbirth, entitled by that latter designation "to the respect given to warriors who have been heroes in fierce battles." Thus: C. A. Burland's account of the myth but also of the myth-become-propaganda of the first great military state in the history of North America.

Page 51   CROW VERSIONS

SOURCE: Robert H. Lowie, *Crow Texts*, University of California Press, 1960.

As with other tribal poetry, these Crow songs & prayers came in visions or at other moments of great urgency. Prayers, like the fourth poem here, were addressed mainly though not exclusively to the sun, & sacrifices of the supplicant's own flesh, etc. were offered to him as a kind of over-all deity superseded only on special occasions by personal gods or special sacred objects. (Said One-blue-bead: "The only thing I prayed to specially was my feather. I might pray to the sun any time.") Old Man Coyote, who figures in the sixth poem, "was at times confounded with the sun, though sometimes he himself figures as praying to him." The same might of course be said for most of the other dream-time beings, especially in a culture, say, where ideology & poetry are responsive to what Cassirer speaks of elsewhere as a "law of metamorphosis" in thought & word. (For which, see page 453, below, as well as the more specific comment on the fifth poem here.)

Crow Text 1. In a narrative of the Medicine Arrow Bundle, one Hillside tells how his brother's son, Cut-ear, went to a mountain-top, chopped off a finger, & fasted in search of a vision. The Seven Stars appeared to him as seven persons, & sang songs to him. This was the song of the third star.

Crow Text 2. In White-arm's vision he tells us: "I slept near Horn's place. During my sleep I saw a person riding a brown horse toward the top of a mountain & singing. He came toward me. I noticed all the feathers & other ornaments tied to his horse. A hawk was painted on his horse's neck. I took a wing of this bird & used it for my necklace." The person then sang this song to him. White-arm adds: "I joined the Church & now the one who gave me the song is teasing me at night, but I won't listen to him." (Lowie, *Religion of the Crow Indians*, page 338.)

Crow Text 3. Addressed to a whirlwind. The words are like those spoken to a ghost, an implied comparison that conveys "a grave insult."

Crow Text 4. The sweat-lodge was conceived as, above all, an offering to the sun. Writes Lowie: "Sweat-lodges were originally ritualistic, & even those who had the relevant privileges would, according to my informant, sweat only when prompted by a dream. On the other hand, tradition tells of a man who constantly erected sweat-lodges & was accordingly named Sweats-regularly. In the construction of the sweat-lodge, the Crow used willows numbering from twelve to a hundred. Plenty-hawks' (full) prayer specifies lodges of 18, 14, 20, & 100 willows respectively." Merwin's version only gives the section of the longer poem dealing with the 100-willow lodge.

For more on sweat-lodges, etc see *Sweat-House Ritual #1*, page 280, above, & commentary, page 448, below; also the sweat-lodge section of *66 Poems for a Blackfoot Bundle*, page 201, above.

Crow Text 5. In a narrative by Yellow-brow, a young warrior named Double-face, enduring the typical *ennui* of a Crazy Dog member pledged to self-destructive madness, wanders feverishly around camp the day before battle with the Cheyenne. He says to his older brother: "There are three things I am now eager to do: I want to sing a sacred song; I want to sing a Big Dog song; I want to cry." Then he paints his horse & himself, fits on medicines, & goes into the camp-circle, crying & making others cry, wailing a prayer, part of which Merwin works into the fifth of these Crow versions.

Events of the Crazy Dog Society (but literally Crazy-Dog-wishing-to-die) appear elsewhere in this anthology (for which, see page 195, above). Actions were extreme & futile but heroic too: a very literal playing-out of older Plains Indian despair over death & old-age—a kind of behavior not that foreign to our own lives lived at extremes, etc. "Why have you done that?" Spotted-rabbit's mother asked. "You are one of the best-situated young men . . . you are one of the most fortunate men who ever lived . . . & were always happy." But, writes Lowie, Spotted-rabbit was bored with life because he could not get over his father's death. Or again, when Spotted-rabbit receives a gift of plums, he says, "I began to be a Crazy Dog early in the spring & did not think I should live so long; yet here I am today eating plums." Comments Lowie, of such as Double-face & Spotted-rabbit: "We have here reached the peak of the Crow spirit." (*Texts* 331–334)

N.B. The reader interested in how men make poetry—i.e. how they use language to take the measure of reality—might also check Lowie's description of the process in Double-face's prayer & elsewhere, by which the man so moved improvises names for a power he feels in the world, not stuck with fixed gods only but making any object he can name a manifestation of that power. Thus, in the section of Double-face's poem that Merwin translates, Double-face is in the act of hypothesizing a location for the power that moves him & which appears elsewhere in the Crow texts in whatever catches the poet's eye & mind:

Hallo, Little Sweat-lodge, 'We are making it for you,' I said: now I have made it.
You, mountains of renown, Big Rivers & Small Rivers, smoke it.
You, Beings Up Above, smoke it.
Beings in the Ground, smoke it.
Earth, smoke it.
Willows, smoke it.
Hallo, Fat: wherever I go I want to come on something fat.
Hey, Charcoal, I want to blacken my face with some charcoal.
Winds, I want you Winds to smoke, I want the Winds to blow toward me.

(*Crow Indians*, page 115)

Not reification, then, & the contemporary sickness of an ecological life-death, but a life-investing process & ongoing deification! And if that ain't the red-hot/white-hot sense-of-the-world that Radin spoke of [for which, see page 417, below], then the present editor is damned if it meant anything at all in the first place.

Crow Text 6. From one of more than six versions of the Crow "Earth Divers" collected by Lowie. Of the considerable variations in the narrative, he writes: "Obviously there is no one standard version: each narrator works into his cosmogony what seem to him suitable incidents." An example of tribal "freedom," etc. as commented upon by Lowie, Radin, Diamond, & many others.

For more on Coyote the reader can check the commentaries on page 422, below. Among the Crows, as in other Indian religions, he appears as the Supreme Trickster but also as the first maker of the earth & all living things. "He was a great trickster & our ruler," says another narrator. "And since he was a great trickster, we are that way also." But he adds: "All the ways of the Indians he made for us. He put us to sleep, he made us dream, whatever he wanted us to do we did. He put the stars into this world in the beginning; they were dangerous." (*Religion of the Crow,* page 320) Thus Old Man Coyote is the imperfect (=dangerous) creator of an imperfect (=dangerous) universe—a view which, being more empirical & rational in the first place, presents fewer problems to rationalize than the Christian view, say, of a perfect god & universe, etc.

Page 56   A POEM FOR CATCHING TURTLES

SOURCE: Frances Densmore, *Music of the Tule Indians of Panama,* Smithsonian Miscellaneous Collections, Volume 77, Number 11, 1926, pages 27–28.

Densmore's recordings were made during a Washington visit by eight Tule Indians in 1924. The typical Tule song (she tells us) is in the form of a "simple, continuous narrative" with hardly any repetitions, etc.—often (as in this turtle charm) acting as a kind of scenario for the actions it accompanies. The way the words are sung "suggests melodic speech" (rather than chants) "in which the rhythm is determined by the accents & lengths of the words." It's also common to improvise, i.e. "the substance of the words & the general character of each song is 'learned,' but . . . each performance of the song is an improvisation. . . . The Tule said they did not intend to 'sing a song always the same.'" All this in contrast to typical North American song practice.

In addition to a second Tule piece (above, page 168) the reader may also want to look at work under the synonymous tribal designation, Cuna (thus, pages 92 & 312, also above).

Page 58   ARCHAIC SONG OF DR. TOM THE SHAMAN

SOURCE: Collected by James A. Teit, in Morris Swadesh & Helen H. Roberts, *Songs of the Nootka Indians of Western Vancouver Island,* Transactions of the American Philosophical Society, Volume 45, Part 3, 1955, pages 230–231.

The words used by the singer (a Thompson River Indian named Nêluk) are in Chinook jargon & "in imitation of those used by

Dr. Tom." In a typical doctoring performance, songs were "sung only by the doctor or his wife or helpers, & the words were mumbled so that usually only the doctor understood what they were. He would breathe on the patient as he sang." The power of the words, then, is clearly more than a matter of their immediate—or even eventual—comprehension.

Addenda. The commentary on Dr. Tom identifies him as "an old Indian from the coast who traveled in the Interior . . . & doctored the sick. He had formerly traveled with a white man's circus (for two or three years) & knew a lot of the sleight-of-hand tricks used by white performers as well as other tricks known to the Coast Indians. These tricks he used to good effect in conjunction with his doctoring. He was driven out of the interior by the missionaries & the police for obtaining money under false pretenses, & was in jail for a while. A favorite trick of his was to show things he claimed he had taken out of the bodies of the sick." About "tricks," though, the reader should note Knud Rasmussen's story of a young Copper Eskimo named Taiphuina who told how she "had once been a shaman disciple but had given it up, as 'she could not lie well enough,'" to which the shamans present responded with much good-natured laughter, knowing (Rasmussen writes) that "the relationship between the natural & the supernatural is in itself so problematic that it is of no consequence if there is some 'cheating' in the ritual during an invocation."

N.B. For a major attack on this concept of poetry & art (namely, that of the trickster-poet), the reader may again check the 10th book of Plato's *Republic;* he may also ponder how Plato's apparent rationality & love-of-the-truth have contributed to getting us where we are today & may devise his own game-theory as a start at extrication.

Page 59   MAGIC WORDS FROM RUN TOWARD THE NIGHTLAND

SOURCE: Jack Frederick Kilpatrick & Anna Gritts Kilpatrick, *Run toward the Nightland: Magic of the Oklahoma Cherokees,* Southern Methodist University Press, Dallas, 1967, *passim.*

Translated from manuscripts written in Sequoyah's Cherokee syllabary, usually in medicine books owned by shamans, wizards, etc., but by interested laymen also. The power, though, remains in voice & thought, the part of the ritual that "consists of what one says (or merely thinks) or sings," of which the written poem is only a reminder. The words, if fixed to a finer degree than in oral tradition, are open to modifications in performance: e.g. "the repetition of a key word the sacred four times, the interjection of the supremely sacrosanct numeral seven; the insertion of the pronoun *ayv* ('I'), & a hiatus in which the reciter thinks intently upon the purpose of the ritual." (*Nightland*, page 7) A master may also improvise a text if the spirit so moves him, but obviously subject to those limits that will make the spell work. The second element of Cherokee magic ritual, i.e. the accompanying "physical procedures" (=events), while often recorded, are clearly subordinate to the words—though a better way of looking at the process (as with other mixed-media situations) may be as a total pattern of events, in which the word-events are themselves physical procedures but with a greater "power" attributed to them as the only elements necessary to each performance.

Some of the language-events also show the level of "abstraction" possible in the poetry-of-magic, as in any poetry that groups words toward the creation &/or implementation of a possible or existing music. For example, the Cherokee use of color is both symbolic & expressive (as all living language tends to be), with fixed associations for color words on the one hand, & on the other a heightened ability to produce & induce "thought-paintings" (the Kilpatricks' term for it), not on the basis of what-the-eye-sees but in "abstract" combinations that may then have image-making functions of their own. (For which, see also the commentary on *The Killer*, page 413, below.) The use of "seven!" as an interjection is another example of words acting apart from their usual meaning: here as a pure power-word that strengthens the whole mix.

Addenda. Even more important in Cherokee is the use of number in determining the structure of the spells. Thus the translators write: ". . . Anyone who can read Cherokee can readily see that religious, medical & magical texts are built upon patterns that take full advantage of the powers resident in the minor sacred numeral four or major sacred numeral seven. This accession to numerological fiat usually results in a given text's being structured into four or seven lines, into four or seven groups of lines, or into major divisions subdivided into units of four or seven." Some such insistence on symmetries & the relevance of abstract detail is, in fact, one of the strongpoints of Indian poetry & performance in general: not as a question of dead metrics, etc. (=literature) but as a key to the living world.

Page 62   THE KILLER

SOURCE: James Mooney, *Sacred Formulas of the Cherokees,* Bureau of American Ethnology, 7th Annual Report, 1891, page 391.

This poem, from the manuscript book of A'yunini (Swimmer), is typical in fact of the Cherokees' use of colors beyond their (mere) symbolic values (for which, see page 412, above) to achieve striking effects by juxtaposition, etc. as with the introduction of the conflicting color in the following:

As the Red Cardinal is beautiful, I am beautiful
As the Red Dhla:nuwa is beautiful, I am beautiful
As the Red Redbird is beautiful, I am beautiful
As the Blue Cardinal is beautiful, I am beautiful

much as in *The Killer* itself for that matter. Says Jack Kilpatrick, who translated the red & blue piece: "Something peculiarly Cherokeean in the unexpected dissonance"; or as Mooney explained it way back then: "As the purpose of the ceremony is to bring about the death of the victim, everything spoken of is symbolically colored black. . . . The declaration at the end, 'It is blue,' indicates that the victim now begins to feel the effects of the incantation, & that as darkness comes on, his spirit will shrink & gradually become less until it dwindles away to nothingness."

N.B. The editor has discussed the "obsessive, single-color imagery" of *The Killer* elsewhere (*Technicians of the Sacred,* page 433) & has compared it to other tribal poetries & to the practice of modern poets like Lorca & Wakoski, among many others. This is not merely to point to analogues for their own sake, but in the hope that all such "devices" & modes-of-thought may be of interest to the reader in considering the possibility of poetry in his own life.

Page 63   THE ARCHER'S DANCE SONG

SOURCE: *El Libro de los Cantares de Dzitbalché,* translated into Spanish by Alfredo Barrera Vásquez, Instituto Nacional de Antropología e Historia, Mexico, 1965, pages 77–78.

Mayan ritual poetry but apparently of later origin than the hymns in, say, the *Chilam Balam.* The order of events would have been in close correspondence to the surviving images: thus "probably chanted" (writes Miguel León-Portilla) "during the celebration of the sacrifice by arrows. The victim was tied to a stake placed up on a kind of stage.

The people gathered round it, & a priest gave the signal to begin the dance & the song. Several warriors with their bows & arrows began to dance round the victim. Synchronized with the song & music, they shot arrows at the one to be sacrificed. The victim's blood dropped on the ground, symbolizing fertilization of the earth," etc. For all of which the song itself is the functional scenario, depicting the actions of the performers, as kachina dolls, e.g., or statues would depict the appearance of the performers & the beings they represent.

Page 66   SNAKE MEDICINE POEM FOR A TOOTHACHE

SOURCE: Frank G. Speck, *Ceremonial Songs of the Creek & Yuchi Indians*, University of Pennsylvania Museum, Anthropological Publications, Volume 1, Number 2, 1911, pages 217–218.

"Obtained in 1905 by purchase from Kabi'tcimała [Leslie Cloud], whose fame as a shaman or doctor was no less than his renown as a leader & town chief." The translated section is spoken, followed by a song that repeats "waiting making a noise" over & over, occasionally varying it with "coiled up making a noise." A prolonged hissing ends the charm.

Words & song strengthen a herbal medicine of the kind used in curing diseases caused by animal powers. In the ritual-event the "shaman . . . steeps (herbs) in a pot of water, produces his blowpipe, a section of cane about 30 inches in length, &, in the secrecy of his private quarters . . . sings a magic song or repeats a formula over the draught, between verses giving the decoction a blowing through the pipe to make it bubble up with air. The virtue of the song is . . . transferred into the medicine."

The snake is the water moccasin, whose distended cheeks resemble the patient's. It's also equated with the medicine—the twigs used in the brew resembling its body, the dried leaves its body's color. Thus, a total picture of the snake as power, presented by whatever means.

Page 67   SNAKE MEDICINE POEM FOR A SNAKE

SOURCE: A. L. Kroeber, *Handbook of the Indians of California*, Bureau of American Ethnology, Bulletin 78, 1925, page 506.

Part of a series of shaman-led SNAKE EVENTS aimed at preventing snakebites in the year to come. (1) A group of shamans approaches a rattlesnake den, coaxing & teasing the rattlers to come out & into their sacks. (2) That evening, while others sing & shake cocoon rattles, the snake shamans walk about whistling, each with a sack of snakes on his head. The shamans wear down-filled head nets & are painted in alternate horizontal stripes of white & red across the body & limbs. From time to time they place their bags on the heads of spectators. (3) The shamans act out the curing of future bites, to prevent them from actually happening. (4) At one point they play with the snakes, throw them about, tease them to anger, allow them to bite themselves, & even hold them out hanging by their fangs from the shaman's thumb or hand. (5) The snakes are put in a small hole outdoors, which other participants poke at with long sticks "from which hang crude imitations of shell money." The participants only desist when the shamans pay each man the equivalent in real money of the length of bark or rag on his stick. (6) In a concluding group event, the entire community files past the hole, "each man, woman or child placing the right foot into or over it."

Page 68   A SONG FROM RED ANT WAY

SOURCE: Hoijer, McAllester, Wheelwright, et al., *Texts of the Navajo Creation Chants*, Peabody Museum of Harvard University, pamphlet to accompany record album, ca. 1950. The original singer was Hasteen Klah (1929).

A version of the Red Ant Way myth begins: "The fact is that the Ant People did not originate here, but their origin is traced below this earth to earth twelve, called the Dark One, on the surface of which they were the very first to come alive." And it adds: "There, you see, many of them began to live in human form . . . & to kill one another by every possible means." But all of that is part of the acute sense the first poets showed not only of the animal world at its farthest morphological remove from us (the Navajos, e.g., identify 35 different types of ant by name, some say as many as 70) but of the use to which it could be put to describe the human world as well. Both in fact as part of a continuum. The Ant people (basically dangerous or "evil" but like all things never completely so) were, especially when molested (e.g. pissed upon or otherwise disrupted in their anthills), the direct cause of a variety of diseases. For these & other sicknesses related to them by an intricate network of symbol & myth, the Red Ant Way chant-event system was a cure.

Like other Navajo ceremonials, Red Ant Way contains hundreds of songs in its various versions, along with other ritual-events such as sand painting, body painting, prayerstick planting, pollen events, herb events, etc. The whole chantway system is so complicated in fact that the individual medicine man or chanter (*hatali*, literally a keeper-of-the-songs) can rarely keep-in-mind more than a single ceremony—the nine-day Night Chant, for example—sometimes only part of one. As with other "mixed media" art of this complexity (& the Navajo includes dozens of multi-layered ceremonials like Ant Way & Night Chant) translation for-the-words-alone may hit certain highlights but never the magnitude of the composite work.

Addenda. An attempt at a more comprehensive (i.e. "total") translation of Navajo poem-songs appears above, on pages 350–353; & the same method (of translating both semantic & non-semantic vocalizations) could apply to the whole range of Navajo song as sound-poetry. But the editor doesn't mean by that to play down the effectiveness of translation that focuses on the words alone, being aware of the special sense-of-things that that kind of isolating technique makes possible. A good next departure in the presentation of American Indian poetry would be a large-scale anthology of the poetry of a single tribe like the Navajo, for which so many partial (often heavy) translations already exist. The work of new translation, etc., would proceed by whatever processes could serve to bring the range & depth of it across.

A further discussion of chant-way as intermedia, etc., appears in *Technicians of the Sacred*, pages 438–440.

Page 70   THE DEADLY DANCE

SOURCE: Angel María Garibay K., *Llave del Náhuatl,* Editorial Porrua, Mexico, 1961. Spanish text: pages 229–230; Náhuatl text: pages 145–146.

Page 75   A MYTH OF THE HUMAN UNIVERSE

SOURCE: Charles Olson, *Human Universe & Other Essays,* Grove Press, 1967, pages 13–15.

Olson was in Yucatan December 1950 to July 1951, & other versions of the sun/moon myth appear in *Mayan Letters,* etc. as a poet's real turn-on to an older (poets') way of ordering things. His own comment at end of this telling (*O, they were hot for the world they lived in, these Maya, hot to get it down the way it was—the way it is, my fellow citizens*) holds true too for new attempts in our own culture "to keep the attention poised," etc. & points to the growing interest in matters of tribal poetics & that search-for-the-primitive Stanley Diamond sees at the center of our post-Romantic development. The reader may also notice how the "hotness" in Olson's description parallels Paul Radin's cry of recognition at presentation of a Pima narrative: *This is a reality at white heat,* & he may consider both against the diminution of said intensity factor among the rulers-of-our-own-lives today & may ponder if the triumph of the American republic didn't in fact accomplish the rub-out of the tribal poets Plato had proposed for all republics, *the way it was—the way it is, my fellow citizens!*

Page 78   THE POPOL VUH: *The Destruction of the Dolls*
Page 83   THE POPOL VUH: *Alligator's Struggles with the 400 Sons*

SOURCE: Munro S. Edmonson, *The Book of Counsel: The Popol Vuh of the Quiché Maya of Guatemala,* Middle American Research Institute, Publication 35, Tulane University, 1971.

"Not the story of a hero," writes Edmonson "(but) of a people." The name, Popol Vuh, means "book of the community" (or "common-house" or "council"), & its theme (like other epic works with which it should share prominence—certainly in this hemisphere we would not only live in as intruders) is the history of all of "us" traced back to the beginnings: in this case "the goodness of Quiché: the people, the place, & the religious mysteries which were all called by that name. It is a tragic theme, but its treatment is not tragic: it is Mayan. The rise & fall of Quiché glory is placed in the cosmic cycling of all creation, & when it is ended, like the cycles of Mayan time, it stops. . . . The next cycle will be something else, perhaps the epoch suggested by the closing line of the work, something called 'Holy Cross.'" Or maybe past that too, to a point where we can again see where they were & can join them toward unknown ends in common—for which, see the "proposal" given below, or consider the purposes of this book in general.

Edmonson's translation gets away from the prose of all earlier ones (including the written Quiché), to assert an original "entirely composed in parallelistic (i.e. semantic) couplets," much of it governed by a process he calls "keying . . . in which two successive lines may be quite diverse but must share key words which are closely linked in meaning. Many of these are traditional pairs: sun-moon, day-light, deer-bird, black-white, (but) sometimes the coupling is opaque in English, however clear it may be in Quiché, as in white-laugh," etc. Such associations—as part of the developed poetry of a language—are discussed below (page 457) in relation to a series of Navajo "correspondences."

The excerpts from the Popol Vuh printed here are from early in the work & depict the end of the first of four creations of the world, marked by the "fall of the puppets carved of wood who didn't learn to worship the gods"; & the beginnings of the career of Alligator (=Cipaena), one of the sons of pride (=7 Parrot =Vuqub Kaqix), before his destruction by Hunter & Jaguar Deer (=Hun Ah Pu & X Balan Ke), etc.

Addenda. An Academic Proposal. For a period of 25 years, say, or as long as it takes a new generation to discover where it lives, take the great Greek epics out of the undergraduate curricula, & replace them with the great American epics. Study the Popol Vuh where you now study Homer, & study Homer where you now study the Popol Vuh—as exotic anthropology, etc. If you have a place in your mind for the *Greek Anthology* (God knows you may not), let it be filled by Astrov's *Winged Serpent* or the present editor's *Technicians of the Sacred* or this very volume you are reading. Teach courses in religion that begin: "This is the account of how all was in suspense, all calm, in silence; all motionless, still, & the expanse of the sky was empty"—& use this as a norm with which to compare all other religious books, whether Greek or Hebrew. Encourage poets to translate the native American classics (a new version for each new generation), but first teach them how to sing. Let young Indian poets (who still can sing or tell-a-story) teach young White poets to do so. Establish chairs in American literature & theology, etc. to be filled by men trained in the oral transmission. Remember, too, that the old singers & narrators are still alive (or that their sons & grandsons are), & that to despise them or leave them in poverty is an outrage against the spirit-of-the-land. Call this outrage the sin-against-Homer.

Teach courses with a rattle & a drum.

Page 89   The Origin of the Skagit Indians
           According to Lucy Williams

Collected & set down by Cary in the narrator's English. About which he writes: "I became aware of this creation myth in 1952 when I was collecting general myths of the Skagit people. Many of the older people denied knowledge of it, or claimed forgetfulness, and I am inclined to believe both because Lucy said very few people knew the myth & very few people cared about it. Even here there appear to be gaps. Lucy didn't remember Swadick or his place of creation and Stoodke has no account. I suspect they belong to neighboring tribes since the Okanagans are an east neighbor. It took Lucy about thirty minutes to tell this story. There were long pauses. The delivery was very slow. But it is restated entirely as it was told to me. I have chosen this form in an effort to maintain her idiom." A recognition, too, that where speech is the vehicle of language, there is no prose, but the speaker's language as it strives towards articulation is forever in the process of becoming a poem. The lack of the old details, etc.—while we would want to have them too—in no sense denies that process, but may in fact intensify it by the nature of the search. Said the Hasidic shaman of my other tribal past: "The fire we can no longer light, the prayer we no longer know, nor do we know the place where it happened in the woods. All we can do is tell the story." And that too, adds the story-teller, proved sufficient.

Page 92   THE CREATION OF THE WORLD
           ACCORDING TO CHARLES SLATER

SOURCE: Erland Nordenskiöld, *Picture-Writings & Other Documents of the Cuna Indians*, Volume 2, 1928, pages 30–35.

Like other Cunas, Slater picked up his knowledge of English (his name too) from sailors he worked with in Panama. He gives the actual source of his narrative as a chief at Aligandi named Iguanigdipipi, & in the absence of better texts, the present editor is offering Slater's written English version as is—& would likely do so anyway, for the high delight it presents of a man mining a language to which he's hardly native. Also that the power's there with very little waste: a power of conception typical (as far as I can tell) of one aspect of Cuna poetry & thought: its ability to arrange all available imageries, etc. toward the geography of a landscape not immediately to hand. This primary surrealism—clear enough here—turns up throughout the various Cuna spirit-journeys now recorded; e.g. the following in *The Journey through the Next World* of Nele Pailibe of Ustúpu (same source as Slater, pages 37—47). Here

——the voyager (=dead man, or shaman as his representative) first goes by canoe on "the mother of all rivers," then on a fast & exceedingly beautiful vessel to a forest where the trees, sand, stones & fruits are all of gold.

——He arrives some time later at the principal water reservoir in the world, with whose manager God communicates by "a sort of telegraph," to warn him of eclipses of the sun, floods, earthquakes, hurricanes, etc.

——At the mid-point between heaven & earth, from which the earth itself looks no bigger than a quarter of a coconut & heaven appears as great palaces off in the distance, he is surrounded by large numbers of eagles, "very sumptuous, of massive gold."

——He later sees a wall made of gold, on which life-sized statues of gold are moving like humans.

——At a house of interrogation, a woman named Ólotilisóbi comes with a bell & summons a group of workers, who arrive by elevator & shut the dead man in a gold chest, first smearing his body with fragrant perfumes. Ólotilisóbi seats herself on the chest; when she gets up, the top of the chest is opened, & the dead man emerges in clothes of gold, & with gold shoes & hat. Even his body is pure gold.

——Ólotilisóbi says to him: "Walk out through that door! Do you see the flag fluttering far away over there? A flag of pure gold." From the top storey he now takes an elevator to the ground floor & goes to the place where the flag was fluttering. This is also a four-storey house, & he goes to its top floor, where he's well received. There are many people there. After a while they show him a large mirror, in which he sees the inside of a human body.

——Later a railroad train takes him to a river where a woman guards a tree, the branches of which are hung with golden necklaces of all kinds & sizes. He sees another tree whose branches & leaves change into golden mirrors.

——The dead man crosses a river of cocoa, then a river of brewed coffee, then a river of pineapple juice, etc.

——On his return journey he takes a train, which brings him to a road, along the sides of which are figures resembling babies. They have a perfectly natural look, & all of them are holding flowers in their little hands.

Then, at the top of a very large building which they reach by elevator, the dead man's helping spirit gives another Cuna account of the creation of the world. The earth began as a hen's egg, he tells him, then shows him eggs of all sorts of colors. Any color may be further divided into eight categories, as blue, say, exists in eight shades, some lighter, some darker. The eggs now change into women, & the spirit fetches a very sumptuous chest, in which are cups filled with human sperm & eggs. When he touches these, they turn into children & from the chest come sounds as if from wailing babies. "Thus," he says, "Our Lord created the earth & the human race. The chest represents the womb of woman. The cup is the mould within which the embryo is formed. In the same way as God created man he also created the earth."

Then he concludes: "At no time does the soul reach God: man will never behold him."

Addenda. The poetic process (of vision & language, myth-making, etc.) stays alive in the narratives, both in pulling basic Indian threads through the thin Christian fabric & introducing elements that are personal to the seer himself as poet (e.g. God creating clothes & ornaments for woman in Slater's creation, etc.). There are also secondary interpretations of many of the images, as Slater's explanation elsewhere that the various colored souls="menstruation in its various aspects," that the table is "woman's bosom" or her labia spread flat from intercourse, that the white soul on the table is God's sperm, etc. But that much may be the elaboration of theologians & not poets, even if the line between is thin.

Page 96   THE SORCERER

SOURCE: K'HHalserten Sepass, *The Songs of Y-Ail-Mihth,* ed. by Eloise Street, Vantage Press, 1963.

The original mimeo edition of the poems—published more than forty years after date of translation—carried this note on authorship:

This cycle of songs was given by Chief Khalserten Sepass [1841–1943] of Chilliwack, B.C., Canada, to Eloise Street, & translated from the original Indian by Mrs. C. L. Street [1857–1942], daughter of the early missionary, Rev. Edward White. Four years were occupied in this work [1911–1915].

Sepass is further identified as "the last hereditary chief of the Lower Fraser" & "Chief of 'Tsilli-way-ukh (Chilliwack), Gathering Place of the People of K'HHalls, the Sun God,' actually the place of Sun Ceremonies held every four years." While the present editor can't even begin to get into the question of the "authenticity" of these poems, it's his judgment that they represent, under any circumstances, an extraordinary convergence of content & means at a time in the history of North American poetry—prior to First World War—when nothing of this accomplishment had come into English from native sources, & it's as a forgotten work of tribal/"modern" poetry that he would first have them seen.

Eloise Street, as intermediary between singer & translator, describes the style of the original (so far as she heard it) as "a sort of free verse, rather like waves washing on a beach, rolling in & withdrawing, rolling in again & again. These lines were spoken in a semi-chant, the singer holding in one hand a small drum, which he palmed with the other hand. A traditional form governed the delivery. As the mood dictated, he would stand still & declaim in an oratorical style, then his chant would turn into a lively falsetto singing, accompanied by dance steps. Sequence followed sequence in this manner, the phrases having always an uplift of voice at the end, which had the effect of drawing the listener on with a sense of continuance—of something never quite finished—again like the sound of waves." In a later note she puts an even greater stress on the accompanying gesture & dance.

Y-Ail-Mihth, whose name figures in the cycle's title, is only identified as the traditional singer-of-the-songs mentioned in the cycle itself. Because of the translator's method of identifying names in her own text, further notes wouldn't seem to be needed.

Page 102   COON CONS COYOTE, COYOTE EAT COON, COYOTE FIGHTS SHIT-MEN, ETC.

Page 105   COYOTE BORROWS FARTING BOY'S ASSHOLE, TOSSES UP HIS EYES, ETC.

SOURCE: Melville Jacobs, *Northwestern Sahaptin Texts,* Columbia University Contributions to Anthropology, Volume 19, 1934.

Coyote appears in the familiar role of primordial shit-thrower, cock-erupter, etc., to satisfy the need for all that in the full pantheon of essential beings. No merely horny version of a Disney character, he is (like other tricksters in tribal America: Rabbit, Raven, Spider, Bluejay, Mink, Flint, Glooscap, Saynday, etc.) the product of a profound & comic imagination playing upon the realities of man & nature. Thus, as Jung writes of the Winnebagos' Trickster in that now-famous essay: he is "absolutely undifferentiated human consciousness . . . a psyche that has hardly left the animal level . . . (but) god, man & animal at once . . . both sub- & super-human . . . an expression (therefore) of the polaristic structure of the psyche, which like any other energic system is dependent on the tension of opposites." Like any genuine poetry system too.

The good-of-him, which should be more apparent than ever to "counter-culturists," etc. is at least three-fold:

(1) to find a place for what—as animals, children, etc.—we were

& are: to be aware of, even to enjoy, the very thing that scares us with threats of madness, loss of self, etc.

(2) to ridicule our ordinary behaviors by breaking (vicariously at least) their hold on us: to punch holes in established authority (=the way things are) so as not to be its forever silent victims;

(3) where Trickster is creator too, to explain the dangers inherent in reality itself—of a world, that is, that must have such gods at its inception: or as an old Ten'a Indian said to John Chapman, "The Creator made all things good, but the Raven (=Trickster) introduced confusion" (for which, etc. see page 409, above).

Page 117　　THE FLIGHT OF QUETZALCOATL

SOURCE: Spanish prose translation in Angel María Garibay K.'s *Épica Náhuatl*, Biblioteca del Estudiante Universitario, Mexico, 1945, pages 59–63. J.R.'s working from *Technicians of the Sacred.*

The present version of the Quetzalcoatl or Birdsnake Man narrative (not the exclusive account by any means but one of many—in the best tribal/oral tradition) comes from Bernardino de Sahagún's 16th Century *Historia de las Cosas de Nueva España,* with the ending from the contemporaneous *Anales de Quauhtitlan.* It begins here after whatever-had-happened to get him on the road. In Sahagún, say, three sorcerers (one with a god name, two without) came to him, got him high on "white wine" (maybe pulque), while working other sorceries to destroy his city, Tollan ("Tula"). But the account is shapeless & lacks the thrust or point of myth-become-poetry.

The *Anales* in this case are more articulate. In brief, the gods Tezcatlipoca, Ihuimecatl & Toltecatl decided to force Quetzalcoatl out of his city "where we intend to live." Tezcatlipoca thought to bring it off by "giving him his body," so showed him a double mirror "the size of a hand's span" & "Quetzalcoatl saw himself, & was filled with fear, & said: 'If my subjects see me, they will run away!' For his eyelids were badly inflamed, his eyes sunken in their sockets, & his face all covered with wrinkles. His face was not human at all!"

The vision is repeated: always the terror of self-recognition, of the man in his dying body, his flesh. And so on, toward the spirit journey that will lead him to apotheosis as the planet Venus, etc. or to the opening of Snake's earthly body & its wing'd ascent-to-heaven. For which, see the fuller note in *Technicians,* pages 444–445, or L. Séjourné's great account of Toltec/Aztec religion in her *Burning Water.*

Addenda. More on the sacred image of Old-Man, etc. common to many Indian & other tribal poetries (i.e. the rotting face we start from in knowing where we are: both the god imaged as man-fallen-with-man-into-rotting-flesh & idealized as man-more-than-man-surviving-death) can be found in the commentary on the Omaha "Sweat-House Ritual" (page 449, below). The reader may also note the power the shaman visionaries had of seeing their own skeletons & undertaking ritual journeys to overcome death. But the editor doesn't mean to suggest that seeing an old face in the mirror is straight ritual symbolism in every tribal context; e.g. the Eskimo "Old Man's Song" (page 161, above) obviously gets the whole thing down in more personal terms, as have many key poems in many different traditions.

Page 125   A BOOK OF NARRATIVES (II): THE BOY & THE DEER

SOURCE: Dennis Tedlock, *Finding the Center: Narrative Poetry of the Zuni Indians,* Dial Press, 1971.

Tedlock's version of *The Boy & the Deer,* along with his other translations, is a primary example of what the present editor has been calling "total translation," i.e. the rendering of *all* sounds & repetitions which the translator can be made to perceive in the original. By doing this with Andrew Peynetsa's oral narratives, Tedlock has also expanded the area of what "we" can recognize as poetry—I mean as any treatment of language in which all particulars (of movement, phrasing, idiom, etc.) count & have to be accounted for in bringing the work across. He has potentially increased the body of oral poetry a thousand-fold through the clear recognition that prose doesn't in fact exist "outside the written page." For which & other comments, his own view-of-the-matter follows.

"[TRANSLATING SOUND & SILENCE IN A SPOKEN LITERATURE]: The spoken narratives of the Zuni Indians (like those of other tribal peoples) are events, not just verbal descriptions of events. They sound like poems and plays, but because they are spoken rather than sung or chanted they have always been treated in translation as if they were equivalent to written prose. If one 'listens' only for *meaning* (in the ordinary sense), it is easy to fall into this trap; but if one listens to the *sounds* (with more than the narrow phonetic ear of the linguist) and to the intervening *silences,* it becomes clear that what has been widely called 'oral prose' is in reality dramatic poetry. Indeed, there is ample reason to believe that 'prose' has no existence at all outside the written page.

"What makes written prose most unfit for representing spoken narrative is that it rolls on for whole paragraphs at a time without hesitating or taking a breath: there is no silence in it. To solve this problem I have adopted line changes, which in contemporary poetry usually correspond to pauses in performance. The noticeable silences in Zuni narrative range all the way from about four-tenths second to three seconds, so I have divided them into two types: ordinary pauses, averaging a little less than a second in length and represented by simple line breaks; and long pauses, two to three seconds long and represented by double spaces between lines. A prose presentation would not be much of a guide to these silences: some of them fall between clauses or sentences, but others do not, and some of the clause and sentence boundaries are not accompanied by silence.

"In passing from Zuni to English it is possible to at least approximate the original contrasts in line length. There is no point in preserving the exact syllable counts in translation [these vary anyway from performance to performance—ed.], but radical changes in the original lengths would distort the pace of the narrative. Line length—or, to put it the other way around, the frequency of pauses—is the major cause of variations in the apparent rate at which human speech is delivered: passages with short lines (many pauses) seem slow, while those with long lines (few pauses) seem fast."

[Other sounds attended to—loudness, intonation, vowel lengthening, etc.—are noted in the "Aids to Reading Aloud" on page 126. Tedlock goes on to say about this translation & the boundaries of translation in general]: "Accidents or 'errors,' when recognized, are eliminated in conventional translations, but they are a natural part of performance: keeping them in translation can help preserve the sound-event quality of the original narrative. In the following passage, the line consisting solely of 'you' was a false start on the part of the narrator:

'Your belly grew large
you
you were about to deliver, you had pains in your belly, you were
    about to give birth to me, you had pains in your belly
you gathered your clothes
and you went down to the bank to wash.'

The repetition of 'you had pains in your belly' might also be considered an error. The narrator is quoting an agitated person and simply gets carried away, making the quotation more realistic in the process.

"In most spoken narrative traditions the audience gives the performer a standardized response. In the Zuni case the response is *eeso*, with the effect of 'ah yes' or 'yes indeed,' given after each of the two introductory lines and otherwise scattered here and there among the pauses in the body of the story. The presence of a tape-recorder inhibits this response, and so it occurs only five times (each marked *audience*) in the present narrative; under more normal circumstances it might have occurred something like twenty times."

The reader should also note that other words in the original—the opening & closing formulas, proper names without meaning, etc.—are brought across (translated, so to speak) without being changed: an optional strategy even in a "total" translation. Kachinas are (as elsewhere among the Pueblos) the ancestral gods impersonated in masked dances; their village "lies beneath the surface of a lake & comes to life only at night." The translated term, "daylight person," refers to all living human beings, while "all other beings, including animals, some plants, various natural phenomena, & deceased humans (kachinas), are called 'raw people,' because they do not depend on cooked food. The boy is partly daylight, since his mother is daylight, and partly raw, since his father is the Sun and since, as Andrew Peynetsa points out, 'he was the half-son of the deer mother, because she gave him her milk.'" On death he becomes completely "raw," thus "enters upon the roads of his elders," going back to the deer forever. This may partly explain why the narrator himself interprets the boy's death as a suicide.

For more on "total translation," particularly in the area of song & sound-poetry, see J.R.'s working on pages 350–353, above, & the commentary thereto on page 466, below.

Page 153   WOLF SONGS & OTHERS OF THE TLINGIT

SOURCE: John R. Swanton, *Tlingit Myths & Texts*, Bureau of American Ethnology, Bulletin 39, 1909, *passim*.

Koller's workings probably deliver much more than Swanton—describing the poems as "highly metaphorical" & hard to understand—thought possible to get across. But good poets have the advantage of not believing in metaphor, therefore not being conned by its presumed presence. What emerges, anyway, is a cumulative picture of Tlingit life & attitudes (given above without a break for singers' names, etc.) that the present editor finds almost unbearable in its clarity & directness.

If it's not otherwise apparent to the reader, note should also be made that many of the animal references (Wolf, Eagle, Crow, etc.)

are to clans in the original, though Koller has chosen to emphasize their natural & totemic significances. "Crow" in the Tlingit is more like "raven." Notes on individual songs & poets follow.

Song No. 1 (I keep dreaming . . .) Composed by Qaqatcguk after his dream on the island.

Song No. 2 (Shaman Song) A spirit song composed by a shaman called Luswat.

Song No. 3 (Throw him into . . .) Spirit song composed by Kasenduaxtc.

Song Nos. 5–8 (Cradle Songs) Sung over a child & used sometimes at feasts. When a man died his brother married the widow— as with the old Hebrew tribes.

Song No. 9 (Funeral Song) Composed by Hayiaku, also called Small-Lake-underneath. "It is used when a feast is about to be given for a dead man, & they have their blankets tied up to their waists & carry canes."

Song No. 10 (That's a rich man . . .) Used by all families of the Wolf phratry, who sing it all together just as they are coming to a feast.

Song No. 11 (We've all been invited . . .) Composed in Tsimshian & used at a great feast. Songs in other languages—like the following one too—were in fact common.

Song No. 12 (How is it all . . .) Composed by a Haida who was popularly called Haida Charlie. A dance song at feasts.

Song No. 13 (I wonder what eagle . . .) Composed by Gaxe (Crying-Wolf).

Song No. 14 (I think about you . . .) Composed by Yuwaku & "addressed to the rest of his group."

Song No. 15 (I know how people . . .) Composed by Andeyek (name means: For-a-town-spirit) to denounce strangers to town who paid no attention to his people.

Song No. 16 (You surprise me . . .) Composed by Nigot.

Song No. 17 (I'm gonna die . . .) Composed by Tsakak.

Song No. 18 (Song on the Way to Jail) Composed by Kakayek about his brother's wife. She does the speaking in anticipation of being sent away by the Whites for drunkenness (her actual rejoinder in fact is two songs down.) Kakayek's own name probably meant something like wolves-howling-in-the-distance.

Song No. 19 (Song for the Richest Woman) Composed by Guxnawu (Dead-Slave) about a woman named Kahantiki (Poor-Orphan).

Song No. 20 (I don't know why . . .) Composed by Toxaoci in reply to No. 18.

Song No. 21 (It's only whiskey . . .) Composed by a shaman named Kagank.

Song No. 22 (My wife went away . . .) Composed by Katda (Around-A-Flat-Basket), whose wife her people took back.

Song No. 23 (If you'd died . . .) "This is sung when peace is being made after a great war." It can be sung for any clan by inserting the clan's name.

Song No. 24 (Before he died . . .) Part of a song composed by a man named Łquena, when he was the only one of his people saved & his enemies wanted to make peace with him. He danced as a deer, singing his song, & at the end of it, cut the man standing next to him in two.

Song No. 25 (It would be very pleasant . . .) Composed by Yełdugu (Raven-skin) when his sweetheart abandoned him.

Song No. 26 (He followed . . .) A mourning song.

Page 158   ESKIMO SONGS ABOUT PEOPLE & ANIMALS

SOURCE: Field's working from Knud Rasmussen's *The Netsilik Eskimos*, Report of the 5th Thule Expedition, 1931; Schwerner's translations from *Poèmes Eskimo* by Paul Emile Victor, Pierre Seghers, Paris, 1958.

The range of Eskimo poetry has easy extensions into the everyday & personal: areas (they used to say) too particular for the likes of primitive hunters & gatherers. But Rasmussen showed long ago how Eskimo songs, etc. got down precisely "the thoughts & moods of people journeying or hunting in solitude . . . hummed at home in the snow hut or tent in the evenings . . . but in company with the drum they are also the central point in the *qagsgé*," i.e. a big house built for the public song festivals, where large groups met after feasting in private homes, to hold song contests, etc.

The reader may also be interested in Orpingalik's song (page 176, above, & the commentaries thereto) for a major Eskimo work in this mode. As a contrasting type, the Eskimo *Magic Words* (pages 45–48, above) are also available.

Page 164   LULLABY

SOURCE: Garfield, Wingert & Barbeau, *The Tsimshian: Their Arts & Music*, Publications of the American Ethnological Society, Volume 18, 1951, page 125.

This lullaby for girls belonged to the family of the singer, a man named Weerhæ, English name: Robert Pearl, he having learned it from his mother who was sister of the woman who was the real owner.

Page 165   TSIMSHIAN MOURNING SONG
SOURCE: ditto.

Sung by the same singer as the preceding, but this one from the other side of his family. The type of song called a *lin* (=lament), it was sung immediately after the death of a relative & again a year later.

Page 166   TWO DIVORCE SONGS

Translated by Cary from his own gatherings in the Kispiox-Hazelton country of British Columbia, summer 1968.

Page 167   INSULT BEFORE GIFT-GIVING

SOURCE: Garfield, Wingert & Barbeau, *The Tsimshian: Their Arts & Music*, Publications of the American Ethnological Society, Volume 18, 1951, page 125.

A potlatch (=giveaway) song of the Eagle clan to accompany gifts of food to the guests at feasts. The singer in this instance was one Tralahæt, also called Frank Bolton; the interpreter was Pahl (Charles Barton). Recorded in 1927.

(1) While the idea was to "roast the guest before making gifts to him" (thus: Charles Barton), the poem isn't an example of N.W. Coast meanness, etc., so much as an indication of the use of language (poetry) to experience & bring-to-surface threats to group stability: why real poets (who even today remember their roots in the primitive) often appear anti-social or (merely) negative to those who no longer understand poetic process & modes-of-thought. But poetry either explores the area of the socially & spiritually destructive or becomes (as it often has) an instrument for its own emasculation.

(2) "Some of the words," writes Barbeau, "are Gitksan & others Niskæ—side by side," a use of foreign languages fairly common in tribal practice & another reminder that "power" & not immediate or total comprehension was the primary poetic value. Expressions like "Now the words!" or "Sing louder!" were usually interjected by the singer himself; "they were meant to call the attention of the listeners to the theme of the song."

Page 168   SPYGLASS CONVERSATIONS

SOURCE: Frances Densmore, *Music of the Tule Indians of Panama*, Smithsonian Miscellaneous Collections, Volume 77, Number 11, 1926, page 31.

"The boy & the older girl are 'doctors' (possessors of mysterious powers) . . . The Tule had seen spyglasses but did not own one." Other Tule (Cuna) journeys were, however, carried on into earth, air & sea, as in the trip of Nele Pailibe (see page 419, above) or that along Muu's way (page 312, above; 458, below). The spyglass, then, is confirmation of powers attested to in other songs; thus:

> Go to sleep & dream of many animals—mountain lions & ocean
> lions
> You will talk to them & understand what they say
> & when you awake you will be a shaman like me.
>
> (Densmore, Tule, page 18)

For more on the writing down of the Tule poems, etc. see page 410, above.

Page 170   NAVAJO ANIMAL SONGS

SOURCE: David P. McAllester, *Enemy Way Music*, Papers of the Peabody Museum of American Archaeology & Ethnology, Harvard University, Volume 41, Number 3, page 80.

A group of moccasin game songs, as given by Son of Bead Chant Singer. When he recorded "wildcat," McAllester writes, "he was so amused he had difficulty finishing the song, & his daughter laughed so loud she had to sit down on the ground. The first line of the song was enough to set the audience laughing in anticipation of what was to come."

Writes Reichard of moccasin game songs in general: "Matthews, in an early work, 'Navajo Gambling Songs,' refers to the large number of songs concerned with the moccasin game. One old man said there were four thousand, & another that there was no creature that walked, flew or crawled in all the world known to the Navajo that had not at least one song in the game & that many had more. The reason is almost certainly that the game originated as a contest for day & night in which all living things participated." (Reichard, *Navajo Religion*, page 287) The reader should remember too (especially if he still tends to equate sacred & sober, etc.) that laughter is itself an old form of religious language, if a dangerous one. Says McAllester about the thin line walked here: "It is interesting that the moccasin game songs which contain laughable remarks about various animals & birds are sung only after the first killing frost when it is safe. There is a minimum of danger from retaliatory lightning, snake bite or damage to crops after this time of year."

For more on comic language, etc., see page 440, below, among other places in the present volume.

Page 172   MORE ESKIMO SONGS ABOUT PEOPLE & ANIMALS

SOURCE: "Boas Eskimo Songs 1889 (?)," Franz Boas manuscript in the American Philosophical Society, Philadelphia. An indication of the number of tribal works collected but unpublished, etc.—in addition to all the published, out-of-print pieces from earlier in the century.

Page 176   ORPINGALIK'S SONG: IN A TIME OF SICKNESS

SOURCE: Knud Rasmussen, *The Netsilik Eskimos*, Report of the 5th Thule Expedition, Copenhagen, 1931, pages 321–323, 324–327.

Orpingalik (the name means man-with-willow-twig) was a shaman, poet & hunter, "notably intelligent & having a fertile wit" (writes Rasmussen), who could move, like other big poets, between personal modes (as here) & "magic words" of the kind given elsewhere in these pages (for which, see pages 45–48, above). Obviously into it up to his elbows, he called this song "my breath" because (he said) "it is just as necessary to me to sing as it is to breathe." That breath, which is all the more visible where he came from (in the language of the Netsilik shamans, e.g., a living person is "someone smoke surrounds"), becomes the physical projection of the process of thought, etc. that goes on inside a man. Thus, Orpingalik describes an order of composition something like "projective verse" as follows:

Songs are thoughts, sung out with the breath when people are moved by great forces & ordinary speech no longer suffices. Man is moved just like the ice floe sailing here & there in the current. His thoughts are driven by a flowing force when he feels joy, when he feels fear, when he feels sorrow. Thoughts can wash over him like a flood, making his breath come in gasps & his heart throb. Something like an abatement in the weather will keep him thawed up. And then it will happen that we, who always think we are small, will feel still smaller. And we will fear to use words. But it will happen that the words we need will come of themselves. When the words we want to use shoot up of themselves—we get a new song. (*Netsilik,* page 321)

As for the extent of his own involvement therein, he says elsewhere:

How many songs I have I cannot tell you. I keep no count of such things. There are so many occasions in one's life when a joy or a sorrow is felt in such a way that the desire comes to sing; & so I only know that I have many songs. All my being is song, & I sing as I draw breath.

The particular circumstances behind "Sickness" were very much as the poem describes them. For other Eskimo poems, etc. about people & animals, see above, pages 158–163 & page 172.

Page 179   A BOOK OF EVENTS (I)

This book of events is presented as a sequel to one in *Technicians of the Sacred*. As there, the editor has taken a series of rituals & other programmed activities & has, as far as possible, suppressed all reference to accompanying mythic or "symbolic" explanations. This has led to two important results: (1) the form of the activities is, for the first time, given the prominence it deserves; & (2) the resulting works bear a close resemblance to those mythless activities of our own time called events, happenings, de-coll/age, kinetic theater, etc. It may be further noted that most of these "events"—like the (modern) intermedia art they resemble—are parts of total situations involving poetry, music, dance, painting, myth, dream, etc. as are many of the songs & visions presented elsewhere in this anthology. But a crucial point of tribal poetry-&-art is precisely that it calls for total performance & participation: a maximization of human activities to allow the world to remake itself at that level of intensity (=reality at white heat) that Radin spoke of.

Having revealed this much, the editor again doesn't wish to obscure by a series of explanatory footnotes the forms that have been laid bare. While absence of such notes may result in some distortion, that surely isn't more than what results from the usual presentation of the words-of-the-event (=poem) apart from the rest. But the work of poets is poetry in whatever medium it takes place!

Addenda. (1) Other presentations of poetry beyond speech- & song-utterances will be found in *A Book of Extensions* (*I*): pages 295–335, above, & in *A Book of Extensions* (*II*): *Soundings,* pages 339–353, above. The editor feels this approach to be vital to an adequate comprehension of the ways in which the "word" (=*logos*) manifested itself among the American tribes in a complex of moves in which word, event & image were generated by a single impulse toward "vision" or whatever term of ours would fit the bill today.

(2) The contemporary word "happening"—as cover-all for these kinds of events—itself has counterparts in, e.g., the Navajo word for their own (intermedia) ceremonials, which (Kluckhohn & Wyman tell us) translates literally as "something-is-going-on"; or in the widespread use by the Iroquois & others of the English word "doings."

(3) Since writing the above, the editor has become aware of new occurrences in contemporary happenings & theater that have gone beyond the mythless presentation of events to first attempts at a redefinition of the content-of-reality itself: in other words, to a renewed willingness to define content before the event rather than after it. This shift from an inductive to a deductive art has often involved some sense of Indian or tribal heritage as model.

Page 181   DREAM EVENT I & DREAM EVENT II

Anthony Wallace's "Dreams & the Wishes of the Soul" (available, say, in *Magic, Witchcraft & Curing,* ed. J. Middleton, Natural History Press) is the going account of Iroquois dream practice back to the 17th Century *Jesuit Relations.* Said Father Fremin: "The Iroquois have, properly speaking, only a single divinity—the Dream." But dream was central to the creative & intellectual experience of most Indian groups —as source of vision & song, & key to that "dream-time" to which the Australian aborigines ascribed all outcroppings of the sacred, etc.

Page 182   A MASKED EVENT FOR COMEDIAN & AUDIENCE

SOURCE: Bernhard J. Stern, *The Lummi Indians of Northwest Washington*, Columbia University Contributions to Anthropology, Volume 17, 1934, pages 57–59. For other comic events, notes on sacred comedy, etc. see above, pages 342–346, & below, page 448, among others.

Page 183   BUTTERFLY SONG EVENT

SOURCE: Leslie Spier, *Yuman Tribes of the Gila River*, University of Chicago Publications in Anthropology, Ethnological Series, 1933, page 231.

Compare not only the construction of mobiles, windworks, etc. in contemporary art, but transposition of voice & other body sounds to visual media.

Page 184   AUTUMN EVENTS

SOURCE: Franz Boas, *The Central Eskimo*, Bureau of American Ethnology, 6th Annual Report, 1888, pages 200–201.

Page 185   TAMALE EVENT

SOURCE: Bernardino de Sahagún, *Florentine Codex*, tr. Arthur J. O. Anderson & Charles E. Dibble, University of Utah, Part 2, page 163. The present version is unaltered from the Náhuatl translation.

Compare the event itself with the poems from it on pages 378–381. Animal events of this sort are notably widespread—& probably no more baroque among the Aztecs, say, than with the Lummi of Northwest Washington, for which see "Animal Spirit Event" on page 196 above.

Page 186   MUD EVENTS

SOURCE: Gladys Reichard, *Social Life of the Navajo Indians*, Columbia University Contributions to Anthropology, Volume 7, 1928, pages 132–133.

For other acts of earth- & body-rootedness the reader may compare contemporary happenings that involve daubings, etc. (as Allan Kaprow's *Soap*: instructions for the 2nd evening bodies dirtied with jam

bodies buried in mounds
at the sea edge

bodies cleaned by the tide)

or more or less spontaneous expressions of some within the "counter-culture"—but remember too the generations of experience that gave these Navajo events their context.

Page 187   DAKOTA DANCE EVENTS

SOURCE: Lewis Henry Morgan, *The Indian Journals 1859–1862*, University of Michigan Press, 1959, page 146.

Highly condensed scenarios as given to Morgan, circa 1860. The ordeal of "Moon Event" more commonly turns up in Plains Indian sun-dances. "Half-Man Event" has numerous contemporary analogues in body painting, polar images, etc.

Page 188   GIFT EVENT II

SOURCE: as originally printed in J.R.'s *Technicians of the Sacred*, based on native accounts in "The Amiable Side of Kwakiutl Life: The Potlatch & the Play Potlatch," by Helen Codere, *American Anthropologist*, Volume 56, Number 2, April, 1956.

Compare Alison Knowles' *Giveaway Construction* (1963):

Find something you like in the street & give it away. Or find a variety of things, make something of them, & give it away . . .

among many contemporary happenings, etc. that involve gift-giving. Part of the redistribution pattern for valued objects, or way of creating new value, but no more sinister (as potlatch or as art) here than there.

Page 189   GIFT EVENT IV

SOURCE: Paul Radin, *The Winnebago Tribe*, originally in Bureau of American Ethnology, 37th Annual Report, 1923, reprinted by University of Nebraska Press, 1970, page 339.

Page 190   LANGUAGE EVENT I

SOURCE: Knud Rasmussen, *The Netsilik Eskimos*, Report of the 5th Thule Expedition, Copenhagen, 1931, pages 307–314. For more on shaman language, etc. see the commentaries (pages 405–406, above) on "magic words."

Page 191   LANGUAGE EVENT II

SOURCE: Gladys A. Reichard, *Navajo Religion: A Study of Symbolism*, Bollingen Series, XVIII, Pantheon, 1950, 1963, page 270.

Among other Navajo forms of "altered language": this one, not surprisingly, for use in the Rain Ceremony. But the reader might take it from there, & see what results would follow the application of the single rule to a wider series of situations.

Page 192   PICTURE EVENT

SOURCE: Washington Matthews, *The Night Chant, a Navajo Ceremony*, Memoirs of the American Museum of Natural History, 1902, page 129.

Compare this to contemporary self-destroying art, say, or to the notion that a work-of-art's survivability may *not* be the real measure of why we bother in the first place.

Page 193   NAMING EVENTS

SOURCE: Ruth Underhill, *Social Organization of the Papago Indians*, Columbia University Contributions to Anthropology, Volume 30, 1939, pages 174–178.

For naming as a fundamental source of poetry, see *Technicians of the Sacred*, pages 392–393, & Gertrude Stein's reminder therein that "that is poetry really loving the name of anything & that is not prose."

Page 194   PEBBLE EVENT

SOURCE: Alice C. Fletcher & Francis LaFlesche, *The Omaha Tribe*, Bureau of American Ethnology, 27th Annual Report, 1905–1906, pages 565–566.

This is the major ritual-event of the Pebble Society, for which *Sweat-House Ritual No. 1* (page 280, above) is a preparation. For more on the accompanying sacred narrative, etc. see commentary, page 448, below. Another example of simultaneous recitation appears above, on pages 342–346.

Page 195   CRAZY DOG EVENTS

SOURCE: Robert H. Lowie, *The Crow Indians*, Holt, Rinehart & Winston, 1935, 1956, pages 330–331.

The events resemble dada activities, say, but also the political gestures of the provos & crazies, etc. of the late 1960s. But the phenomenon was also a deep-seated aspect of Plains Indian warrior life, not unlike traditional patterns of the Japanese & others. For more on this, see page 408, above.

Page 196   ANIMAL SPIRIT EVENT

SOURCE: Stern, *Lummi*, as above, pages 63–64.

An immediate comparison is to the Aztec event ("tamales," etc.) above, but the experience of another animal's nature (or even that of an inanimate *thing*) was one of the major achievements of Amerindian poets & visionaries. Not a masquerade either, for when Lowie, say, writes in a passage that my eye just now lights on, of a Crow man who "could not eat a cherry without going into an ecstatic condition & acting like a bear," there is a level of experience & an utterly sane blowing-of-the-mind, so to speak, that transforms events into vision & from which the words will then emerge as song or narrative, etc.

Page 197   VISION EVENTS I, II & III

SOURCES: (I) & (II) from Peter Freuchen, *Book of the Eskimos*, Fawcett World Library, 1961, pages 158, 159; (III) a highly condensed version of the Plains Indian "vision quest" as initiation into manhood, etc.

Page 201   SIXTY-SIX POEMS FOR A BLACKFOOT BUNDLE

SOURCE: Clark Wissler, *Ceremonial Bundles of the Blackfoot Indians*, Anthropological Papers of the American Museum of Natural History, Volume 7, Part 2, 1912, pages 215 et seq.

Imperfect scenario based on Wissler's incomplete description, but a lot of poetry anyway & gives you some idea of what else was going-on. The bundles themselves were "wrapped-up aggregations of sacred objects" (thus: R. Lowie): medicines whose powers were put to a number of curative & other religious ends. The principal item in the present beaver-bundle was the *natoas,* a ceremonial bonnet made of turnip leaves, etc. but also the other objects handled in the ritual-event or mentioned in the accompanying myth-of-origin (below ↓). Much obviously remains untold here, but the sheer action of the piece may be sufficient news to us outsiders.

AND NOW THE MYTH—one version anyway—in which this bull elk went out looking for his wife who'd run off with a second bull elk. So he filled his pipe & went as usual to ask some other animals for help. He offered them a smoke (tobacco in those days) but they all said no they didn't care to. So he had to go on a ways before he came to Moose & Raven who said yes & smoked it. Now, in the woods it isn't easy to find elks who fuck your wife, & Raven said: That's true enough but it's easier for me to cover ground so I'll go on alone & you two wait. When he was out four days he found that old bull elk & saw he had some real big power, so then he spooked the two of them so that they couldn't get away.

Then Raven went back to Elk & Moose, but when he did he found Elk was scared of that bull elk, then he asked Moose what power Moose had & Moose said: I can really hit them hard. Then Elk said: I've got horns so powerful I really can hook hard. When Raven heard that he knew that someone was secretly afraid of that bull elk, so Raven said: I'd say his power was greatly overrated, maybe we can knock him off without much trouble.

So they all headed out. Raven flew ahead of them & Moose said: Old pal Raven sure talks big. But what's he got but wings? That's not going to help us fight no elk. A good argument too, but after some distance through those woods they ran into a clump of cottonwoods. So Raven got back to them & said: You look out yonder, you'll see that bull elk & your wife down by those cottonwoods. So Elk looked now & saw them, he was in the lead & Moose was close behind him. You bet that they were singing, & every step Moose took, his great power made him sink deeper & deeper in that very hard ground.

Elk was the first to approach the tree where his wife & that bull elk were standing. He just hooked that tree three or four times maybe until he knocked some big chips off of it. He was angry by then & wanting to kill that other bull elk, & being angry he kept hooking at that tree. Moose struck it a few times with his feet & managed to dislodge a few chips too, but then that bull elk who had been fucking Elk's wife, remember, he just hooked that tree & knocked it down. Which was really enough for Elk & Moose, who lost their taste for fighting then & there. That's how it was. Moose said to Elk: I think we should just make friends with him, I think he's got power left to spare. But Raven said: What you guys scared of? His power ain't so much, why we three could just gang up on him &. . . . Pretty good idea you'd think but not to Moose, he said: I'd rather just be friends with that big guy. Anyway, he said, I don't see what help Raven would be, all he's got's a pair of wings & that heavy curvey bill of his. So Elk said: You bet, & I think I'll give him my robe & my bonnet. Then Moose said: I think I'll give him my hoofs, & Raven said: I guess I'll give him my tail feathers. But I know sure as shooting we could beat him & wouldn't have to give it all away. My secret plan was I would land right on his head & peck his eyes out one by one. Then you & Moose would go & get him & being he was blind you could have run all over him. But hell, said Raven, Moose is such a coward & you decided to go easy & give him all those gifts to get him off your wife, so that's the way it is.

And that's the way it was too. Sorry as Elk & Moose were now & even itching to get in & fight, Raven still said: No shit you better do just what you said. Also that bull elk who had been fucking old Elk's wife turned out scared of Raven: Yes, he was thinking to himself, I'll take what I can get & let him have his wife. You bet he did. That one wife cost an elkrobe & a dress, a bonnet, wristlets, moose hoofs, raven feathers, & not just any bonnet either but the holy turnip bonnet with feathers like the prongs of old Elk's horns. But most of that was woman's things, see, & that bull elk didn't have a wife so one day he was going past a tipi & he thought he'd give them to whoever was inside. Good idea, he thought again & changed into a man, that way he went into the tipi & gave it all away & taught the man inside it all about that ceremony. Yes, he would give his wife that robe & dress & bonnet for the ceremonies of a beaver bundle that he had & would let the women borrow it besides when people gave a sun dance. And for that ceremony of his they'd chop down a small cottonwood & would plant it & go through the hooking motions at it that that elk & moose had done when they were testing their own powers.

Lots of other things he might have told them but the story doesn't have them, & some say anyway that all of that was from the woman who married the star & not those elks. And others say that Scar-face gave a little & that Scabby-robe did & the beavermen—& probably they're all at least half right.

Page 214   THE TEXT OF THE RAINGOD DRAMA

SOURCE: Vera Laski, *Seeking Life,* American Folklore Society, 1958. J.R. has adapted the verses & has reworked the dialogue toward creation of a mock clown-style in English. The rest is essentially Laski's.

The Raingod Drama (Nu·hi) is from the Winter Moiety's version at San Juan Pueblo. The "goddess" addressed early along is the one through whom the Winter Cacique [=religious leader of the Winter Moiety] receives his strength; sometimes in fact the Cacique himself is called O·yi·ka, the root meaning of which is "ice." Neither the Cacique nor any of the people present are an audience for the dramatic event, but all are active participants: something that distinguishes theater as ritual from theater as spectator sport.

The comic as religious form is central to tribal practice & reminds us that laughter may have been the first religious language, that it may in fact be latent in much religious experience as we know it or overt among those contemporaries of ours who are still tribal or living closer to their tribal roots. The "sacred clowns" (as Al Ortiz calls them) keep man down-to-earth while acting as intermediaries for powers that reach beyond (if not above) the human. So do the masked dancers (the kachinas of the present work), but with the balance tilted toward the more-than-human, whose language we don't understand & don't dare laugh at. Both reflect the ambiguity of the sacred (dream)-life as it incredibly attempts to reach us, charged as it is with the danger of something that goes against our (waking) sense of how-things-are. But in the spirit world (they sometimes tell us) everything appears reversed, as it does too in the speech & actions of the Clowns, in the incomprehensible "language" of the kachinas, in the silence of the last kachina who is also the old man doing the thing that young men do best, etc. In response to this, the laughter that fills the people's throats & is itself convulsive & uncontrollable, may be felt as a force speaking through man: the language of the gods deflected in the medium of our human world. (A language too that poets in our own time may again be learning to speak!)

The pivot of the god-comedy, as it reveals itself in these terms, is the Man Ceremony. The Silent One reaches the extreme of the raingods, going from their grunts & whistles to his own total silence, but playing that too against the restlessness of his stalking, which is both that of the hunter & of the fiercely sexed old man. He is called either Yeŋ sedó=Old Man or Povi yen=Flower Man, & his name in turn becomes a joking term for penis, just as Man Ceremony itself may be a synonym for fucking—at least where unexpected or especially exciting. Ambiguous enough all by himself the old man is further set against the young virgin, like two extremes of nature brought together, as opposites are always joined in that fusion from which the sacred comes to life in poem or other such implosion. This "uniting of opposites" is for the Pueblos (Laski writes) "a symbol of harmony," just as sex is in general.

Says the formula of the Initiation Ceremony: "Be a man & be a woman," & the words are repeated in other aspects of Pueblo life, wherever the supernatural intervenes.

Addenda. Laski gives the following description of the full (if "non-musical") exploitation of sound in the present work, which links it too with many discoveries & rediscoveries in contemporary music, etc.: "The Raingod Ceremony is essentially different from most Pueblo ceremonies as it is a ritual drama, with both pantomime & spoken word, yet without music . . . neither singing nor drumming, nor are there any rattles. Still, besides the spoken word there are many sounds which form an essential part of the drama. Most of them are the sounds of nature represented by the Raingods. There is the churning of the excited water; thunder produced by stomping feet; & the roaring wind imitated by bullroarers. . . . Other noisemakers used are the turtle shells attached to the Clowns' moccasins & the many jingling bells (formerly pieces of deerhoofs or pig knuckles) attached to the ankles & waists of the Kachinas. The most important sounds of the Raingod Drama are the voices of the Raingods themselves; voices that utter weird sounds which belong to no human language; they are in the language of the gods. Each Raingod has his own particular vocal sounds that identify him, & these many weird sounds, deep & shrill, resounding & piercing, reflect the multiple aspects of nature's threats & blessings, which are the threats & blessings of the gods." (Laski, page 142) The silence of the final kachina & the silence that surrounds his entrance, must be included with all of that as well—part of an ongoing modulation of sound that represents a high conception of the boundaries of noise & silence.

Page 236   RABINAL-ACHÍ: ACT IV

SOURCE: Translated from the Quiché & French edition of Brasseur de Bourbourg, Paris, 1862, & the Spanish edition of L. Cardoza y Aragón (from an unpublished French version by Georges Reynaud, 1928): *Anales de la Sociedad de Geografía e Historia,* Volume 6, Numbers 1–4, Guatemala, 1929–1930. Translation © 1971 by Nathaniel Tarn.

One of three great Maya classics from highland Guatemala—along with the *Popol Vuh* (see above, pages 78 & 83) & the *Annals of the Cakchikels*—the *Rabinal* is a dance-drama, virtually the only Maya one in existence. Except for the absence of religious ritual, which may have been deliberately excised, this version seems by most accounts to be authentically pre-Hispanic.

(Writes Tarn): "The *Rabinal* was found in the town of that name in the Verapaz region of Guatemala by the pioneer Americanist, the Abbé Brasseur de Barbourg. After hearing from some servants of the legendary Knight of Rabinal, Brasseur cured the wife of one Bartolo Ziz who, in gratitude, visited the Abbé and declared himself ready to reveal the text of the drama he had performed thirty or forty years before on his father's and grandfather's orders. The dictation took twelve days. After this, Brasseur worked to obtain a performance, frightening the Indians into it by quoting lines from the drama at them and pretending to know everything there was to be known of their customs better than they did themselves. On January 25th, 1856, with financial aid from the Abbé and with his blessing in Church, the *Rabinal-Achí* was performed in Rabinal. . . .

"The play itself concerns the capture by the Knight of Rabinal of a neighboring Knight of the Quiché, his bringing before Rabinal's father and his ultimate sacrifice by Rabinal's soldiers after consuming his captor's food and drinks and dancing with his captor's wife. Georges Raynaud has suggested that, but for truncating of the text, the sacrifice would have included the presentation of the heart to the gods and the cardinal directions.

"I have tried for a straight, text-faithful but colloquial translation, setting the text out to exploit the parallelisms and stylistic redundancies. There has been no attempt, or little, to get rid of the repetition by one speaker of what his interlocutor has just said. The salutations alone are an invention of mine based on a mixture of Quiché and English phonetics: I think they give something of that solemn, almost harassing, repetitiousness characteristic of the *Rabinal* as I read it."

While translations exist in French, Spanish & German, Tarn's is the first significant go at it in English—& the first, certainly, as verse.

GLOSSARY (of Maya words not translated in the text). *Ahau*: Chief. *Achí*: man, in the sense of Latin *vir* opposed to *homo* (=Maya *vinak*). *Galel Achí*: Eminent *Achí*. *Balam*: Sorcerer; also: Jaguar. *Cala*: a hailing term, as also *yeha*. *Cavek-Quiché*: one of the tribes of the *Quiché* people. *Cot*: Eagle. *Hobtoh*: Five-Rains, alluding to birthday of the Chief. *Ixtatzunin*: meaning uncertain. *Ixtaz*: frog. *Oyeu*: Brave, Valiant. *Rahaual*: High Chief, Governor, Prince. *Tun*: two-tongued wooden drum, like Náhuatl: *teponaztli*. *Toltec*: a Mexican (plateau) culture which had great influence in Highland Guatemala.

SOURCE: Prose text in William Jones, *Fox Texts*, Publications of the American Ethnological Society, Volume 1, 1907, page 79.

The present working is from a narrative Jones translated as "The Little-Creatures-of-Caprice Ensnare the Sun," which creatures themselves turned up (he noted) in various other stories not recorded in *Fox Texts*. Of interest too to the reader who wants to keep track of the diversity of modes in Amerindian poetry, etc. is Jones' stress on the great preference shown by Fox narrators for brevity & a kind of "rapid narrative" —an almost opposite technique from other North American story-tellers (for which, e.g. see Tedlock's total translation of a Zuni narrative, etc., page 127, above). Thus, Jones' description of a Fox narrative performance: "When the weather begins to chill & the nights become raw, the fire of the lodge is then the center of a circle of men & women, some sitting & others lounging, with the feet always toward the fire. By & by someone spins a tale; the next person tells another, & so round the circle. . . . They soon get under way & hurry on with little or seldom any by-play, & come up at the end with a suddenness that is often startling. The result is a tale generally so elliptical that it would not be altogether clear to an outsider who was not familiar with its setting." If such condensation is a general characteristic of "poetry" (it isn't always, but let it go, by Pound's definition, at that), the Fox narratives would clearly so qualify. But then the reader should remember that in an oral culture (where the movement of the voice carries all the language & where justified margins just don't exist) there's no such thing as prose in the first place.

Addenda. NARRATIVE EVENT (Fox)

Sometimes a man goes into a fast to tell stories. He paints all his face black. This is at night, & when he begins to tell stories it is to be for all that night.

Often he does not eat in the morning, nor for the whole day. His eating is at midnight. He shells off two rows of white corn from a cob of eight rows. The corn he makes into *tagwahani* & cooks in a small kettle. The amount that he eats at this time is very small.

All this is that he may have good health & that he may have long life.

—*From William Jones,* Ethnography of the Fox Indians, *page 109*

SOURCE: Frances Densmore, *Yuman & Yaqui Music,* Bureau of American Ethnology, Bulletin 110, 1932, pages 130–141. Singer: Alfred Golding.

One of the principal cycles of Yuman songs & said to be the only one with dancing, it described Deer's journey & his power over certain animals—to bring all that to man! The songs in effect were a schematic of the narrative, a little like those highly developed aboriginal cycles from Australia as described by R. M. Berndt & others (for which, see *Technicians,* especially pages 363–375). The dance event, which took a full night to get through, was usually held (Densmore writes) "in summer at the time of a full moon. . . . The men are usually painted & usually wear an animal's tail or the head of a deer. Sometimes a man wears the whole skin of a wild cat on his head with the paws hanging on each side of his face. The animal's tail is hung at the back of the dancer's belt." The songs for Water Bug come early in the night, the others further into it. After the songs for Deer given here, Densmore describes the narrative as follows:

"The road made by the spider was a long thread of spider web. The deer travelled on this until he got out of the darkness. He rolled & shook himself when he reached the daylight. . . .

"Then he asked various birds & animals to sing or do something characteristic for him, & after each had performed he said, 'That is all right, that is all you can do.'" (Densmore, page 141)

Various animal events follow. (For other such events, the reader can check pages 185, 187 & 196, above, among many other places in this book; but obviously they'll appear everywhere in cultures where totemism remains alive.)

Addenda. Some Deer Dance songs of the nearby Yaqui are worth a look at also. Thus:

1.
Way out there in the brush
the deer are playing

2.
The Deer looks at a flower

3.
The rain comes in summer & the grass grows up
That's the time the deer gets his new horns

4.
The bush is sitting under the tree & singing

5.
A man said he'd damn sure get the deer
& hang it on a tree
6.
The deer is dancing in a circle.

The reader might also check the *Huichol Peyote Songs* with their figure of Blue Stag (above, pages 362–365, plus commentary) & notice that the line between Mexico & the U. S. Southwest is by no means an aboriginal demarcation.

Page 266   THE EAGLE ABOVE US

SOURCE: Konrad Theodor Preuss, *Die Religion der Coraindianer,* Volume 1, 1912, page 43.

Sung by one Santiago Altamirano for the eagle whose eye is the sun. Hollo has translated about half the original text.

Page 268   A SONG OF THE RED & GREEN BUFFALO

SOURCE: William Whitman, *The Oto,* Columbia University Contributions to Anthropology, Volume 28, 1937, page 109.

The song was taught to him as a boy. He had been "painted up with mud & dressed in a little buffalo hide with the tail round (his) middle," & so taken on a long walk to the Buffalo Medicine lodge for his induction. Along the way the older men taught him by speaking & singing. Would later become a good doctor & famous hunter—also a leader of the Peyote religion among the Oto.

BUFFALO DANCE EVENT, *for men & women.* (1) Dress up like buffalos. Let some of the dancers wear buffalo caps; let others wear buffalo robes or tails; & let some be plastered with mud & clay. Have some of the dancers blow whistles of cane, & certain women shake rattles of buffalo hooves. (2) Have everyone paint up. Let the kinds of painting come from visions. Use red paint freely but also use dirt from the earth. When someone has been painted have him sing a paint song of his own. Let him sing a set of buffalo songs, & let others join him when he calls on them. Feast on meat. Then have each member sing a separate quitting song together. Then quit.

BUFFALO NARRATIVE
A journey through the seasons
                    came in summer
        to a field of buffalos
        saw
old buffalos were covered   head & back
with goldenrods
        & some   with sunflowers
                    wrapped around their horns
in winter
it was gone
                    he changed
                    along with it
        had been a boy
        that spring
        that same day maybe
        or that evening
was an old man now
a doctor

& it began to snow

    — *Origin myth of the Buffalo Medicine Lodge, after Whitman (pages
    107–108)*

Page 269   THE SONG OF THE ROLLHEAD OWL

SOURCE: Albert S. Gatschet, "Songs of the Modoc Indians," *American
Anthropologist*, Volume 7, 1894, page 27.

Song & narration are in the person of "a small species of prairie owl
(which) . . . draws its body up until it appears almost ball-shaped,"
traveling like a "light-colored ball rolling rapidly over the ground."
This resemblance, then, links the owl to the young man who becomes
a rolling head & who (also like the subterranean prairie owl) will
take up an underground residence. In the full Modoc song there's a
further stage in which the man's sister is the one who follows him,
carrying the cast-off parts to his lodge, where she sees the severed head
eating, drops his things, & runs off in a fright. And that, says the
narrator, is as far as it goes.

Page 271   ONE FOR COYOTE

Translated by Cary from material he collected around 1951. He writes of it: "When Harry told it to me he chuckled & poked me slyly. His wife, Jessie, big woman, shook her head unhappily. Harry moved quickly to an ending in which Coyote threw bumblebees at the woman & ran away laughing. It's taken a long time for the story to grow to what I feel is Coyote, as the transformer according to Radin & the trickster cycle he set down. Anyway I do feel it true according to every sensitive groping backwards. The 'primitives' had their jokes & the creator carried the burden. I won't do it, but I think there's a definite similarity between Loki & Raven-Coyote etc."

More on Coyote turns up in the present "service," but the narratives on pages 102 & 105, say, are particularly relevant to the present working.

Page 272   THE GREAT FARTER

SOURCE: Prose text in Knud Rasmussen, *The Netsilik Eskimos*, Report of the 5th Thule Expedition, Copenhagen, 1931, page 448.

More scatology turns up, say, in the Coyote stories on pages 102 & 105, above, & it's almost needless to say that the recovery of all of that today opens the possibility of digging a highly developed, highly surreal aspect of the tribal imagination that earlier generations would have dismissed as mere barbarism or would have translated into dead Latin. Which dismissal, in its various aspects, has left its mark too on those Indians who are doubtful of where the power lies or has its public limits.

Page 274   HOW HER TEETH WERE PULLED

SOURCE: Isabel Kelly, "Northern Paiute Tales," *Journal of American Folklore*, Volume 51, 1938. Ramsey's working "synthesizes several versions of the story."

Elsewhere the toothed-cunt may turn up as one with thorns, even (among the Pomos, say) as one filled with live rattlesnakes—like that very medusa-head-as-pubic-hair-tangle of Sigmund Freud's nightmares. Among the tribes, too, it isn't merely expressive of fear but of the "power" (always ambivalent & dangerous) a man must take the teeth from, to make it amenable to his life.

For other versions of that female aspect, its place among the powers, etc., see above, pages 282–283, & commentary.

Page 275   THREE SONGS OF MAD COYOTE

SOURCE: From Herbert J. Spinden, "Essay on American Indian Poetry," in his *Songs of the Tewa*, 1933, page 21.

Spinden identifies the first as a "dream song of Silu-we-haikt (Eyes-around-the-Neck), first revealed in the annual Guardian Spirit Dance, where each dreamer costumed himself according to the nature of his vision." For more on Nez Percé visions of Coyote, myths about his eye-balls, etc., see pages 102–116, above, & commentaries. Coyote material from elsewhere also appears in the present gathering.

Page 276   THE EVIL SONG OF TAWEAKAME PEYOTE GOD OF LUSH

SOURCE: Fernando Benítez, *En la Tierra Mágica del Peyote*, Biblioteca Era, Mexico, 1968, page 251.

Trickster (one of the geniuses of tribal religion & poetry) is shown on the road to being (d)evil, but he can still say, here, that the point is no simple division like that & can ask for his place as a power (of subterranean urges, laughter, etc.) among the other powers. Songs like this come on "the third night of drunkenness" within the Huichol peyote ceremonies & alternate with "good songs" for the gods —for which, see above, page 362, & the commentary below here on page 470.

Page 278   THE INVISIBLE MEN

SOURCE: Prose text in Knud Rasmussen, *The Netsilik Eskimos*, Report of the 5th Thule Expedition, Copenhagen, 1931, pages 245–246. Nakasuk's narrative about "the great farter" appears on page 272, above.

Page 280   SWEAT-HOUSE RITUAL NO. 1

SOURCE: Alice C. Fletcher & Francis LaFlesche, *The Omaha Tribe*, Bureau of American Ethnology, 27th Annual Report, 1905–1906, pages 571–573.

The sweat-lodge in question was used as a preparatory rite by the Pebble Society [lit. "they who have the translucent pebble"], & the words of the ritual belonged to Waki'dezhinga, a former Society leader, who used them "as he entered the sweat lodge to make ready for his duties toward the sick." Membership in the society followed a dream or vision of water or of its representative, the pebble, or a dream or vision of the "water monster." Devices indicating such dream animals, etc. were painted on the bodies of participants. [For a scenario of other events in the ceremonial, see above, page 194.]

The old man of the poem is the "primal rock" of the Omaha dream-time: an aged being sitting in the midst of water that's impossible to traverse, spoken of as having "persisted through all time since the gathering of the primal seven, to have sat at the center where the paths converge, & endured the shock of the four winds, those mighty forces which bring life & can destroy it," etc. The sacred narrative of the Pebble Society—at least in Waki'dezhinga's telling of it—places the dream-time history as follows:

> At the beginning all things were in the mind of Wakonda. All creatures, including man, were spirits. They moved about in space between earth & the stars. They were seeking a place where they could come into a bodily existence. They ascended to the sun, but the sun was not fitted for their abode. They moved on to the moon & found that it also was not good for their home. Then they descended to the earth. They saw it was covered with water. They floated through the air to the north, the east, the south, & the west, & found no dry land. They were sorely grieved. Suddenly from the midst of the water uprose a great rock. It burst into flames & the waters floated into the air in clouds. Dry land appeared; the grasses & the trees grew. The hosts of spirits descended & became flesh & blood. They fed on the seeds of the grasses & the fruits of the trees, & the land vibrated with their expressions of joy & gratitude to Wakonda, the maker of all things (*Omaha*, pages 570–571)

In the actual ritual (see description, below), the stones in the sweat-house represented the old man & were so addressed, while the steam was equated with the primal water, etc. The "children" of the poem are the patients about to be ministered to, & the winds are "the messengers of the life-giving force, winds of the four directions, into whose midst the child is sent, to reach the four hills of life." What we have here, in short, is a religion & poetry at a point of high & complex development.

Addenda. (1) SWEAT-HOUSE EVENT (Omaha)

A framework of slender poles is bent so as to make a small dome-shaped frame; this is covered tight with skins. Stones are heated over a fire, then placed in the center of the tent. The bathers enter, carrying a vessel of water with them. The coverings of the sweat-house are then made fast, & the participants sprinkle water on the heated stones & sit in the steam while singing songs & chanting the words of the sweat-house ritual. After a sufficient sweat has been experienced, they emerge from the sweat-house & plunge into cold water, after which they rub themselves dry with artemisia or grass. (*Omaha,* page 585)

(2) The movement of the poem, in its cumulative juxtaposition of divine attributes, etc. is typical of that tribal poetry which attempts to realize a form & shape for powers that have been experienced in dream & vision before or during the event. While the poem's contents may finally be fixed, as here, there are other instances where it involves an ongoing activity, e.g. in the Crow sweat-house poem (above, page 53, commentary, page 409) & Lowie's description of the process by which the supplicant (=poet) articulates his sense-of-reality, etc. through language.

(3) A cross-reference of a very different kind is to the avatar of Quetzalcoatl as old-man in the Aztec myth of his transfiguration:

. . . And it is said, he was monstrous.

His face was like a huge, battered stone, a great fallen rock; it (was) not made like that of men. And his beard was very long —exceedingly long. He was heavily bearded.

Thus, Sahagún's informant in the *Florentine Codex* (for which, see above, pages 423–424), to say nothing of the Ancient-of-Days & those primal rocks of our own tribal poetries, etc.

Page 282   A POEM TO THE MOTHER OF THE GODS

SOURCE: Sahagún's 16th Century gatherings, as rendered into Spanish in Angel María Garibay K., *Poesía Indígena,* Ediciones de la Universidad Nacional Autónoma, Mexico, 1952, pages 11–12.

For the power of the imagination (Indian, Aztec, etc.) to give a face to its gods, the reader should check again the art of the ancient codices (for which see e.g. page 296, above) & such overwhelming statues as *la Gran Coatlicue,* that "Lady-of-the-Serpent-Skirt" & mother of the gods, "whose head is twin serpents, whose necklace human hands & hearts, whose feet & hands are claws, whose skirt is made of writhing snakes," etc. but depicted elsewhere as a mother carrying a baby in her arms. Garibay's note to this poem gives the name of the mother goddess as Teteo innan, but he points also to her many other names & aspects. Her worship was *sumamente antiguo* in Anáhuac.

The *holy thigh* of the goddess (another version has the thigh skin painted on her face) probably goes back to a sacrifice for the goddess Toci in which the victim was flayed & her thigh worn as a conical cap by a young priest acting as her son, Cinteotl. *Tamoanchan* is, literally, house-where-they-come-down or where-they're-born: the Aztec place-of-emergence. The *Nine Plains* (probably "high arid regions") are part of the imagery of subsequent Aztec migrations into Mexico, on one of which she was said to have manifested herself as *obsidian butterfly* (Itzpapalotl) on rounded (melon) cactus. *Xiuhnel & Mimich*, who witnessed her avatar as deer, were likely gods of that place & seem to have played a key role in the wanderings. The deer itself was sacrificial victim before they turned to humans (thus: Garibay), but a later form of human sacrifice involved daubing of victims with white plaster & feathers. The poem itself may represent a fusion of goddesses—easy enough in mythic thought.

Addenda. (1) While such information as here given has its uses, the reader should not be discouraged from focusing his own mind on the actual image-of-the-god, to follow that wherever it may lead him; or, as Mr. Joseph Peynetsa of Zuni said to our friend Dennis Tedlock: *When they tell those stories do you just write them down, or do you see them with your mind as well?* The poem, then, as a process of bringing-the-image-forward.

(2) "And the costume of Teteu innan was as follows: there was liquid rubber on her lips & a circle of rubber on each cheek. She had cotton flowers. She had a ball with palm strips. She had a shell-covered skirt, called a star-skirt. She had the star-skirt. Eagle feathers were strewn over her skirt—it was strewn with eagle feathers; it had white eagle feathers, pointed eagle feathers. Her shield had a golden disc in the center. She carried the medicinal herb, *totoicxitl*. She used a broom; she carried a broom." (Sahagún, *Florentine Codex*, Book Two: "The Gods," 8th Chapter)

Page 284   A POEM TO XIPE TOTEC

SOURCE: same as *Poem to the Mother of the Gods*, preceding; pages 21–22.

One of the Aztec gods of vegetation & fertility, though apparently a late-comer to the area. His "drinking of night" would seem to involve an offering of blood at midnight, while the "golden clothing" is the flayed skin of Xipe's victim worn by the officiating priest. The sun as snake, etc. is part of the imagery of the war- & sun-god Huitzilopochtli, whose birth will lead to that liberation from matter that the sacrifice—worked out with the typical literalism of the Aztec political state—may represent at its best. Or so Séjourné would encourage us to believe.

Addenda. "He was the god of the sea-shore people, the proper god of the Zapotecs.

"His gifts, which he dealt out, his particular creations, his attributes, with which he visited people, which he gave them, were blisters, sores, smallpox, ophthalmia, maladies causing watery eyes, infected eyelashes, lice about the eyes, fogging of the eyes, filling of the eyes with flesh, withering of the eyes, cataracts, glazing of the eyes.

"Those who were affected, we men thus sickened, would thereupon vow to him, saying that therefore we would keep on, having donned it, his skin, on the celebration of the Feast of the Flaying of Men.

". . . And the young men garbed like Xipe totec, wearing human skins, then went everywhere from house to house, begging. They were placed on *zapote*-fibre seats; bunches of corn were hung on them like jewels; they placed garlands on their shoulders, they covered them with flowers. They gave them to drink.

". . . Xipe's garb was thus: he had the quail-painting on his face. Rubber divided his lips in two parts. On his *Yopi*-crown was placed a band with forked ends. He wore a human skin, the skin of a captive. He had a wig of loose feathers, golden ear-plugs, a *zapote*-leaf skirt. He had rattles. His shield was red & had circles. His rattle stick was in his hand." (Sahagún, *Florentine Codex*, Book Two: "The Gods," 18th Chapter)

Page 285   BEFORE THEY MADE THINGS BE ALIVE THEY SPOKE

SOURCE: Constance Goddard DuBois, *Religion of the Luiseño Indians*, University of California Publications in American Archaeology & Ethnology, Volume 8, Number 3, 1908, page 138.

An excerpt from what she labeled "Luiseño Creation—4th Version," it was narrated by Lucario Cuevish, "an old man blind from his youth." DuBois herself pointed to the "tendency to variation in the (telling of) myths," which we can now recognize as part of the frequent *de facto* freedom of the tribal/oral poet, whose sacred "texts" are in a constant process of self-correction & transformation. The mode of the narrative (lost in the carry-over) involves the extensive use of gesture language & a "groaning style" in (especially) the dialogue; i.e. that utterances are often drawn out &/or punctuated with a groan-like sound, han-n-n-n-n—though it's not clear from her own notations that that would be the case with the lines excerpted here. At any rate the present editor has restricted himself to compressing (on basis of the apparent Luiseño text & notes for a literal reading) what seemed to be heavy paraphrases & expansions in the original.

About the basis for such expansions & the implications of just such passages as this one, she writes: "Much of this mythology is abstraction, belonging to the domain of metaphysics." With which the present editor would likely agree, being reminded too of abstract/concrete workings from the other India; lines, say, like these from the Brihadaranyaka Upanishad:

In the beginning there was nothing to be seen here . . . but it was all concealed by death—by hunger, for death is hunger. Then Death was first & thought to have a body. Death moved about & worshiped & his worship produced water.

And what was there was froth of water, it was hardened & became the earth. Death rested on the earth & being rested he grew warm, & Agni flared up full of light

who was the sacred fire, etc.—as in the Luiseño, the union of the earth & Death (but after a detailed exploration of each other's bodies) first generates the sacred objects: nets & baskets, red paint, thorny plants, salt grass, & woman's menses. All of which would indicate, perhaps, where some of that was headed at the point of its disruption.

Page 286   SIOUX METAMORPHOSES

SOURCE: Frances Densmore, *Teton Sioux Music,* Bureau of American Ethnology, Bulletin 61, 1918, *passim.*

(1) ". . . Life is not divided into classes and subclasses. It is felt as an unbroken continuous whole which does not admit of any clean-cut and trenchant distinctions. The limits between the different spheres are not insurmountable barriers; they are fluent and fluctuating. . . . By a sudden metamorphosis everything may be turned into everything. If there is any characteristic and outstanding feature of the mythical world, any law by which it is governed—it is this law of metamorphosis . . . the deep conviction of a fundamental and indelible *solidarity of life* that bridges over the multiplicity and variety of its single forms. . . . The consanguinity of all forms of life seems to be a general presupposition of mythical thought." (From E. Cassirer, *Essay on Man*)

(2) On the PLANET, EARTH, September, 1969

The unanimous Declaration of Interdependence

When in the course of evolution it becomes necessary for one species to denounce the notion of independence from all the rest, and to resume among the powers of the earth, the interdependent station to which the natural laws of the cosmos have placed them, a decent respect for the opinions of all mankind requires that they should declare the conditions which impel them to assert their interdependence.

We hold these truths to be self-evident, that all species have evolved with equal and unalienable rights, that among these are Life, Liberty and the pursuit of Happiness.—That to ensure these rights, nature has instituted certain principles for the sustenance of all species, deriving these principles from the capabilities of the planet's life-support system.— That whenever any behavior by members of one species becomes destructive of these principles, it is the function of other members of that species to alter or abolish such behavior and to re-establish the theme of interdependence with all life in such a form and in accordance with those natural principles, that will effect their safety and happiness. Prudence, indeed, will dictate that cultural values long established should not be altered for light and transient causes, that mankind is more disposed to suffer from asserting a vain notion of independence than to right themselves by abolishing that culture to which they are now accustomed.—But when a long train of abuses and usurpation of these principles of interdependence, evinces a subtle design to reduce them, through absolute despoilation of the planet's fertility, to a state of ill will, bad health, and great anxiety, it is their right, it is their duty, to throw off such notions of independence from other species and from the life support system, and to provide new guards for the re-establishment of the security and maintenance of these principles. Such has been the quiet and patient sufferage of all species, and such is now the necessity which constrains the species Homo Sapiens to reassert the principles of interdependence.—The history of the present notion of independence is a history of repeated injuries and usurpations all having in direct effect the establishment of an absolute tyranny over life.—To prove this let facts be submitted to a candid world.—1. People have refused to recognize the roles of other species and the importance of natural principles for growth of the food they require.—2. People have refused to recognize that they are interacting with other species in an evolutionary process.—3. People have fouled the waters that all life partakes of.—4. People have transformed the face of the earth to enhance their notion of independence from it and in so doing have interrupted many natural processes that they are dependent upon.—5. People have contaminated the common household with substances that are foreign to the life processes which are causing many organisms great difficulties.—6. People have massacred and extincted fellow species for their feathers and furs, for their skins and tusks.—7. People have persecuted most persistently those known as coyote, lion, wolf, and fox because of their dramatic role in the expression of interdependence.—8. People are proliferating in such irresponsible manner as to threaten the survival of all species.—9. People have warred upon one another which has brought great sorrow to themselves and vast destruction to the homes and the food supplies of many living things.—10. People have denied others the right to live to completion their interdependencies to the full extent of their capabilities.

We therefore, among the mortal representatives of the eternal process of life and evolutionary principles, in mutual humbleness, explicitly stated, appealing to the ecological consciousness of the world for the rectitude of our intentions, do solemnly publish and declare that all species are interdependent; that they are all free to realize these relationships to the full extent of their capabilities; that each species is subservient to the requirements of the natural processes that sustain all life.—And for the support of this declaration with a firm reliance on all other members of our species who understand their consciousness as a capability to assist all of us and our brothers to interact in order to realize a life process that manifests its maximum potential of diversity, vitality and planetary fertility to ensure the continuity of life on earth.

(Signed) ECOLOGY ACTION

(3) For everything that lives is holy.—W. Blake.

Page 293   A BOOK OF EXTENSIONS (I)

The two "books of extensions" present an exploration of other-than-speech or -words (the non-verbal, conceptual, pictorial, graphic, etc.) as the medium of poetry or as part of a continuum with poetry itself. Such merging of arts & shifting of boundaries ("our" arts & boundaries, I mean) are not beside the point, but directly at the heart of the great tribal poetries of North America—to see which at its fullest, it's no longer possible to stick with the limited categories of western poetics. In the first book of extensions, the work explored includes: (1) the extension of language into non-verbal media, but especially through pictures & writing where these aren't merely a shorthand for speech & aid to memory but develop from that as distinct (but never isolated) activities; (2) poetic process as observed in the movements of language itself or the ways in which particular cultures construct or associate words & concepts; & (3) games that program words & utterances toward particular realizations as play, etc. (for which, see also the "language events," pages 190–191, among other items in this book).

Page 295   THE TABLET OF THE 96 HIEROGLYPHS

SOURCE: Enrique Juan Palacios, "Inscripción recientemente descubierta en Palenque," *Maya Research*, Volume 3, Number 1, New Orleans, 1936, facing page 3.

(Wrote poet Charles Olson, back 1951 or so): "Christ, these hieroglyphs. Here is the most abstract & formal deal of all the things this people dealt out—& yet, to my mind, it is precisely as intimate as verse is. Is, in fact, verse. Is their verse. And comes into existence, obeys the same laws that the coming into existence, the persisting of verse, does." (*Mayan Letters*)

Page 296   FROM A BOOK OF THE MAYA

SOURCE: From the pre-Conquest Dresden Codex, as given in Eduard Seler, *Gesammelte Abhandlungen zur Amerikanischen Sprach- und Alterthumskunde*, Berlin, 1908, Volume 3, page 683.

"According to the early sources" (thus: Michael Coe) "the Maya books contained histories, prophecies, songs, 'sciences,' & genealogies . . . : thousands of books in which the full extent of their learning & literature was recorded." The three which survived the onslaught of the Spanish civilizers "are written on long strips of bark paper, folded like screens & covered with gesso. . . . (Of these three) the most beautiful & earliest . . . (is) the Dresden codex."

Page 297   THE CALENDARS

SOURCE: Leona Cope, *Calendars of the Indians North of Mexico*, University of California Publications in American Archaeology & Ethnology, Volume 16, Number 4, 1919. A selection, from which the present group is taken, appeared in Richard Grossinger's *Io*, the "ethnoastronomy issue" of Summer 1969.

The present editor suggests (1) that giving a name to something is a fundamental act of poetry, & (2) that a language in which names convey real information may be superior because of that to one whose proper nouns, etc. have been stripped of all significance. But the reader might consider the possibility of using the Indian ones as models toward construction of his own calendar of names by which he & his children could govern their lives.

For another aspect of naming, see the "naming event" on page 193, above, & the commentaries thereto.

Page 301   LEAN WOLF'S COMPLAINT

SOURCE: Garrick Mallery, "Sign Language Among the North American Indians," *Bureau of American Ethnology*, 1st Annual Report, 1880, pages 526–528.

"The whites have had the power given them by the Great Spirit to read & write, & convey information in this way. He gave us the power to talk with our hands & arms, to send information with the mirror, blanket & pony far away, & when we meet with Indians who have a different language from ours, we can talk to them in signs." Thus: Iron Hawk, a Sioux Chief, as quoted back in 1885 in William P. Clark's *Indian Sign Language*.

Page 304   ZUNI DERIVATIONS

More searchings for the poetic processes inherent in the language itself—or how it goes about its work. A question then arises of the degree to which language or its elaborations may have been the invention of "poets," i.e. of people hot in their seizing of reality through language, their willingness to play therewith, etc. But instances of specific tribal inventions, e.g. of shaman language (page 190, above), water language (page 191, above), etc.—not only Indian but world-wide—point to this as a distinct possibility in the self-transformation (=evolution) of man.

Page 309   NAVAJO CORRESPONDENCES

SOURCE: Gladys Reichard, *Navajo Religion*, Bollingen Series, XVIII, Pantheon, 1950, pages 518–521. Selected from sixty-five such groupings & arranged in sets by J.R.

Reichard speaks of such correspondences ("associations" her word for them) as "key to the Navajo system of symbolism" & maintains that they "are by no means 'free,' but are held together in a stipulated pattern which only the details that compose it can explain"—details, however, which she finds impossible to get at, therefore no "explanation" presently possible, etc. While the present editor accepts all that as "true enough," it seems to him that there's also a level at which the combination of images (poised between languages & cultures) has a way of opening *our* eyes to possibilities of relationships it would be hard to reach by following our own set habits-of-thought. And while it's interesting to learn in relation, say, to the fifth group in the third set, that the "ax which destroyed anyone who took hold of it, other than the owner, was possessed by Frog, Gambler & Old Age," it seems obvious that the matter didn't end there but might itself be changing under the influence of transmission through succeeding generations or as touched by the vision of a single seer (="poet")—which is something that is always going on.

Page 312   MUU'S WAY OR PICTURES FROM THE UTERINE WORLD

SOURCE: Nils Holmer & S. Henry Wassén, *The Complete Mu-Igala in Picture Writing: A Native Record of a Cuna Indian Medicine Song*, Etnologiska Studier, Number 21, 1953, Göteborg (Sweden), pages 71–75, 144–146.

The transposition of song to picture writing was the work of Guillermo Hayans, who was mostly using the "less evolved type" of Cuna writing "according to which sentences or situations are represented rather than single words or parts of words." Where single words are shown, "this is done according to phonetic rather than to semantic principles"— punning, for example, as bird (*nuu*) in the pictures =teeth (*nuka*) in the text, worms (*nusu*) in the pictures =penis (*nusupane*) in the text, etc. But the man who makes the pictures is not only a transcriber but an active intelligence.

The song (657 lines in this version from Nele de Kantule, the shaman who was Hayans' teacher) is used to cure whatever complications of childbirth follow capture of the pregnant woman's soul by Muu, the power who "forms the fetus in the womb of the mother & gives it its characteristics, or talents, *kurgin*." In this case the archetypal shaman journey (to free the soul, etc.) is understood as a uterine voyage, in which the road to the goddess Muu is also the vagina of the sick woman, her home the woman's uterus, etc. To get there the shaman & his helpers (carved dolls, in fact, that he's turned into "shamans") enter a world, writes Lévi-Strauss, of fantastic animals & monsters, etc. "darkened & completely covered with blood . . . (through which they find their way) by the white sheen of their clothing & magical hats," to come on her at last in her dark whirlpool (of the "woman's turbid menstruation" & place-of-the-fetus). A reconciliation is then accomplished, but even so the way out of Muu's world must be blocked, the vagina "sealed" after birth, etc.—thus the nets, entanglements & striking-with-sticks of the passages given here.

All of which the reader may want to set against other images of the subterranean goddess, lady-of-birth who eats back her young, etc.—for which see the Aztec Teteo innan (pages 282–283, above) or Eskimo Nuliajuk (page 405) or even, say, the great toothed mother (page 274). The danger of precisely these necessary (=natural) forces is fundamental to the outlook of much tribal poetry &/or religion, which may be at home with the Earth all right, but aware too of the void on the other side of the rise.

Addenda. Lévi-Strauss' description of the technical accomplishment of the *Mu-Igala* is worth a look at as further testimony to the powers latent in poetry & language, "effectiveness of symbols" that aren't read as such, etc. Thus he contrasts the detailed frame-by-frame description of movement in the early sections of the poem ("as if . . . filmed in slow-motion") with the use in the uterine voyage itself of "an appropriate obsessing technique" to bring across the "lived experience" of the body in its sickness, i.e. "a rapid oscillation between mythical & physiological themes, as if to abolish in the mind of the sick woman the distinction between them." In doing which, the songs "relate in detail a complicated itinerary that is a true mythical anatomy, corresponding less to the real structure of the genital organs than to a kind of emotional geography . . . (giving a) picture of the uterine world peopled with fantastic monsters & dangerous animals" like a "hell à la Hieronymus Bosch." The shaman who does this "provides the sick woman with a *language*, by means of which unexpressed, & otherwise inexpressible, psychic states can be immediately expressed . . . (towards) the reorganization, in a favorable direction, of the process to which the sick woman is subjected. . . . Thus" (he concludes) "we note the significance of Rimbaud's intuition that 'metaphor' can change the world." (For more of which, see his essay, "The Effectiveness of Symbols," in *Structural Anthropology*, Doubleday Anchor, 1967, pages 181–201.)

Page 320   THE WINTER REVELATION OF BATTISTE GOOD

SOURCE: Garrick Mallery, *Picture-Writing of the American Indians*, Bureau of American Ethnology, 10th Annual Report, 1888–1889, page 289.

Introduction to a copy of a Dakota Winter Count, made circa 1880 by Battiste Good, a Brule Dakota, whose Dakotan name is given as

Wapoctanxi, translated Brown-Hat. The main text of his book is a picture history of events from 900–1880, to which this drawing is an "introduction," the words his own synopsis of its contents.

Page 322   THE MYTH OF ATOSIS

SOURCE: same as the preceding, page 470.

Page 323   STRING GAMES

SOURCE: Franz Boas, *Bella Bella Texts*, Columbia University Contributions to Anthropology, Volume 5, 1928, pages 151–155.

String games with verbal read-outs like these (as songs, chants, narratives, etc.) were fairly widespread—thus the possibility that the game may have been played under circumstances conducive to the sacralizing (="poetic") process. Which wouldn't be at all surprising. But with read-out or not, it can be seen as a (damn near) universal game-of-changes not far from the activity of magicians & poets.

Page 326   THE STORY OF GLOOSCAP

SOURCE: Garrick Mallery, *Picture-Writing of the American Indians*, Bureau of American Ethnology, 10th Annual Report, 1888–1889, page 474.

Page 327   OJIBWA LOVE POEM

SOURCE: Same as the preceding, page 363.

Page 328   POEMS FOR THE GAME OF SILENCE

SOURCES: Frances Densmore, *Chippewa Music-II*, Bureau of American Ethnology, Bulletin 53, 1913, page 303; & Densmore, *Mandan & Hidatsa Music*, B.A.E., Bulletin 80, 1923, page 171.

The "game of silence" consisted of keeping still as long as possible in the face of songs whose non-sequential & far-out expressions were meant to cause laughter. Here directed at children, the mind's activity reflects the same energy present in more serious tribal poems: for the pleasure of the game, say, or as a simple exercise for developing & keeping all those faculties alive.

For a sacred version of the above, check out the "masked event for comedian & audience" on page 182 of the present work.

SOURCE: Frances Densmore, *Chippewa Music*, Bureau of American Ethnology, Bulletin 45, 1910, *passim*.

Recorded circa 1907, the "song pictures" (as she called them) are ideographs recorded on birch bark, representing individual songs & extended series of songs that can be read-out from them. According to Densmore the pictures use certain "established" (but apparently very open) symbols common to Midē drawing (see below) & rearranged & elaborated for each particular occasion. But W. J. Hoffman's earlier readings show departures from the mere representation of the songs' contents to the presentation of new information not supplied by the words.

The songs so depicted are almost all from the *Midēwiwin* (Society of the Midē or "shamans"), the basic organizational form of the tribal religion. The artists—Odenigun (numbers 82–87), Debwawendunk (number 17), Becigwizans (numbers 66–69), & Nawajibigokwe (all the rest)—had all been initiated through the various grades or degreees of the society, toward a gradual opening-up of sense perception, powers to heal, etc. Again & again Densmore tells us that even in the recording of songs for her information, singers & artists treated the events, i.e. the singing & drawing, as an experience of some intensity, an occasion for prayer, tobacco offering & (sometimes) meditative withdrawal. There are 107 song pictures in *Chippewa Music*; I follow Densmore's own numbering therein.

Song Picture 17. For initiation into the sixth degree of the Society. Before singing, Debwawendunk ("an old man . . . & a most devout adherent of the Midē") smoked in silence, then made a speech as follows: "I am not doing this for the sake of curiosity, but I have smoked a pipe to the Midē manido from whom these songs came, & I ask them not to be offended with me for singing these songs which belong to them."

Song Pictures 27, 29, 30, 34. All relate to the water spirit (manido)— his dwelling, his actions & his manifestation as male beaver. To induce visitations from such "in the form of water animals, mermaids & mermen . . . it is not unusual for a member of the Midēwiwin to sit beside the water for hours at a time, singing Midē songs & beating the Midē drum or shaking a rattle."

Song Pictures 54, 56, 58, 64. All sung after a man has been initiated & given a medicine bag corresponding to the degree he's taken. (54): Again a water spirit, this time in form of a *migis*=white shell used in initiation, shot into candidates & then removed; its purpose was "cleansing." [See *Pebble Event*, page 194, above, & accompanying commentary.] (56): The double line at left divides the series in half on the birchbark strip; participants dance during the second part.

Song Pictures 66, 68, 69. Sung during the dance which follows the initiation ceremony, when members sing songs for their special medicines. "It is said that a man whose hunting medicine is particularly strong may rise & dance & sing his hunting-charm songs" joined by others who know them. Sung otherwise at the start of a hunt. (68): refers to a midē bag made of marten skin with "power to drive together animals from all parts of the earth."

Song Picture 71. Not used ceremonially.

Song Pictures 82, 83, 85, 86, 87. All deal with "rare medicines" & can only be sung by those who purchase the right to sing them. (82): Composed by a starving man, who then tried it out himself in hunting bear. (83): Sung in a "round dance" around the grave of a person whose death had been avenged by a war. At the end, poles with scalps were stuck into the ground at the head of the grave, "to stay there until the poles should decay & fall." (85): Two women had "crab-skin" medicine bags that let them hold on to everything good—like crab-claws, etc. (86): Song of a man who put medicine on his feet & body, so could walk on fire without being burned, hold hot stones in his hands, etc. (87): Of a man starved out by people from another camp; a midē sends a woman to steal a small bone, puts medicine on it & sings this song until the people in that camp can get no game. "But the man whom he was helping could get all the game he wanted."

Page 337   A BOOK OF EXTENSIONS (II): SOUNDINGS

An exploration in this section of poetries where the sound heard at surface is stripped of apparent meaning, or where words are absent or are distorted from their normal forms. Otherwise the conventions of song & poem are followed, toward the creation of a sound-poetry that has been brought to a high development in the Indian Americas, but has been aimed at in divergent ways by other poets in the contemporary culture.

If meaning-as-explanation or for the sake of convincing an audience, etc. is absent here (or beside the point of the whole process), it's hardly that the poems are "meaningless." Rather that they develop an immediately functional language—a special language, of magic, etc. in which the power of sound & breath & ritual is used to move an object toward ends determined by the poet-magus. Such special languages, extraordinary in their nature & effect, unite the user (through what Malinowski calls "the coefficient of weirdness") with the beings & things he's trying to influence or connect-with for a sharing of power, participation in a life beyond his own, beyond the human, etc. Or, from a somewhat different point of view, what's happened here can be seen as a system of native American mantras—for those for whom that kind of comparison would bring it closer.

What follows, then, is a selection of ways in which the older American poetry has moved beyond words toward a redefinition of language itself or to the discovery of those deeper sources from which language comes. An earlier discussion of tribal & contemporary sound-poetry (on a worldwide level) appears on pages 386–391 of *Technicians of the Sacred*. Further commentaries—on special languages, etc. —are scattered through the present work.

Page 339   SOUND-POEM No. 1
Page 340   SOUND-POEM No. 2

SOURCES: Number 1 from Washington Matthews, *The Night Chant, a Navajo Ceremony*, Memoirs of the American Museum of Natural History, 1902, page 152; Number 2 transcribed from an original composition by Richard Johnny John & set on the page by J.R., July 1968.

The first of these functions in the old sacred (tribal) context, with some possibility of words interjected in the 13th & 15th lines (translated: the rain comes down / the corn comes up) but with considerable distortion. The second is a contemporary woman's dance ("social") song, but with distinct echoes (Johnny John tells me) of older, fixed sounds taken from their original places & collaged into the new works. An ongoing tradition of wordless songs (=sound-poems) throughout native America—& still hasn't played itself out.

Page 341   A POEM FROM THE SWEATBATH POEMS

SOURCE: Truman Michelson, *Contributions to Fox Ethnology*, Bureau of American Ethnology, Bulletin 85, 1927, page 77.

SOURCE: Francis LaFlesche, *The Osage Tribe: Rite of the Chiefs*, Bureau
of American Ethnology, 36th Annual Report, 1921.

Presented here in simulation of the actual method-of-performance
are "two of the twenty prayers recited simultaneously by the twenty-three
clans present during the initiation of a new chief." Of these twenty-
three, twenty (namely, the Elder Water People, White Water People,
Star People, Deer People, Bow People, Hidden People, Golden Eagle
People, Black Bear People, Mountain Lion People, Elk People, Craw-
fish People, Wind People, Sun People, Sun-carrier People, Night
People, Red Eagle People, Last Sky People, Buffalo-back People, Men
of Mystery, & Bull Buffalo People) recite their particular prayers,
while three clans (Turtle, Cattail & Buffalo-face) remain totally silent.

Writes Barbara Tedlock, after LaFlesche: "The candidate and all
the totems mentioned are located in the center of the House of Mystery
with the clan members, arranged in the three main divisions Sky,
Earth and Water, surrounding them. After the candidate distributes
all his fees—buffalo meat, sweet corn, dried squash, lotus roots, horses,
clothing, weapons—to the individuals present, all the clanspeople (with
the exception of the three silent clans) begin reciting their prayers.
This recitation is not in unison but is simultaneous" [a type of
performance not uncommon in Plains Indian ritual-events, as also in
those contemporary "happenings," etc. in which (writes John Cage)
"everything will eventually be happening at once: nothing behind a
screen unless a screen happens to be in front"]; "the prayers vary in
length from 17 lines to 179 lines."

She writes, too, of her own translation: "The phrase *said'nth'house*
on the left hand margin is a refrain or burden said after each of the
longer phrases on its right . . . I've written it as a vocable phrase
because of its natural collapsing from *said in this house* during recitation.
The Hidden People are in regular type while the Star People are
indented and in italics. The double spacing in the second half represents
the silence of the Star People who've already finished."

SOURCE: Charles L. Boilès, "Tepehua Thought-Song," *Ethnomusicology*, Volume 11, Number 3, 1967, pages 267 et seq.

Songs without words or other vocalizations but with a built-in system of "semantic signaling" that permits all the participants to read-out texts, etc. from melodies played on guitar & violin. Nor is it a case (as with us, say) of silently thinking the words to an instrumental version of a song we know, but that the musical phrases themselves are codes for concepts that can be further modified or expanded in combination. The songs presented here are from a collection of forty-five recorded in Pisaflores, Veracruz, in 1966. The accompanying read-outs were provided by Pedro Hernandez, a Tepehua priest, & were translated by José Marquez, one of the village elders. Also, writes Boilès, these are long versions, whose "wealth of detail" goes beyond the "basic message content" of the song, to "explain the subliminal context in which the song is heard & understood." But the thought process & resulting composition have been directly generated by the music.

The ceremony itself is called Halakiłtunti (literally, the moving-of-things, or priest's manipulation of sacred objects at an altar) & can be turned to purposes of curing, invigorating, "restoring harmony to daily life," etc. But beyond that, too, communion is established with Thought itself; namely, with the "seven sacred thoughts of god" represented by the Marijuana goddess, lakatuhún hatupasdíqał (Spanish: Santa Rosa). This takes place in the second part of the ceremony, when the participants have all taken on otherworldly roles: priest has become a spirit priest; tables, altars & all other objects have turned to gold; priestess has become the Great Midwife ("our-grandmother-of-the-vapor-bath"); two men & two women have become the four guardians of the great table which is the world, etc. Through the thought-songs, then, & by chewing marijuana leaves, the participants come to know the thoughts of the goddess Thought. She "enters" finally & order is restored to the world, ending when "the four guardians seize the corners of the table & begin to dance, moving the table around, causing the earth to resume its proper movement."

In all of this the songs are so central that (as Boilès points out) the "songs associated with the marijuana spirit can induce euphoria even without actual use of the drug. Any time that the songs are played, it is believed that the physical and spiritual worlds are drawn together & that candles & incense must be burned & a libation poured for the spirits."

SOURCE: Jerome Rothenberg, *The 17 Horse-Songs of Frank Mitchell: Nos. X–XIII*, Tetrad Press, London, 1970. Recording of Songs X and XIII in *Alcheringa*, Number 2, Summer, 1971.

[A NOTE ON TRANSLATION AS "TOTAL TRANSLATION"]: This is my almost final working (the "final" one would *not* be written down) of the twelfth & thirteenth of 17 "horse-songs" in the blessingway of Frank Mitchell (1881–1967) of Chinle, Arizona. Their power, as with most Navajo poetry, is directed toward blessing & curing, but in the course of it they also depict the stages by which Enemy Slayer, on instructions from his mother Changing Woman, goes to the house of his father The Sun, to receive & bring back horses for The People. The Navajos, of course, had no horses before the coming of the Spaniards, but a short time after the actual delivery, the myth had already taken shape, translating history into the Eternal Dreaming. The 12th Song marks the point in the narrative where Enemy Slayer contemplates returning home with his father's horses & other good gifts; the 13th Song is his prevision of their beauty on the earth.

I've been attempting total translations of all the horse-songs, accounting not only for meaning but for word distortions, meaningless syllables, music, style of performance, etc.; &, since translation is at no time mere reproduction, even the music isn't free from changes. The idea never was to set English words to Navajo music, but to let a whole work emerge newly in the process of considering what kinds of statement were there to begin with. As far as I could I also wanted to avoid "writing" the poem in English, since this seemed irrelevant to a poetry that had reached a high development outside of any written system.

Under the best of circumstances translation-for-meaning is no more than partial translation. Even more so for the densely textured Navajo. Right from the start, then, the opening line of the first horse-song, reading something like this:

dzo-wowode sileye shi, dza-ŋa desileye shiyi dzaŋadi sileye shiya'e

is really a distortion of the phrase "dzą́ądi sila shí" repeated three times. A literal translation (i.e. "for meaning") would say something like "over-here they-are-there (&) mine" three times over, which would fail to get the sense of one statement presented as three distinct oral events. To do more than that, a total translation must distort words in a manner analogous to the original; it must match "meaningless" syllables with equivalents in our very different English soundings; it may begin

to sing in a mode suitable to the words of the translation; & if the
original provides for more than one voice, the translation will also.

The translation of the 12th Horse-Song follows some such program.
David McAllester provided me with tapes of Frank Mitchell singing, &
with texts that included transcriptions of the words-as-sung, indications
of how they would be sounded in normal Navajo speech, literal & general
translations, footnotes, & ready answers to such questions as I still had. I
translated first for meaning & phrasing in English, adding small words
to my text where the original had meaningless syllables; then dis-
torted, first the small words so that they approximated to "mere"
sound, then within the meaningful segment of each line toward more
or less the density of the original; e.g. "& by going from the house
the shining home but some are & are gone to my house" >"& by
going from the house the shahyNshining hoganome but some are & are
gone to my howinow *baheegwing*." Most of the distortions were
carried out on the tape recorder, & as part of the process I went from
speaking toward singing, moving rapidly from Mitchell's version to
soundings of my own. Since the opening of each song (typical of
Navajo) is a string, small or large, of meaningless syllables, I let my
equivalents for these introductory sounds serve as "key" to which I
could refer in determining my moves within the poem. Similar sounds
& distortions had naturally to be carried over from song to song.

The final step in the process (realized so far for the 12th & 13th
Songs) was a departure from the Mitchell tape, but in line with
McAllester's description of how the songs would be sung ceremonially.
The typical Navajo performance pattern calls for each person present
to follow the singer to whatever degree he can. Thus group singing
is highly individualized (only the ceremonial singer is likely to know
it all) & leads to an actual indeterminacy of performance. Those who
can't follow the words at all may make up their own vocal sounds—
anything, in fact, for the sake of participation.

To simulate this in recording, I used a four-track system, on which I
laid down the following:

TRACK ONE. A clean recording of the lead voice.

TRACK TWO. A voice responsive to the first but showing less word
distortion & occasional free departures from the text.

TRACK THREE. A voice similar to that on the second track but
provided with significantly less information—i.e. recorded without
written text while listening to a playback of the first two voices at a
barely audible level.

TRACK FOUR. A voice limited to pure-sound improvisations on the meaningless elements in the text, recorded under circumstances like those for the third voice.

When I had recorded the four tracks, I had them balanced & mixed onto a single monaural tape.

In all this what matters to me most as a poet is that the process has been a very natural one of extending the poetry into new areas of sound. Nor do I think of it as poetry plus something else, but as *all* poetry, *all* poet's work, just as the Navajo is all poetry, where poetry & music haven't suffered separation. In that sense Frank Mitchell's gift has taken me a small way toward a new "total poetry," as well as an experiment in total translation. And that, after all, is where many of us had been heading in the first place.

N.B. For more on "total translation," particularly in the area of spoken narrative, see Dennis Tedlock's working of the Zuni *Boy & Deer* (pages 126–149; commentary, page 424). J.R.'s versions of *Shaking the Pumpkin* (pages 15–41, above) are attempts at "translating" words, sounds & (to some extent) "melody" onto a visual field.

Page 357   THE NET OF MOON

SOURCE: Prose text in Alexander Lesser, *The Pawnee Ghost Dance Hand Game*, Columbia University Contributions to Anthropology, Volume 16, 1933, page 96.

Told by Mark Evarts in a narrative full of good visions. The man who cried was Louis Behaile.

With the coming of the Ghost Dance in the 1890s, the Pawnees revived many old activities, e.g. the hand-game being played here, which was (a) sacralized & (b) delivered in various new forms through individual visions—much in the manner of song-transmission through dream, etc. Writes Lesser: "Once the games were begun, whether it was by [Tom] Morgan or by [Joseph] Carrion, by direct inspiration or through borrowing from the Arapaho, the idea of learning Ghost Dance hand games in visions spread like wildfire & the games sprang up like mushrooms. . . . For a game to persist after it was once created, the owner had to be well thought of by his people . . . & the public had to believe in the supernatural sanction of the game. Many games were probably demonstrated briefly & then forgotten.

". . . The game visions were supposed to give full directions to the visionary as to the details of the game. This included the essentials of the ritual aspects (such as offerings & ceremonial arrangements), the character of the hand game set, the way to play the game." (Lesser, pages 155–156) Unlike sacred games elsewhere, no actual gambling was involved.

Addenda. (1) THE HAND GAME VISION OF JOSEPH CARRION. . . . *Saw a large circle of people above. In a vision on the fourth day . . . saw things whirling round in the sun, crows flying round the sun & flying over him, & an eagle feather in the whirling sun. Then he saw a black sun streaked with white coming toward him, & fell over. When he stood up he saw a buffalo bull stick his head out of the sun, & just before sundown Jesus standing in the western sun with one hand extended toward him.* (Lesser, 233) INTERPRETATION: as a gift of the hand game. The circle of people were the players, & Christ held the set of sticks in his extended hand. As he held them extended downwards toward Carrion, so in the intervals of Ghost Dance hand games the beneficiary must hold them aloft toward the heavenly bestower, etc.

(2) The vision of the moon comes to the man who was ready to be caught by it. Everyone was having visions in those days, as Evarts tells it: the air was heavy with them, the process one of a continuing re-creation & renewal through dream—as with so much tribal activity in the absence of a final text. Anything—a song, a stone, a gamblers' game, an odd way of walking—could be made sacred thereby & renewed, which was also the essential "freedom" within the great Plains culture, that man was not only bound to the tribal unit by cultural forms, etc. but could develop his special take on them through the poetics of his own mind. It is this respect for the details of individual behavior, this as much as anything else, that the tribal way holds temptingly before the minds of many at the time I write this down.

(3) For more on the Ghost Dance, see the poems on page 398 & the commentaries thereto.

Page 358   PEYOTE VISIONS

SOURCE: Paul Radin, *The Autobiography of a Winnebago Indian,* University of California Publications in American Archaeology & Ethnology, Volume 16, Number 7, 1920, *passim.*

Peyote use among the Winnebagos dates back to John Rave's conversion "during 1893–94 (when) I was in Oklahoma with peyote eaters"— i.e. with the probable Kiowa & Comanche founders of the religion. The present lines are from a man identified as S.B., who wrote down his "autobiography" in Winnebago. Many of the visions (Radin points out) are similar in content & structure to those experienced by older methods of fasting, suffering, etc.—to a greater extent here than in other accounts from the Native church with its strong Christian under-pinnings. But the "vision quest" is a persistently Indian value, & peyote itself has been used back to pre-Conquest times in Mexico.

See the Huichol poems that follow for a thoroughly aboriginal imagery-of-peyote.

Addenda. Of the Native American practice, Ruth Underhill writes: "The Peyote religion teaches an ethical doctrine much like those of the monotheistic religions. However, it eschews specific Christian theology, its exponents often stating that while Christ came to the whites, Peyote came to the Indians. . . ." [Or, says a Comanche to J. S. Slotkin, himself a member: "The white man talks *about* Jesus; we talk *to* Jesus," etc.] "(Their meetings) are held in a tepee strewn with white sage in the Plains manner & with a half-moon shaped earthen altar as in some Kiowa ceremonies. During the evening, a drum & rattle are passed around clockwise, one man singing a song, supposedly of his own composition, while a man on one side of him drums & one on the other side rattles. Meanwhile heads of the cactus, usually dried, are passed around, each person expecting to eat eight during the evening. After midnight, when the round has been made once, there are testimonials from individuals who have been helped to follow the 'straight road,' giving up liquor & other faults. At dawn comes a token meal of old Indian foods, then prayers asking God's help for Indians, whites & all the world."

Page 362   FOR THE GOD OF PEYOTE

SOURCE: Spanish versions by Marino Benzi in *Correspondencias*, Number 1, Mexico, May–June 1966.

Aboriginal images & transformations within the Huichols' localized (tribal) religion. Blue Stag is Tahumatz Kauyumari, culture hero of the Huichols, messenger between the gods & man. Stag-Peyote-Maize form the Huichols' mystic trinity: the three are one. Roses, wind, etc. are symbols of the same. Blue Stag's home & place-of-origin (Wirikota) is in the East.

Continuity of sun-&-flower images from ancient Mexico, for which see the following set. An additional Huichol peyote song (for the "evil" god, Taweakame) appears above, page 276. The Peyote visions directly before the present set are, by contrast, from the widespread intertribal Peyote church in the United States.

Page 366   THE FLOWERING WAR

SOURCE: Angel María Garibay K.'s Spanish versions in his *Poesía Indígena*, Ediciones de la Universidad Nacional Autónoma, Mexico, 1952. Poems are Aztec but earlier too.

The "flowering-war" image in Mexican poetry becomes one of the basic symbols of Náhuatl spiritualism. As Laurette Séjourné summarizes it in her book *Burning Water:* "To reconcile the matter & spirit of which he is formed, individual man must all his life keep up a painfully conscious struggle; he is a battle-ground in which two enemies confront each other pitilessly. The victory of one or other will decide whether he lives or dies; if matter conquers, his spirit is annihilated with him; if spirit wins, the body 'flowers' & a new light goes to give power to the Sun. . . . This 'flowering war,' continually renewed in every conscious creature, is symbolized by two divergent currents, one of water, one of fire—which at last unite." The actual military orders of Eagles & Tigers (Jaguars) would then be taken as prototypes of those enlisted in that struggle: on some "real" battleground (in the latter & grotesque Aztec view of it) or in man as "meeting ground of opposing principles, which die in isolation when they are removed from it."

For more on this, see *Technicians of the Sacred*, pages 437–438. The imagery & ritual of flowers continues into contemporary Mexico, e.g. in the Huichol peyote songs, pages 362–365, above.

Page 375   WHAT HAPPENED TO A YOUNG MAN IN A PLACE WHERE HE
            TURNED TO WATER

SOURCE: Pliny Earle Goddard, *White Mountain Apache Texts*, Anthropological Papers of the American Museum of Natural History, Volume 24, Part 4, 1920, pages 128–131.

Hollo's condensation & working from prose-&-song texts given by Goddard. Not only did the boy come back to hunt deer but brought back water-songs (like the second section here, etc.) for a new water ceremony:

> He asked for a sweathouse to be built. When it was ready the boys went in & were singing inside. The young man who had been turned into water started to sing water-songs. Inside he wove lightning together again. There had been no water-songs & now they existed. That's how medicine men for water came to be.

> (Goddard, page 131)

The story, writes Goddard, "was told by Frank Crockett's father who practiced the ceremony." It was for the recovery of those made ill by the floods due to thunderstorms.

Page 378   POEM TO BE RECITED EVERY 8 YEARS WHILE EATING UN-
            LEAVENED TAMALES

SOURCE: Eduard Seler, *Gesammelte Abhandlungen zur Amerikanischen Sprach- und Alterthumskunde*, Berlin, 1904, Volume 2, pages 1059–1061.

"Thus was respite given the maize every eight years. For it was said that we brought much torment to it—that we ate it, we put chili on it, we mixed salt with it, we mixed saltpeter with it; it was mixed with lime. As we troubled our food to death, thus we revived it. Thus, it is said, the maize was given new youth when this was done." (Sahagún, *Florentine Codex*, Part 2, page 164)

Of the parties named in the poem, Tlaçolteotl was patroness of all that ecological renewal—"goddess Desire" certainly but also our-Lady-of-the-Bunghole, in which earth-fertilizing guise her name (as Seler tells it) was Tlaelquani=Lady *Dreckenfresser*—& was equated with that same Teteo innan (see above, page 450) who mothered maize-god Cinteotl & must later have had an eye out for him as Kid Fertility (= Piltzintecutli=Xochipilli, flower god) though he was on his own by then & busy shagging Xochiquetzal=Flower Bird, etc. A story & cast-of-characters, then, that touches all bases on the fecundity front & goes to show you how the Nahuatl poets, etc. saw earth's life transfigured into beings "without check with original energy" (Whitman)— before the advent of prose redactions & the secularization of dreams.

For a scenario of part of the eighth-year ceremony, see page 185, above.

Page 382   HEAVEN & HELL

SOURCE: Prose text in Knud Rasmussen, *The Netsilik Eskimos*, Report of the 5th Thule Expedition, Copenhagen, 1931, pages 315–317.

Page 384 *From* The Book of Chilam Balam

Source: Ralph L. Roys, *The Book of Chilam Balam of Chumayel,* University of Oklahoma Press, 1933, 1967, pages 125–131.

Chilam Balam (but literally the Prophet Balam or Prophet Jaguar) was the "last & greatest" of the Mayan prophets, in the line of Ah Kauil Chel, Napuctun, Natzin Yabun Chan, & Nahau Pech. He "lived at Mani during the reign of Mochan Xiu" & made the great prophecy that "in the Katun 13 Ahau following, bearded men would come from the east & introduce a new religion"—by which he meant the Mexican god-king Quetzalcoatl (Mayan: Kukulkan) & his white-robed priests. But the actual appearance (in his own lifetime) of the Christian conquerors did in fact "so enhance his reputation as a seer that in later times he was considered the authority for many other prophecies" both before & after him, & his name was put to various books (of prophecies, chronicles, rituals, almanacs, catechisms, etc.) written in the Mayan language but in European script. Besides the present version from the town of Chumayel, the two major books of Chilam Balam are those from Tizimun & Mani; but no collection now extant was compiled earlier than the last part of the 17th Century & most are from the 18th.

The mix of Christian & Mayan things in the present chapter is typical of the work as a whole: a natural enough process for the mind operating under pressure of conflicting imageries. Apparently, in this catechism, "the details of the crucifixion of Christ . . . recalled to the Maya mind some of the ceremonies connected with human sacrifice, in which the victim was probably considered the representative of the god. Like the crown of thorns, a paper crown was placed on his head, & the spear which pierced Christ's side appears to have reminded the Maya writer of the arrow with which the priest struck blood from the thigh of the sacrificial victim. It is also possible that the legend of the stone arrow-points, which entered the mythical rocks at the four corners of the world, was associated in the mind of the writer with the rocks which were rent at the time of the crucifixion." Anyway, from the ninth or tenth line, say, the imagery is almost pure Maya, in a process of generating sacred riddles, etc. that's poet's play & verbal vision at its wildest.

Page 388   HER ELEGY

Source: Prose account in Ruth Underhill, *Papago Indian Religion,* Columbia University Contributions to Anthropology, No. 33, 1946, page 266.

The divining crystals, common to shamanism not only in North America but in other tribal cultures as well, were the Papago shaman's "most precious possessions." They shed light " 'like your car lamps' on the seat of disease. . . . According to legend these flakes of quartz"— usually four in number—"are the solidfied saliva of I'itoi"—child of Earth & Sky, & creator of life along with Coyote & Buzzard—"who spat on the head of the first shaman so that saliva entered the man's heart." In general the crystals didn't come from outside but grew within the shaman's body, "lots of them" (said the informant to Ruth Underhill) "like honey in a honeycomb." But the possibility existed too of their withdrawal (as in the present poem) or loss. Thus the same narrator told of her brother who was a shaman "but had a bad wife who came to sleep with him while she was menstruating. That killed his crystals so that they rotted away, & another shaman who looked into his heart, saw it like an empty honeycomb." (Underhill, page 271) Said yet another shaman, when asked to show his crystals: "I keep them in my heart. I never show them."

The delivery or creation of a song or special words as part of the shaman vision should be noted too, & is obviously a key to that link between shamans & poets commented on elsewhere (for which, see in the first place the commentaries on shamanism in J. R.'s *Technicians of the Sacred*, pages 423–430, as a quick review of all of that & an attempt to connect the experience to tribal & contemporary views of basic poetic process).

Addenda. Though Papago girls like this one sometimes had the unbidden initiatory visions typical of shamanism, "most women were discouraged from practicing shamanism until after childbearing age, & the prowess they could attain after such a late start never gave them important standing." Adds Underhill: "As in White society, women doctors usually confined themselves to obstetrics & children's diseases." (Page 267)

Page 389   DANCE OF THE RAIN GODS

SOURCE: Konrad Theodor Preuss, *Die Religion der Coraindianer*, Volume 1, 1912, pages 48–49.

Page 395   A KALAPUYA PROPHECY

SOURCE: Free working after materials in Melvile Jacobs, *Santiam Kalapuya Ethnologic Texts*, University of Washington Publications in Anthropology, Volume 11, 1945.

SOURCE: Prose text in Knud Rasmussen, *The Netsilik Eskimos*, Report of the 5th Thule Expedition, Copenhagen, 1931, pages 138–139. Part of a longer account by Samik.

Page 398   THREE GHOST DANCE SONGS

SOURCE: James Mooney, *The Ghost-Dance Religion & the Sioux Outbreak of 1890*, Bureau of American Ethnology, 14th Annual Report, 1896.

The late 19th-Century messianic movement called the Ghost Dance was not simply a pathetic reaction to White rule or confused attempt to suck-up Christian wisdom. The ritual use of ecstasy & the dance is clearly more Indian than Christian, & the movement's central belief that the present world would go the way of all previous worlds through destruction & re-emergence had been (for all the Christian turns it was now given) widespread throughout North America & at the heart, say, of the highly developed religious systems of the Mexican plateau.

The "messiah" of the religion was Wovoka, also called Jack Wilson, who circa 1889 was taken up to heaven by God & there given the message of redemption, invulnerability, return of the dead, etc. In trance or dream, dancers would receive the words & music of songs, which they would ecstatically project: "no limit to the number of these songs" (writes Mooney) "as every trance at every dance produces a new one. . . . Thus a single dance may easily result in twenty or thirty new songs." This intense existence at the level of poetry was an abiding characteristic of those nations of poets who were defeated or driven onto reserves by armies of European businessmen & farmers. But, writes Gary Snyder: "The American Indian is the vengeful ghost lurking in the back of the troubled American mind. Which is why we lash out with such ferocity & passion, so muddied a heart, at the black-haired young peasants & soldiers who are the 'Viet Cong.' That ghost will claim the next generation as its own. When this has happened, citizens of the USA will at last begin to be Americans, truly at home on the continent, in love with their land. The chorus of a Cheyenne Indian Ghost Dance song—'hiniswa'vita'ki'ni'—'We shall live again.' "

Or the need for something like that toward our common recovery & survival.

POST-FACE

I am not doing this for the sake of curiosity, but I have smoked a pipe to the powers from whom these songs came, & I ask them not to be offended with me for singing these songs which belong to them.

(1907) / 1971

JEROME ROTHENBERG was born 1931 in New York City and was educated through the New York public schools, City College and the University of Michigan. His first book of poems appeared in 1958, since then he has published over twenty volumes of poetry and translations, which include *White Sun Black Sun, Between, The Gorky Poems, New Young German Poets, Poland/1931*, and *Poems for the Game of Silence*, as well as the playing version of Hochhuth's *The Deputy* and the groundbreaking anthology of primitive poetry, *Technicians of the Sacred* (AO-6). He has also edited several important poetry presses & magazines, from Hawk's Well Press in the early 1960s to *Alcheringa: Ethnopoetics* ("a first magazine of the world's tribal poetries") in the '70s. In 1968 he received a Wenner-Gren grant-in-aid for a two-part experimental project in the translation of American Indian poetry, and in 1971 he held a regents' professorship with the University of California at San Diego, where he led a first seminar-workshop in the translation and extension of tribal poetry into contemporary art and life.